Under the editorship of

LEONARD CARMICHAEL

FRED McKINNEY

University of Missouri

Understanding Personality

CASES IN COUNSELING

Houghton Mifflin Company • *Boston*

*To those who, in their
search for self understanding,
have provided these studies
to serve as guideposts
for other searches*

EDITOR'S INTRODUCTION

In this book an experienced psychologist and expert clinical counselor presents a series of case studies based on the lives of persons seen during his counseling career. The descriptions given are not a cold recital of external characteristics or a mere transcription of tape-recorded interviews or dull "facts of record." Rather, in these pages we see living people, with the same variety of problems that might be found in any randomly selected group. These cases do not illustrate bizarre or grotesque behavior. They picture people that a college student can recognize and understand. They are not very different from the people with whom one comes into daily contact. This may permit the reader to identify with, or to become vicariously involved in many of the cases.

As these cases are read and studied, the student cannot fail to see that a knowledge of the inner lives of individuals is basic in understanding the public, overtly observable aspects of human behavior. Modern psychology is sometimes accused of being too *nomothetic*. That is, it is said to be too preoccupied with a scientific effort to arrive at general abstract laws about human nature and human mental life; thus, it seems to sacrifice an understanding of the intellectual and emotional growth that makes up the unique character of each individual. In the present book this imbalance is redressed. The student sees here the importance of considering the emergent characteristics of each unique personality.

These case presentations do not depend primarily on test results or on the analysis of records or personality inventories. These approaches have not, however, been neglected by the author in his analyses of the dynamic organization underlying the behavior that is recorded. The usefulness of the client-centered approach to counseling is emphasized, but the book also has much to offer those who espouse different approaches to the clinical interview. An eclectic point of view is assumed in explaining the complex motivational patterns of each individual, and in the suggestions that are given concerning diagnosis and therapy.

This book's main function is to help the serious student of psychiatry, mental hygiene, clinical and general psychology, and related fields to gain a first-hand knowledge of what people who need counseling are like. Here the student is shown typical fellow human beings who need sympathetic help from those who know and practice modern clinical techniques, so that he can begin to understand how counseling assists individuals in gaining better educational adjustment and in living happier, more productive lives.

Washington, D. C.   LEONARD CARMICHAEL

PREFACE

There is a need today, among students of behavior, for more immediate contact with real personalities involved in the total process of development and adjustment. The relatively brief case history has its greatest value in this connection. It is almost universally satisfying as reading material; it makes human experience more vivid, permits identification, and presumably arouses personal insights leading to a broader perspective. This collection was written with the hope that it might fill these needs and also furnish materials which can be used with groups in active learning situations.

Much of the instruction in higher education currently is given in large groups and emphasizes abstractions. The exclusion of meaningful realities, particularly of extended illustrations, may well force the student into passive acceptance, perhaps even rejection, of course material. There seems to be, then, a particular place for such resources as the case studies presented here. The instructor can achieve a better balance of materials and encourage greater involvement on the part of the student by relating the cases to both theoretical abstractions and personal experience. Reading of the cases may be used as the basis for discussion in small groups or for individual evaluative papers. In addition to the thought-provoking questions at the end of each case, there is a concluding chapter suggesting ways to use the cases. A sophisticated critique on the case of Lewis, written by a clinical graduate student, is included to show how the volume might be useful to advanced students.

These cases are designed to arouse insights in the undergraduates as well as to provide a point of departure for the more advanced student of personality and counseling. They may be suitable for a wide variety of courses or learning situations and for individual bibliotherapy (reading for insight into one's own personal adjustment). Specifically, they may serve as collateral reading with many textbooks in personality, development, personal adjustment, abnormal and clinical psychology, counseling and guidance, social casework, or in introductory psychology courses that emphasize social and emotional adjustment. We have suggested with each case interpretive concepts, which represent a broad theoretical horizon, but which may permit the instructor to illustrate particular theoretical positions. An attempt has been made to assist the reader in exploring these concepts further by directing him to a sample of widely used references in the bibliography.

I have selected most of these cases from a file of approximately 2,500 folders representing interview notes, personal documents, and records concerning students whom I had occasion to see in the course of twenty years of counseling. They include a variety of patterns in personality, background, and dynamics. They vary in degree of "normality," completeness of report, sources of information, techniques of counseling, and in the number of persons reporting on the individual. In making the selection, I gave preference to those files which contained the greatest amount of information, both from personal documents and from sources other than the interviews.

Most of the cases concern young people who sought help with emotional, social, or identity problems. Five can be classified as average or better in adjustive potential, two were hospitalized for psychiatric reasons, one was severely neurotic and needed constant medical reassurance, one was of borderline intelligence, one was a troubled psychology student in the Near East, one came from a family of several known schizophrenics, and another had paranoid trends but was never hospitalized or given psychiatric treatment.

It is hoped that the cases will induce involvement but not threat; and that they will illustrate both general principles and specific aspects of personal development rather than specialized techniques or esoteric concepts. Most of the persons were known rather well to the counselor during their college years and some were followed, informally, for as long as fifteen or twenty years. Such long-term follow-up is somewhat rare and is, in fact, one of the novel aspects of this book. The long-term cases may have value in indicating possible outcomes, or prognoses, for clients in counseling.

The fact that more males than females are represented presumably does not affect the attempt to present human dynamics in a broad scope nor should it limit the potentiality of any student to identify in some way with these cases. An experimental study on involvement in a case history (that of David) gives evidence that young women can become involved in at least this particular young man's case.

My orientation toward these individuals was a consistent effort to understand the whole person and to produce an environment nurturing self-understanding and self-control. Many of the cases, then, lack elaborate diagnostic work-ups or material collected from sources other than the client himself. I have attempted either to present or to suggest the basic dynamic factors involved in the development and adjustment of each individual. Lack of completeness in many of the cases, from a formal diagnostic standpoint, may even furnish a combination of structure and ambiguity which can enhance the reader's understanding of important personality concepts and methods. A skillful group leader can exploit this factor to stimulate discussion and involvement, and to broaden individual perspective. Although I have attempted to give accurate portrayals of dynamic patterns, I have altered some of the presumably non-dynamic identifying details in every case, to assure anonymity. The details so modified include names, places of origin, some aspects of physique or complexion, and specific vocation. Factors thought to have significance in the development or adjustment of the individual remain unchanged. Although most of the cases focus on the developmental years represented by the late teens and early twenties, I have attempted to expand their scope with information about earlier and later individual adjustment, whenever possible.

I am indebted to many of my students for their reactions to the cases as they assumed their final form. Mr. Shahe Zenian and Mr. Richard Pallazza read all the cases and wrote commentaries on them. Mr. Edmund J. Machenberg also assisted with one of the cases. Some of the commentaries are included after the discussion questions, so that the reader may compare his reactions with those of a student in clinical training. Much credit goes to my wife, Margery Mulkern McKinney, for a final reading and editing, and to Norma Matzenbacher for typing and proofreading parts of the manuscript.

Columbia, Missouri   Fred McKinney

CONTENTS

Introduction

In these pages you will find a psychologist's attempt at understanding persons during a process of personal growth through counseling. This is not primarily a book on counseling but rather a collection of narratives about a number of different and real people as they face problems and make consequent adjustments. The counseling context is a good milieu in which to observe individuals in the process of growth and readjustment. Not all of the cases provide full information on the individuals presented, because of the voluntary nature of the counseling situation; but it is hoped that each can be seen as a person. These cases show the individuals' unassisted attempts at adjustment, as well as the changes that occur in behavior when each is permitted to explore the motives underlying his behavior in a secure, accepting environment.

This introduction is designed to provide the reader with a frame of reference so that he may better understand the attitudes of the counselor and the methods he used in understanding individuals, interacting with them, and helping them in their endeavors to adjust to life. This introduction should make more meaningful the techniques used to gain information about the clients and the procedures of counseling them. More detailed information is available in these references on counseling: Bordin (16); McKinney (74); Pennington and Berg (91); Snyder (107, 108); Thorne (114); Tyler (117).

Aspects of personality

The individuals described here were not selected as "ideal cases"; rather, they illustrate a wide range of people with varying personality organizations and varying personal needs, who are functioning on different levels of development toward maturity. The book deals with persons as they actually are, effective as well as ineffective, and with development as it typically occurs, showing progress as well as retrogression. The counseling of these individuals was sometimes successful and sometimes of moderate or little success. Here are studies of persons showing different *dynamics* (motivations and adjustment to them), varied personality *structures* (enduring inner organization), and varied *development* (levels of maturity) — three important aspects of personality.

In addition to the differences among individuals upon first entering the counseling situation, we also find variations in their *relationships* with the counselor; the duration, continuity, and effectiveness of the counseling interaction; and the development of new perspectives and new interpersonal relationships.

We shall emphasize particularly these psychodynamics: the degree to which individuals can explore their *conflicting motives*, their *anxieties*, the *defenses* they use against anxiety, and the *self-defeating traits* they have adopted in attempting to make an adjustment. These self-defeating activities are often satisfying for a time but later are disturbing. We can observe also the extent to which exploration of motives leads to *problem solving*, greater *satisfaction* of important personal needs, growth in *self-esteem* or confidence, and *control* of themselves in their environments.

The emphasis throughout these cases is to some extent nonclinical. Diagnosis is employed, but it is seen at less important than the creation of a climate which stimulates the individual's growth in problem solving and self-control.

Source of cases and viewpoint of counselor

When the first of the persons described in these pages was counseled, practically none of the books listed in the bibliography of this volume was available. Relatively little was available in the psychological literature on personality, clinical or counseling psychology. Psychiatry dealt mainly with psychotics and the severely neurotic. Psychotherapy was hardly encompassed by the concept of treatment at that time. The psychologist had developed few of the techniques now known to be effective and used today for diagnosis and therapy. Nevertheless, students with emotional problems sought help; and their instructors in general psychology seemed to be the logical and most available source of understanding and help.

The persons seen over the longest period were interviewed in a "Personality Clinic" of a university Student Health Service. They were followed informally over a period of years. Many of the individuals came to the clinic on their own initiative; others came on the recommendation of persons interested in their welfare. Voluntary referral was a central aspect of the service.

The psychologist who counseled these students had an eclectic approach to diagnosis and therapy, with special interest in the individual as a person and in his ineffective means of handling his conscious and unconscious motivation. This emphasis anticipated to some extent the present existential movement in the behavioral sciences (Maslow, 76; May, 77).

The counseling climate was largely permissive or client-centered, although directive and nondirective counseling techniques were also employed in understanding and accepting the client as a person searching for his own identity and trying to become a purposeful, self-respecting individual. The emphasis throughout was on understanding and on the promotion of self-understanding (McKinney, 73, 74). This theme runs throughout the interviews, the inquiries, and the suggestions.

Methods of understanding

The counselor attempted to assist each individual in exploring his background and dynamics, the resources open to him for becoming the kind of person he could best be in terms of his unique constitution, his past experiences, and his self-organization. Specifically, he was encouraged to discover — at the rate at which he could accept it — his own psychodynamics. This involved understanding the client's strong persistent needs, his frustrations, conflicts, and anxieties; his self-defeating defenses, which blocked him in satisfying these needs; and his strivings to become a resourceful, creative, self-actualizing individual. This was done largely through social interaction in reality situations rather than through a more mechanical diagnostic procedure. Presumably in this manner the individual could discover who and what he was, what he might (realistically) become, and what appropriate creative resources were open to him for learning self-fulfillment and self-control.

This position, although implicit from the beginning, was not developed into a theoretical structure during the early counseling period. The concepts mentioned at the end of the cases were not necessarily explicit in the counselor's thinking during the period of active interaction with the client.

Theoretical position

The point of view espoused by the counselor prompted a relationship of understanding and a program of growth-oriented psychotherapy which is dynamic in character rather than one which pivots on diagnosis and testing. A client-centered approach predominated in the sessions. All information that was available to the psychologist was used — not to manipulate the client, but to assist him in understanding and controlling the forces within himself, and in using the resources open to him. The psychologist did not limit himself to a single theoretical reference as a background for understanding the client, but rather, he utilized the insights derived from several systems. Understanding of the total person was facilitated by obtaining and encouraging the client to collect all the records that were available on his development, in order to see his uniqueness in the widest possible scope.

Not all counselors would proceed in the manner shown by the various techniques used in this book.* Some writers in this field would not be entirely satisfied with the *eclectic theoretical structure* that this counselor used. However, most of them would agree on the goals — namely, helping the individual to become a more effective person, gaining more satisfaction from life, and making some sort of compromise adjustment between his needs and tendencies on the one hand, and the demands of his environment on the other. There are many views as to how this may be achieved. The procedures to be used are dictated by the counselor's theoretical position regarding the best means of assisting persons to make a more effective adjustment (see Allport, 3; Ford and Urban, 37; Hall and Lindzey, 47; Jourard, 54; Leeper and Madison, 61; Rogers and Dymond, 94; Snyder, 107; Thorne, 114; Tyler, 117).

Resources for personal growth

The interviews emphasized the natural outlets available to the individual and encouraged him to seek other appropriate ones. Together the counselor and client explored campus resources which might provide sources of security and avenues of personal growth, in terms of their availability and relevance to the client's traits and needs. These consisted of volunteer services or extracurricular activities. Hobbies and special interests were inventoried as possible avenues for further personal development. In addition, all efforts on the part of the client to extend the problem-solving and personal-growth aspects of counseling during the days intervening between interviews were reinforced. Some students found free writing or talking with friends of value in supplementing the counseling. Others

---

* The counseling and personal adjustment viewpoints of the author are presented in greater detail in McKinney (73, 74) and in some chapters of Pennington and Berg (91).

utilized their special interests, such as dramatics, sports, writing, religious activities, and other creative outlets in reducing tension and gaining perspective.* This approach is today described as social-learning or milieu therapy.

Tests, inventories, and ratings

Understanding the person was achieved not primarily by tests and inventories, but through interactions with the individual during the interviews. However, this was supplemented by such information as could be gained from the *Pre-Interview Blank,* records, tests, and personality inventories.

It was essential to have some idea of the student's *intelligence* or *college aptitude* level. Practically all of the students had been given a general intelligence test when they entered the university, and this was a part of the permanent record available to the counselor. In some cases, it was important to know more than the general level of intelligence. When vocational selection was a central problem, the student's strengths and weaknesses in relation to verbal and quantitative aptitudes were significant. Such information was usually obtained by referring the student to the Testing and Counseling Bureau, which then furnished a profile of ability-test scores for the counselor's use.

The student's academic records in high school and college were another source of information on how well he had used his abilities. This record represented his achievement pattern.

The Testing and Counseling Bureau was also a resource for obtaining the student's *interest* pattern. Usually the *Strong Vocational Interest Blank* was given to him and thus a profile was available, indicating how his interests compared with those typical of persons employed in particular occupations.

The counselor occasionally used the *Thematic Apperception Test* — a projective technique employing ambiguous pictures about which the client creates a story. From this the counselor was able to get supplementary information on the dynamic pattern of the individual's motivation, some information about satisfying and unsatisfying motives, and other aspects of the student's dynamics mentioned above. In the cases of Joe, Phyllis, and Pearl, we have examples of the use of the TAT and the counselor's interpretation of the patterns revealed.

* See McKinney (74) for a discussion of free writing and other adjuncts to counseling.

Scores on personality inventories that the client had taken were sometimes available. Some clients took these inventories in connection with their work in psychology courses. They revealed the student's status in reference to common personality traits. The *Minnesota Multiphasic Personality Inventory* was available in the cases of Phyllis and Pearl. It consists of a number of items describing personality traits which the subject designates as descriptive or nondescriptive of himself. The resulting profile reveals the subject's normality in respect to the syndromes or personality patterns characteristic of selected criterion groups of hospitalized patients.

On rare occasions the results of the *Rorschach Inkblot Test* were available on the person seen in the clinic, as in the case of Phyllis. This test is described briefly in her case presentation, together with some of the trends revealed by it.

Some psychologists place much more emphasis on *batteries* of tests assessing ability, interests, and personality in understanding the individual than is shown in this group of cases as a whole.

The reader can obtain further descriptions of these tests, the kinds of data they yield, and the interpretations of these data from a number of standard books on general psychology or personality. See, for example, Guilford (46), Hilgard (51), McKinney (72), Munn (84), Pennington and Berg (91), and Sells (102).

On occasion, when the counselor saw that a client did not perceive himself as others regarded him, he distributed to the client's acquaintances (through the client) a set of *acquaintance graphic rating scales* to be completed and returned anonymously to the counselor. The forms solicited ratings of the client on efficiency, emotional stability, social adjustment, appearance, leadership, integrity, and motivation. This furnished both the individual and the counselor with some information as to how the client was perceived by those with whom he came into daily contact. The average range of the ratings on the traits listed was reported to the client during a subsequent interview. This device was used in the cases of Harry and Ralph.

Of all the techniques, the author's *Pre-Interview Blank* was used most frequently, usually after at least a preliminary interview. Customarily, the counselor handed the blank to the client at a propitious time with a statement such as, "This will help you to summarize some of the events in your past and present life and to think about some of the trends in your personality. I think you may enjoy filling it out. Do it in your own way, writing as much or as little as you desire." The client usually accepted the Blank without resistance and almost invariably returned it at the next interview. It was very helpful in orienting the client toward information which would have taken many exploratory interviews to reveal. Although information about most aspects of the individual's life was tapped by the specific but open-ended questions in the blank, the client was free to use it in a manner dictated by his own psychodynamics. It revealed both subjective and objective content as well as the intensity and character of the client's defenses. It had, then, a projective as well as an inventory aspect. For further discussion, see McKinney and Wertheimer (70); and McKinney (71, 72, 74).

The *Pre-Interview Blank* consists of nine mimeographed pages and solicits facts and attitudes about ability and achievement, physical health, college activities, interests and plans, present living conditions, attitudes, problems, personality traits, and history prior to college, including information about parents, health, recreation, sex, social life, school, experiences outside of school, inner life, and religion. The cases of Harry, Ralph, Frank, and Paul, among others, illustrate how the counselor and client were aided by information made available through the use of this blank. A resume of the blank appears on pages 314–316.

With some of the individuals counseled more briefly and more recently (e.g., Tom and Robert), the counselor used the self-oriented *Sentence-Completion Blank* which he had developed. The sentence completions are classified in terms of dynamic categories indicating self-actualizing (coping and propriate striving), self-defeating (defense mechanisms), and self-immobilizing (or anxiety-flavored) responses.

Use of the cases

The individuals are presented as cases to enable the reader to become involved vicariously in their lives, with the hope that he will gain a better understanding of a variety of personalities. This can be achieved not only by reading these cases and noting the wide variety of personality organizations and adjustments they represent, but also by discussing among peers your personal reactions to these persons, to their behavior, and to their experiences. A second objective is to make more meaningful some of the concepts that psychologists of all persuasions have evolved to explain complex behavior. A few of these concepts are listed after each case, with specific reference to representative books readily available to the student.

It is assumed that more detailed discussion and definition of these concepts will be presented by the basic text used in the course. The final chapter, "Use of Cases," gives detailed suggestions for effective use of the cases.

BEN

The Sad Under-Achiever

This is a case involving a few interviews at a college mental-hygiene clinic, supplemented by correspondence with a parent. Ben sought out the counselor on occasions when he was unusually disturbed by anxiety symptoms and when he could not resolve what seemed to him an intolerable situation. Counseling was discontinued when Ben withdrew from college. A self-initiated follow-up interview twelve years later provided information about his subsequent vocational, family, and emotional adjustment. The case illustrates the nature of conflict and anxiety in an academic setting and the long-term effects of an expedient withdrawal from college.

IDENTIFICATION

Ben was a tall, thin, dark fellow with curly hair. Despite a poor complexion, his overall appearance was that of a good-looking fellow. The impressions he gave his associates were many and varied. Sometimes he might be found with a group, telling jokes and playing the clown; at other times he might be seen walking into a class or a fraternity meeting with his head down and a shy, sad look on his face, as though he had just been whipped. He was a pledge in the most prominent Jewish fraternity on the campus, but he had never been able to attain the minimum grades required for initiation.

Ben's family lived in the suburbs of a neighboring city. His father had been successful financially as a real estate broker; he belonged to the country club and was quite active socially. He and his wife had had aspirations for their son to attend one of the best eastern colleges and to distinguish himself in some way. Ben felt he had been a disappointment to them.

9

OCCASION FOR INTERVIEW

Ben came in to see his psychology teacher after class one day and requested an interview. He explained: "I have been quite upset. I just got a telephone call from my father, and he was very angry. I think he is ready to disown me. He can't understand why I am not making satisfactory grades, and I can't either. I have just about lost confidence in myself. I used to be the life of the party, but now it takes an effort just to be civil. Sometimes I feel that there really isn't much to me inside, that I have no character. I am continually disappointing my parents, and they are counting heavily on my success. They both seem to love me very much but I am not living up to their expectations. My father is so disgusted that he hasn't written me for a long time. My mother is the kind of person that gets nervous and goes to pieces when anything like this happens. I can just see her when I get home — screaming and crying and saying things that will hurt me and make her feel very sorry when it is over. I can and should do better, but for some reason I just let things go. That is the problem. I don't seem to have any will power."

Ben said that everything seemed to rest upon his making satisfactory grades, so that he could be initiated into the fraternity. Even his girl was secondary to this goal. "It is not so much that I must be a member of that fraternity; it is just that if I don't get in, it will be another sign of failure. I have failed continually in the past, and I am afraid that means a life of failure."

Analysis of Ben's conflict

The preceding quotation is an example of the narrow, all-or-none kind of thinking that is typical of the anxiety state Ben had been experiencing. In his thinking the goal of achieving high grades was synonymous with the total of life's strivings. Since he conceived of himself as failing in this goal, he therefore considered himself a total failure. He was worried and fretful and could not face his problem realistically. This is a typically non-adjustive reaction.

FAMILY BACKGROUND

It is understandable how this kind of anxiety state can be built in a situation such as existed in Ben's home. Ben's mother seems to have been quite unstable emotionally. She tended to create violent emotional scenes, attacking the very roots of his character, and then expressing her regret, while at the same time declaring her love for him. This kind of climate is conducive neither to developing a stable, consistent, mature personality nor to performing efficiently in pursuit of goals.

Since these emotional scenes followed every unsatisfactory grade report, they made school work very distasteful to Ben. If Ben tried to avoid the memory of the unpleasant scenes, as he undoubtedly did, he must also have tried to avoid anything closely associated with them — most particularly, studying. Since he could not afford the consequences of neglecting his studies indefinitely, he was perpetually stirred up by memories of his mother's scenes and fearful of arousing still more displeasure by his continued failure. He showed the extreme *anxiety* and *vacillation* typical of an *avoidance-avoidance conflict*. The times when Ben could not study were times when he was overwhelmed by the fear and distaste associated with the memory of his mother's scenes. Only when his fear of failure occasionally took precedence was he able to study at all, and then not productively. Ben did not understand the nature of this conflict or that it was the source of his anxiety.

Persons plagued by such a conflict (that is, an avoidance-avoidance conflict), faced with what seems an insoluble problem, frequently seek to escape rather than cope with the problem. Such an escape seemed very attractive to Ben, but at the same time it would have exposed a "weakness" in him, nearly as intolerable as the problem itself. Seeing no alternative (he could not escape; he could not study; he could not face the consequences of not studying), Ben seemed to regress to the state of a helpless little boy. This regression had gained unconscious satisfaction for him in the past. At such times, seeing Ben tearful and despondent after her tantrums, his mother became regretful and showered affection upon him, making him feel better.

Although Ben had said repeatedly that he loved his parents and was proud of them, he was rarely frank in dealing with them. He dreaded the effects of his negligent behavior on his parents — he feared his mother's wrath in particular — so he withheld any bad news. One of his characteristic patterns of behavior, when difficulties occurred in an area in which his parents had a major interest, was to hide the information and try to escape from the situation. This illustrates wide *suppressive tendencies*, *defense* against unpleasant situations that he could not handle, and *anxiety*.

There is evidence that Ben's parents placed greater emphasis upon outward appearances than upon realistic underlying conditions that defined what their son was like and what he could best do. At one time Ben said, "I know one reason why I am not doing too well here. This is a state university and I look down upon it. I have the intelligence to go to one of the Ivy League schools in the East, but because of my lack of will power, I am here, and I can't get enthusiastic about it." He claimed that his parents often praised him and encouraged him, but that he knew their praise and enthusiasm were intended to "build him up," and that disappointing them would be all the more inexcusable.

COUNSELING EVENTS

During the initial interview the counselor had done little more than listen with understanding as Ben expressed his feelings freely. If Ben gained a somewhat better perspective on his situation, it was probably a result of seeing his predicament understood by someone else and reflected back to him more clearly.

About a week after the first interview, in which the foregoing information was revealed, Ben appeared at the counselor's office with a more confident outlook. He told the counselor he was beginning to get a broader perspective on his family situation and on himself. He had talked to all of his teachers to find out where he stood in his courses. He felt that he was studying more effectively than he had for a long time. He admitted that this was a change in attitude and behavior; he was looking at his predicament and attempting to deal with it rather than running away from it. He saw that he tended to retreat from problems because there was always a possibility of failing, and failing was something he very much dreaded. He said he didn't yet understand why he often felt superior to the people around him. He did not seem to be aware of the disparity between feeling superior and worrying so much about failure. In fact, he was unable to perceive himself as a mixture of assets and liabilities. He apparently had difficulty evaluating his mistakes or facing the situations in which they occurred. This is one of the reasons why he so often "couldn't study" when he knew he must. Specifically, books and the study room were associated — largely without awareness — with poor grades, parental disappointment, and personal failure. This second interview, in which Ben appeared more confident, occurred just before final examinations, when many of the students who lived around him were spending long hours in study. In fact, the climate of the campus at this point in the semester, unlike that of preceding weeks, was one of frantic cramming. Perhaps Ben found it easier to study at that time because his motivation was bolstered by the activity of everyone around him.

After examination grades were known, Ben wrote the counselor a note saying that he had earned ten credit-hours of satisfactory grades, six of above average (but not superior), and three of inferior grades. The inferior credits prevented him, once again, from being initiated into the fraternity. He ended the note by saying, "I feel very low and at sort of a loss to know what to do." When he delivered this note to the office secretary, he told her he had to have an appointment immediately. The secretary described him to the counselor as being extremely nervous and upset — almost in a panic.

In the interview that followed, Ben said he had moved out of the fraternity house. He was not concerned about this, he said, because he felt so ashamed in not making his grades. He was probably relieved not to have to face the other members. His shame was intense despite the fact that a number of other boys in the fraternity had also failed to make satisfactory grades and were not initiated. Moreover, he had not failed miserably, but rather had barely missed the standard requirements for initiation. In the interview he talked about fearing the effect of this on his mother's health. He said he could just see her going to pieces, crying and shouting. "My father will be aloof to the whole thing, but he will make me tell my mother," he said. During the interview he became tearful and confessed that he, with some other fellows, had run up a bill at the country club, which his father would have to pay. He left the interview feeling better than he had felt when he came in.

A few days later he returned, saying that his mother had called him about another matter, and he had "got around to" reporting his grades to her. She had taken it calmly. He was pleased about this and acted as though his problems were over, thanked the counselor for his help, and left. This rapid apparent recovery represented yet another cycle in the behavior pattern he had exhibited previously — great concern, then relief when external pressures were removed.

Free writing*

The counselor had suggested to Ben on several occasions that when he felt disturbed, he might find it helpful to engage in some free writing. Specifically, it was suggested to him that he write out his

* The technique of free writing is explained in greater detail elsewhere (72).

feelings vigorously, trying to do it as rapidly as his thoughts arose —
using a kind of personal shorthand or abbreviation of words, if he
wished, or just writing ideas rather than words. Such unrestrained
writing would doubtless have the effect of relieving tension, and it
might also help him to gain some insight into the nature of his conflicts. The counselor believed such understanding might help Ben to
direct his own behavior more effectively. Ben attempted to do this
and left the following with the secretary in the office:

"Why can't I study? Is it fear? No. Is it laziness? I don't
know what the hell it is.

"I'm so restless. I'm tired, yet I can't go to bed. Why can't
I go to bed? It's hopeless. I get nothing done.

"I must study. I must make my grades.

"Can't make them, too late. Oh hell, I'm even failing — I
don't know. Grades are trivial except in their relationship to
your home life.

"I feel nervous but can't seem to do anything about it.

"Oh, what am I going to do? Study, but I can't.

"What happened last week? Nothing much, except I studied
a little more Saturday night, basketball game, complete break-up
with Betsy.

"Tired now!"

What do you think was the effect of this first attempt at free
writing? Did Ben get relief or insight into his situation? What effects
do you think more such writing at other times might have had?

After an interval — panic, then broader perspective

Several months later, Ben came into the counselor's office, quite
tense and excited, at an hour when the counselor could not spend
much time with him. Before many minutes had passed, he became
tearful and said he felt he would have to leave school. The counselor
gave him an appointment for that afternoon. When he returned in
the afternoon he was much more calm. "I have been analyzing myself since I saw you this morning. Again this semester I am not making high enough grades to be initiated into the fraternity. I am
terribly ashamed of this. Everybody knows about it, and when I
meet them, I feel that they're thinking about it. As you may remember I moved out of the fraternity house and now I am rooming in
a private home with another fellow. We are not getting along. This

morning I was homesick and wanted to see my little brother. I know now that going home is not the answer. My problem is inside of me.

"I wouldn't be able to talk this matter over with my mother. She would just say I have failed again and make me feel once more that I have let the family down. She has always talked about me as though I were a 'case.' I feel so lost inside. Even though I have a close tie with my family, I can't sit down with them and talk about the things that I feel inside."

Ben had gone to a fashionable private high school; but for some reason he had never felt accepted as one of the group. His grades had never been as high as those of which he was thought to be capable. He couldn't be open and frank with his family; instead he was underhanded and sneaky, and a disappointment to them. He had gotten to the point where he could hardly face the people with whom he had been associated for so many years. "That is what was bothering me this morning. I really felt that I couldn't go on any more because I couldn't face people, feeling the way I did."

Ben never mentioned the effect upon him of being Jewish in a high school where there were few Jews. This may have been one contributing factor, but it certainly was not the sole cause of Ben's problem.

Thus Ben described in his own way the strong conflict and anxiety that he was experiencing. He was verbalizing it and seeing it in rather broad perspective for perhaps the first time. It is interesting to see what time and acceptance by the counselor did in helping him, between the morning hours and the afternoon appointment, to convert a siege of panic into a verbalization and understanding of his problem. He had even found a solution. He had decided to move into the dormitory where he would meet a new and entirely different group of students. The prospect of living in a dormitory with students who were new to him seemed to break the mental set which had been limiting his outlook.

Ben leaves school

A few weeks later, Ben left school and went home. His father called the counselor at that time and later wrote the following letter:

Dear Doctor,

Let me begin by repeating my gratitude to you both for the interest you have shown in Ben and for the kindly, understanding efforts you have put forth in his behalf.

I think that you should know the developments subsequent

to our phone conversation. Ben received exactly the welcome I promised. He explained fully the whole course of events, recent and more remote, to his mother and me. No detail within immediate recollection was omitted, and in the ensuing sympathetic discussion neither his mother nor I held anything back. The exchange of views, attitudes, and thinking was done as objectively and unemotionally as could have been expected. The result was understanding and agreement that Ben's stand was appreciated and that his decision was logical.

May I again tell you warmly how very grateful Mrs. Hess and I are to you for all you have done for Ben — and, may I say, I feel that was a great deal.

Ben will begin working shortly. Several people have already offered him jobs suitable for a beginner. He will have an interview tomorrow and I feel rather certain he will find employment in a fairly large, well-organized Chicago company with what I believe to be a bright future. Ben will probably end up in sales activity, and there are great opportunities in the company for significant accomplishment along these avenues.

With heartfelt thanks to you and all good wishes.

Sincerely,

HORACE HESS

The counselor replied immediately to the above letter from Mr. Hess, as follows:

Dear Mr. Hess,

I appreciate your writing me after Ben arrived home. I felt sure after talking with you that matters would adjust themselves when Ben returned home. He may want to talk with you quite frankly from time to time, especially about his relationship with his mother. May I suggest that you merely listen and let him say whatever he cares to say, even though he may not deeply mean everything he says. This sort of catharsis is highly therapeutic. Very often the individual doesn't feel the same way after he has gotten it out of his system.

Ben is a very likeable fellow and I am glad to know that he is away from the school situation which was disturbing him so greatly. Would you say to him that I would be glad to hear from him at any time. He may feel free to write as much as he wishes.

Cordially yours,

This is the final letter the counselor received from Mr. Hess:

Dear Doctor,

I have just received your letter of November 16 and do appreciate your continuing concern for Ben. Of course, I shall be delighted to follow your suggestion. I will be a ready and sympathetic, but noncommittal listener to those concerns of Ben that you have indicated. I am most grateful for your advice.

Ben is starting "at the bottom," in the warehouse of a big company, a wholesale cosmetics concern. He hopes ultimately to get into sales work and is quite happy with his decision and activity.

I shall happily convey your message to him with gratitude.

Sincerely yours,

HORACE HESS

OUTCOME

Follow-up twelve years later

Ben dropped into the office unexpectedly after a twelve-year interval. He said he was passing through town and the counselor was the one person he wanted to see. He had married and had a child, of whom he was very fond. He pulled out a picture and displayed it proudly. He said, "I am doing very well. I am in sales work and I like it. I have had several promotions. I am much better adjusted now than I was in school. That was a turning point in my life, and you were very helpful to me. I want to thank you for all you did."

Ben had many of the same shy, withdrawing characteristics that he had when he first came to the counselor's office; but as he talked at greater length, he showed more confidence and ease than the counselor remembered seeing in him as a student. He gave the impression of having more control over his own destiny, of seeing his life more in perspective. He seemed hopeful of the future and less a trapped victim of inner conflict.

BEN: Trends, Life Factors, and Relationships

What do you see in the life of Ben that is most outstanding? Respond in your own way before turning to the following suggestions.

Outstanding life patterns

  a. Do you see certain characteristics as clearly identifying his attempted adjustment?
  b. What factors or influences in his life were most responsible for his salient characteristics?
  c. What role did his religion, social class, and parents' attitudes and motivations seem to play?

Influences in personal relationships

  a. Did the roles of his mother and father remain the same after he left school as they had been before?
  b. Could you suggest reasons why his role as a working man was different from his role as a "student"?
  c. What aspects of the counseling situation were helpful to Ben and what aspects were not explored sufficiently?

Concepts helpful in understanding Ben

  a. Conflicts, especially avoidance-avoidance (31, 80)*
  b. Anxiety and defense mechanisms (22, 96)
  c. Anxiety reduced by the counselor's intervention and the father's understanding (11, 74)
  d. Identity, and commitment to some task; success in sales work (3, 76)

BEN: Comments by a Graduate Student

It is aptly pointed out that Ben is in a conflict situation and experiences anxiety. However, he attributes these feelings and experiences to something inside himself — i.e., a "weakness" within his own

---

* The numbers in parentheses refer to references in the bibliography containing discussions of the topic. The topic may be located in the reference cited through the use of the index in that reference. The reader may also find many of these concepts listed in the indexes of other standard books on psychology and behavioral science.

personal framework. His difficulty lay in being preoccupied with his "weakness" rather than attributing his anxiety and its consequences to the conflict he was experiencing.*

Ben's self-involvement is so great that he sees the fraternity only in terms of what it can do for him. He has not demonstrated how he could be of value to the fraternity.

Ben's difficulties are "ego-syntonic." Like the alcoholic or drug addict, he enjoys his *behavior* and feels regret or anxiety only for the unfortunate *consequences* of his behavior. Having discerned his parents' ambitions for him, he is doing his best to "torpedo" them — for example, by failing to get high enough grades and by running up a bill at the country club. Should the case be formulated or interpreted in terms of a characterological problem (passive-aggressive) rather than in terms of anxiety neurosis?

Did Ben manipulate the counselor? The counselor gave in and saw Ben after the secretary reported that he was distraught and in tears.

---

* We might ask: At his level of maturity and with his anxiety, can we expect any more effective behavior than defensiveness, seeing himself as weak? Only as the anxiety is reduced, and his security as a person increases, can he come to grips with the conflict objectively.

FRANK

The Indebted Son

Frank represents the rather serious individual with a wide range of interests and activities, who seeks supportive counseling as he tries to discover who he is and what he might become. He represents the student from a small community who meets conflicting values and pressures in college. He was followed through his self-initiated contacts with the counselor, over a period of twenty years, to his present status as a happily married, professional man and contributor to society. The case presents the customary test results and biographical information obtained in counseling as well as a cursory glimpse of his motivation and adjustment patterns.

IDENTIFICATION

Frank was tall and well proportioned, not very different in appearance from other freshmen except for the thick glasses which he had worn since he was a small boy. Although his features were symmetrical and he might be regarded as good looking, his glasses and rounded face gave the net effect of "just another big boy." He had grown up in a town of about 4,000 population in the Middle West. He had been a superior student in high school and probably outranked the class in academic potential, although he had never used it to its fullest. It might be hypothesized that he had a reputation as a good, solid boy in his community.

Frank had pledged one of the better-known fraternities on the campus and had made a fairly good adjustment to it. The boys liked him, kidded with him, and coined an affectionate nickname for him. He was not considered an outstanding leader, but he was certainly not a "loser." He spoke his mind at fraternity meetings if he thought he had a contribution to make, but did not jump up to address himself to every issue. When he took a position on an issue he could be very serious, but a few minutes later he might laugh at a joke or even at his own seriousness.

Frank would like to have been more outstanding in his fraternity. Among the star athletes, "big daters," boys with handsome cars, and "activity men" he felt unimportant, and he contrasted his situation unhappily with his popularity in high school. Moreover, Frank had come from a conservative, almost puritanical community, and although he did not specifically say so, he *felt uncomfortable* at times with the other fraternity members' freer behavior and attitudes toward religion, sex, and drinking.

OCCASION FOR INTERVIEW

While Frank was taking a course taught by the counselor, he came into the office one day and said, "I'd like to talk with you some time about tests that I might take to find out what would be the best field for me to enter." He went on to relate some of his ideas about a possible vocation. He had enjoyed studying science in high school and had considered the possibility of going into medicine or some phase of biological research. He was taking a course in physiology and leading the class. His teacher was strongly encouraging him to think about graduate work.

Early in the interview and in filling out the *Pre-Interview Blank,** Frank came to grips with his search for personal identity. He felt somewhat guilty about not getting better grades. He said, "Naturally, in a small high school I won some scholastic honors, and I got started early as a debater, so I learned to speak readily on my feet. This helped me. I also participated in athletics; in fact, I went out for almost everything and did fairly well. But I never was the superior student that I should have been and I realize it now."

EARLY LIFE

Frank showed no reluctance to explore his relationship to his parents. "My parents are spending a lot of money sending me to college. Because I am the only child, they are expecting me to amount

* See pages 314–316.

to something, and I just can't let them down. My parents have a wonderful attitude. They have said that my future is the most important thing in their lives. They are not going to dictate it. They are going to leave it up to me to do whatever I want, and they will assume full financial responsibility for my education. I know that I am always on their minds and in their daily conversation. When I go home and walk down the main street, everyone I meet seems to know details of my life at school and reflects the hopes and expectations of my family."

Frank was highly appreciative of his family's support, but felt overwhelmed by the heavy responsibility of it. "My parents are making sacrifices for me, and sometimes *I wonder whether I am worth it.* I am certainly not making the grades right now to merit their hard work and hopes."

Frank described his father as quick-tempered and hard to know. He said, "I guess he is the typical, small-town merchant. He knows a number of people, he is a good businessman, and he is aggressive." He described his mother as broad-minded and talented, one who mixed well with people and who had created a fine home.

Frank had enjoyed good health and physical vigor throughout his life, except for poor eyesight. He had always been an athlete and had won letters throughout his school years. He played in all major sports and was captain of several teams. He dated about as much as the average high school student, went to all the proms, and enjoyed being a part of teen-age groups.

COUNSELING EVENTS

The counselor reassured Frank and encouraged him to continue to explore in the interview his interests and attitudes, his previous accomplishments, and the avenues open to him for future achievement.

Frank was the kind of student who appreciated the interest his instructors showed in him, and he often raised questions, both during and outside of his classes. Although he was not at all fawning in manner, he sometimes walked with the instructor back to his office to talk about an issue. He was one of the few students on the campus who seemed to like their teachers as well as their contemporaries.

In describing his relationships with girls in a *Pre-Interview Blank*, Frank wrote,

> *My intentions have always been honorable. I have dated widely, and I have no regrets. I have had some warm friendships among members of both sexes. I have traveled about as much as any American boy my age, usually in the summers with my family.* [He was doubtless the "clean-cut regular fellow," who participated in extracurricular activities and sports, with whom mothers could trust their daughters, and whom the other fellows accepted.]
>
> *I think I am more serious than most people my age and I don't know why. I seem to fear myself most of all and I worry about my future. I am normal in my attraction to girls and, like most people, I have tended to go overboard a couple of times — that is, I've liked a girl more than she liked me. Athletics have been of great value in my life. I have gone to Sunday school since early childhood, and I guess religion means more to me than it does to the average college student, although some things about it are rather vague.*

Frank wrote this statement and many of the other quotations on a *Pre-Interview Blank* calling for a survey of contemporary activities, attitudes, and a brief but broad survey of his early history. It is the best glimpse we are able to get into his inner life. There is the intimation of some feelings of insecurity and anxiety, but apparently the anxiety is channeled through planning and good work habits, and acts as constructive motivation. In this sense he represents the large segment of our Western culture that regards introspection as unwholesome and turns to activities to achieve success and satisfaction.*

Frank continued to participate in intramural athletics in college, was active in his fraternity, and represented them in a few campus-wide groups. He dated less than the average fraternity member, but this was in line with his preference. His score on the *Thurstone Personality Inventory*, containing items concerned with psychoneurotic symptoms, indicated that he was aware of more symptoms than the average college student. However, in counseling sessions he talked less about symptoms than about plans and intentions for the present and future.

* See Riesman (92).

OUTCOME

Frank's grades improved steadily during his college years. He was on the Dean's List and did well enough in his junior and senior years to be encouraged to pursue graduate work. For a time he could not decide whether he should continue as a graduate student in physiology or go into medicine. He earned a Master's degree in physiology, then switched to medicine, received his M.D., served his internship, and went into medical research. He then pursued a Ph.D. degree in physiology while teaching in a medical school. He was an average graduate student — not brilliant, but a good, careful laboratory worker, productive of scientific publications.

Post-college life

Frank spent several years in military service during World War II, adjusted to it better than the average man, and served with a medical outfit in combat zones. When he returned to the States, he rejoined the staff of a medical school, was married, and continued to do research and publish his findings. This led to eventual recognition in his field, and today, at forty years of age, he is not only a respected medical educator, but an established and publishing scientist.

His wife is an outgoing, attractive woman of about the same age as Frank. She has a college education and seems intelligent and alert and interested in current events. She evidently enjoys the roles of companion to her husband, mother, and homemaker. Their values seem to be based less on status and conformity than on living a satisfactory, meaningful life in terms of the roles for which their backgrounds have prepared them. Their home is built around their children, three boys and one girl. The living room boasts a few relatively inexpensive original paintings, but the floor and furniture show the wear of hard daily use by the children in play. Any time Frank takes off from his work is devoted to family activities. His wife assumes most of the home responsibilities, such as budgeting, banking, purchasing, and chauffeuring the children around. Their activities are like those of many suburbanites, frequently shared with small groups of friends who have similar interests and values; their attitudes, however, are more like those of a faculty couple. They have a daily cocktail while the children are having their supper. Little information is available about the details of their marital life, but on the surface it seems to run smoothly, with neither member being overly dominant. There seems to be a sharing of responsibilities, and their roles in the home seem to be well integrated.

Frank continues to show a *serious attitude* with a strong emphasis on *achievement*. He works hard, and apparently continues to show a certain amount of the *tension* which was seen in him as a college student. When under stress he has a slight nervous facial twitch. However, he also has a good sense of humor, which allows him to relax with friends and to enjoy the pranks of his children. He says he does not get enough time for physical recreation — something that had meant so much to him in college — but he is trying now to discover the best division of time between hard work in the laboratory, play with his family, and association with his friends. He is more interested in current affairs than the average individual — even more so than most members of his profession — and maintains a liberal political outlook. At present he is looking forward to sabbatical leave. He hopes to apply for a research or teaching grant with an academic or scientific foundation so that he may go abroad, possibly to Japan for a year. He plans to take the whole family for the educational value it will afford them. His wife is equally enthusiastic about the places they will visit. They are busy reading about the Far East and collecting travel brochures.

Interpretive remarks

Frank is similar to many middle-class individuals in our American culture — he places strong emphasis on achievement, sports, social activities, and on solving problems of identity by action and achievement. Frank would be seen by many Americans as a success.

FRANK: Life Patterns and Influential Factors

What personality patterns are evidenced in Frank? Give your spontaneous reactions before turning to the questions below.

Outstanding characteristics

a. How would you describe Frank to someone who was about to enter a personal or professional relationship with him?

b. Were his positions as an only child and as a small-town boy important influences?

c. What constancies and changes do you see in him from the time he sought counseling to his role as scientist and father?

Salient interpersonal influences

   a. Was Frank affected by the heterogeneous values and forces represented in a college fraternity?

   b. Did sports and high-school achievements play a significant role in Frank's life?

   c. What was the value of educational and vocational commitments in Frank's life?

Concepts helpful in understanding Frank

   a. Compulsiveness channeled in the normal range of personality adjustment (*103, 121*)

   b. A compromise between some of the conflicting values in American culture (*26*, particularly pp. 301–317; *92*)

   c. Repression of certain conflicts and defensive use of activity within non-pathological bounds (*2, 74*)

   d. Existential commitments which make his life meaningful to him and his family (*3, 77*)

   e. Achievement motive (*68*)

HARRY

The Father Fighter

Harry was a youth who had suffered from epilepsy since childhood. He had experienced rejection by his peers and felt a lack of understanding by his father. He received non-directive counseling periodically during his college years, usually at times when he had experienced an interpersonal crisis. He was not given special psychological tests, but intelligence-test scores and grades were available. Peer rating scales were used to help him obtain a realistic view of the attitudes of his contemporaries toward him. Discussions of his relationships with college peers and authority figures are augmented with a paraphrased autobiographic short story. The presentation contains a brief report by a college psychiatrist and data from two follow-up interviews, at ten- and twenty-year intervals after graduation. The follow-up data shed light on his later adjustment, financial status, and personal attitudes. A reaction to the case by a graduate student in clinical psychology is appended.

IDENTIFICATION

When Harry walked into the counselor's office, he immediately created a good impression. Although tall and thin, he was well proportioned and conservatively groomed. He had sandy hair and freckles, and wore glasses. He introduced himself in a mature manner, but after he had talked for five or ten minutes, the counselor saw that his first impression had been misleading. When Harry began to talk, he spoke in a whining monotone, looked off into space, and paid no heed to his listener. He seemed overly conservative, self-centered, somewhat aloof, and highly sensitive.

27

OCCASION FOR INTERVIEW

Harry came to the attention of the counselor when he was referred by the Speech Clinic to the Mental Hygiene Clinic of the University. He made the appointment immediately and was frank in relating his problem. He had suffered convulsions throughout childhood and up until a few years before college. He had recently undergone a brain operation, and now had disturbed hearing. He added that earlier in life he had been highly irritable and had temper tantrums. He said that he maintained very high intellectual and moral standards and was not sympathetic with the typical student. One of his problems, he stated, was a social one; he had come away from home to college mainly to meet new people and to broaden his social life. He talked briefly about his very unhappy childhood. He was sure that his convulsions had set him apart from others, that he had been regarded as a queer individual. He had participated in none of the activities that the others normally enjoyed, and consequently felt awkward and somewhat alone. Harry was one of three children, having a younger brother and sister.

Interview with the speech therapist

The speech therapist who had referred Harry met with the counselor and presented some of her findings about Harry. She indicated that Harry had a severe hearing loss in one ear, but that his speech was improving, and that he took suggestions well. She was most concerned about his total adjustment. She said he had become quite friendly with a slightly older student named Bob, whom "he seemed to worship." They shared a common interest in music. Bob would enter a campus beer hangout, go to the piano, and play ostentatiously; Harry would tag along with Bob to these places. The speech therapist had been told that Harry was generally disliked because of his behavior in class. He had a condescending attitude and made himself unpopular by playing up the errors of other students. She felt his association with Bob would only alienate him further. She also felt that Harry's strong tendency to want sympathy and to talk about his problems might stand in the way of working out realistic solutions to them.

Harry said that Bob had done a great deal for him. Bob had taught him methods of study, brought him out of his "shell," and helped him to lose some of his narrow-minded prejudices. Bob was helping him to formulate his beliefs more clearly. He had been spending more time with fellows his own age, fostering hope that he might become "more like the other guys."

PERSONAL HISTORY

Ability, achievement, and test scores

Before Harry arrived for his first interview with the counselor, records were obtained on his scholastic ability and previous achievement. Harry's percentile score on the *Ohio Psychological Test* placed him above 92 per cent of the freshmen taking the test. His high school grade rank, indicating achievement, was at a similar level — 87th percentile. He clearly had ability superior to that of the average college freshman. While he was a freshman he completed the *Thurstone Personality Inventory*; his answers placed him definitively outside the normal range in terms of psychoneurotic symptoms. His grades the first semester ranged from A to D; the D was in French, a course he disliked, largely, he said, because he could not get along with the teacher. His methods of study, as he described them, were regular and quite systematic.

In referring to his health, he said he had about 50 per cent of the visual and auditory capacity of the average person. He admitted feeling inferior and apprehensive about the future. He had begun to spend time in bull sessions with friends, but he tended to schedule these as he did his study time. He had a strong aversion to wasting time — an example of the extreme emphasis he placed on *controlling* his life, which we will see again in other contexts.

Traits and attitudes

Harry indicated that he thought he had certain assets, such as his appearance, his reputation, his musical and mechanical abilities, his sincerity, and his determination. He had already decided to enter the field of accounting and to work toward becoming a Certified Public Accountant. He stated that he was consciously trying to compensate for his inability to get along with people his own age. He rated himself as average in happiness and emotional stability but below average in ability to get along with other people. He felt quite confident about the ultimate fulfillment of his ambitions and gave himself a superior rating on this. He indicated the following areas of marked sensitivity: evaluation of mistakes, self-control, and sex control.

The following are some of the adjectives, from a checklist of traits, that he underlined as descriptive of himself: ambitious, over-conscientious, industrious, nervous, quick-tempered, persistent, individualistic, contemptuous, too serious, sensitive, hard-boiled, dependable, stubborn, often lonely, easily discouraged, and easily hurt. The counselor felt that the above listing reflected an accurate estimation of Harry.

Parents and childhood experiences

Harry described his parents as strict, almost puritanical. He said his mother had always encouraged him to live according to his own standards, but his father had imposed standards upon him which alienated him from the average youth. He was aware of his father's ambivalence toward him: on the one hand he felt his father was very proud of doing everything he could for him; on the other, he felt his father had tried to mold him too rigidly in his own image. Harry believed, however, that this molding by his father had caused him to mature earlier in life. He expressed appreciation for the thousands of dollars his father had spent on his health and training. Despite the violent conflicts he had with his father, he maintained that he admired him and would give his life to protect him. He felt that he had disappointed and disgraced his father by not being better able to control himself. Harry regarded his siblings as sympathetic and admiring, although he rarely mentioned them. He saw them in terms of their response to him rather than as individuals with needs and desires of their own.

He gave a long history of accidents, including two broken limbs, a brain condition, impaired vision and hearing, and being struck by a delivery truck when he was a child. These physical defects had kept him from participating in athletics. He had played very little with other children. The only dates he had had all occurred within the previous year. He felt he had few friends and many enemies. According to Harry, he had argued with teachers and was "mean and stupid" during the primary grades. Although he later grew less antisocial and became a better student, he was still stubborn in dealing with teachers. He was not a member of any organized religious group; he professed belief in personal worship. He ended this survey of himself by saying his physical condition had caused him to feel inferior and depressed all his life, but more acutely so in high school.

COUNSELING EVENTS

The counselor supported Harry in his program of social growth and in his attempt to work out his own standards of conduct. Several interest groups that had open membership were suggested to Harry and within a month Harry had shown considerable social growth, largely the result of his own initiative. He had gone to a dance and felt he was getting better acquainted with more typical students. Harry had joined several small groups around the campus, including a "leadership group." One of the projects of this group was fingerprinting students, and Harry was quite enthusiastic about it. He also attended the social meetings of a student religious group.

During each interview Harry expressed and examined his strong feelings, occasionally relating details of traumatic events in his early life. For example, he talked about several physical encounters that he had had with his father, in which both of them were bruised for a week. His father had rigid rules — for example, he prevented Harry from driving the car or going places where he might meet people his own age. A visit at home made Harry realize how much he had been developing socially while he was away at school and how strongly he tended to be in conflict with his father.

In one session Harry described the kind of boy he regarded as an ideal, but said he had met few such individuals. He described this ideal person as quiet, well-mannered, studious and capable, socially oriented but controlled in social situations, and conservatively dressed. He described himself as "a Ford with a Cadillac carburetor," whereas his image of the ideal fellow was "a Cadillac with a Cadillac carburetor." (It is interesting that he used a machine analogy in talking about himself and describing his personality.)

In grade school he was humiliated when the other children labeled him with disparaging nicknames, such as "bottlehead" to ridicule his haircut. He had wanted to fight back; but since he couldn't, he became very angry. He had violent disagreements with teachers, at which times he was sent to the principal's office for discipline. Several times in school he had had epileptic seizures during which he lost consciousness. He once had a seizure while driving a car, resulting in damage to his own and two other cars. He added that the medication he had been taking since the brain surgery had made him much calmer, and he had had fewer attacks.

Ratings by associates

Harry expressed an interest in knowing how his friends saw him, so that he might use this information for self-improvement. The counselor cooperated by giving Harry some rating scales which he could distribute among his friends. They were to be filled out and sent anonymously to the counselor's office. Harry was not to know who had said what, but some of the comments that were made about him were read to him. A sample scale is given below.

Emotional stability — Consider whether his desires and purposes are unified, if he is consistent, acts with ease and self-confidence, is emotionally controlled or has major conflicts between ideals and behavior, is irritated by or sensitive to many matters, has numerous fears and worries or peculiarities.

5%	20%	50% of students		20%	5%
Very poor	Poor	Below Average	Above Average	Good	Excellent

He was rated by two acquaintances as low in emotional stability, social adjustment, and leadership; average in appearance; and superior in integrity. There was considerable agreement among the raters as to his traits. These ratings were not appreciably different from his own, except on the matter of emotional stability; he regarded himself as being more stable than others did.

Harry seemed to have considerable insight into his own difficulties — and strong motivations concerning the course of future development, based on a fairly clear view of his needs. This observation is important in light of the follow-up (to be presented later), after Harry had been out of school a number of years. During that time he had been active in the workaday world, and had become a husband and father.

Harry mentioned several times that many of his attitudes were changing; he even pointed to the specific persons and events that had helped him. He mentioned Bob especially. He had also met another boy who was helping him with his botany, a subject with which he was having great difficulty. Part of the difficulty stemmed from conflict with his teacher.

Harry felt that he was not as narrow-minded as he had been in the past. On several occasions he talked about going back home to show people how much he had developed, or in his words, "to throw my accomplishments in their faces." This achievement need was also the motive behind his desire to organize a campus-wide club, with himself as leader.

By the end of the first semester the counselor noted that Harry had shown considerable progress in his social adjustment. He had discovered that some students could respect him, although he retained a certain amount of *ambivalence toward most other students.* On the whole, the counselor felt that Harry had become less tense and more at ease with people his own age.

Harry was somewhat in conflict about whether he should stay in school for the summer term. His mother, who seemed to be a very accepting person and who understood his relationship with his father, visited him before the semester closed. Apparently, one reason he wanted to stay and attend the summer session was that his friend was going to be in school. In addition he felt he could consolidate some of the gains he had made during the second semester if he remained away from his father. He decided to enroll in the summer school.

As it turned out, Harry did not stay for summer school but instead got a job selling bus tickets. When he returned in the fall, he felt that he had merely coasted, in terms of his development, during the summer. However, his dread of school had definitely been reduced with the success of his last semester. In addition, he had made a few discoveries about himself during the summer, such as his tendency to exaggerate his accomplishments in talking with people, and his great inability to lose himself in the activities of a group. He realized that most of the time he was with other people was spent thinking about himself and his own needs. On the other hand, he also noted that he was more comfortable with them than ever before.

When Harry returned in September of the following year, the counselor met with him at the request of a doctor in the student infirmary. Harry had entered the infirmary complaining of severe headaches. The physician gave him aspirins, and he felt better almost immediately, although he remained in the infirmary overnight. After the student health physician looked at Harry's medical history, she had a conference with the counselor. It was the physician's impression that this was a functional syndrome.* Harry described his symptoms to the counselor as follows: "Something seemed to click in my head and my eye all of sudden became blind; then I got a terrible headache. I had been worrying about registration, what courses I

* Physical symptoms with apparent psychological origin.

should take, and how well I would do in them." He added that he had been thinking seriously about entering law school, with the idea of handling the legal side of his father's business, but had decided against it.

Early in the conversation he jumped from the reason for his "hospitalization" to a review of the accomplishments he had made during the previous summer and his present subjective status. He indicated that he was less afraid of his father, that he now openly told his father where he was going and how long he planned to stay. Previously he had been afraid to go out of the house without getting permission.

He went out beer-drinking with the boys — something of which his father strongly disapproved. He also associated with some of the boys in a fraternity that was known for its drinking parties, although he had not yet attended any of their parties. He said, "I don't yet feel I have come far enough socially to ask a girl for a date. I still feel pretty miserable at a dance. I come home feeling like I've plowed the fields all day long. I still don't think too much of myself and I certainly don't want to date a girl who is like me, because it would have a bad effect on both of us."

He talked at some length about his friend Bob and what Bob had done for him in the past year. He said, "Once when Bob was drinking heavily, he told me he had used me for a guinea pig. I don't mind it, because he has done me a lot of good. He taught me how to study; he took me to places where I wouldn't have gone otherwise; he helped me to meet other people; and he broke down some of my prejudices. I am a less narrow person because of him. I guess other boys have tried to do this for me in the past, but I was not able to follow their lead. I know I have made progress in my relationships with fellow students, but I still have a long way to go."

The counselor noted that Harry seemed to view the social world as a hierarchy, and to admire, at least from a distance, the glamorous, superficial person as one at the top. Moreover, Harry realized and frankly stated that he was very much unlike the kind of person he placed on this pedestal, had very little in common with him, and felt awkward in his presence. This statement and his attitude about dating a girl like himself give us some information about Harry's *self-concept*.

At a later interview he talked about a double date which was arranged for him by a new friend, Jim, who seemed to have an easy relationship with girls. This new friend had also had some brain surgery. He was a fine-looking, somewhat outgoing, bright, but unstable fellow, with many conflicts. He did not make the grades he wanted to achieve. It was not difficult to see why Harry chose him as a friend. The double dating, however, was not satisfactory. They went out in Jim's car, and before they had driven very far Jim had his arm around his girl. When they later parked, Harry found himself uncomfortable and awkward and constantly contrasting himself with Jim, who seemed to be completely in command of the situation and thoroughly enjoying himself. Harry said, "I got so nervous I wanted to scream. When the girl who was necking with Jim in the front seat turned around and said, 'What's the matter with you-all?', I just didn't know how to respond. It upset me so I couldn't sleep that night. To top this off, I went to a meeting of a church group that Sunday, and there were the two girls who had been on the date. I just about decided then that I wouldn't date for a year or so. This experience also strained the relationship that I had with Jim, a relationship that I had looked upon hopefully." During this counseling session Harry talked about his high ideals, about the way he was brought up and how difficult it was to reconcile this with Jim's behavior and the double-date experience.

Several "crises" prompting further counseling

Harry made a special appointment and came in quite depressed, following a period of six months during which the counselor had had practically no contact with Harry. As far as the counselor knew, Harry was adjusting rather well. Harry reported that he had had a major argument with the woman who ran the boarding house where he ate. He said, "I was talking to several of the boys in my normal manner, and she came in and said, 'What can't you do, Harry? You think you are a big shot and this and that. You really think you are great, don't you? You are always boasting and talking so loud they can hear you downtown.' I lost my temper and told her this was none of her business and to keep her nose out of my affairs. I don't know exactly what I said, but it wasn't very polite. Her husband came out and the boys had to separate us. Her husband told me among other things, to stay out of the house and not to come back again. I replied that if a friend of mine lived in this house and I wanted to visit him, I would come back.

"This happened Friday," he continued, "and I was depressed through the entire weekend. I could not help thinking about my faults and defects. My grades are going down, and my epileptic fits are getting worse. I don't know what I'll be like when I am middle-aged. I am not making any social progress. I can't date."

He continued in this vein for fifteen or twenty minutes. Then he began to talk about trying to get back into social life by learning how to bowl and by going more often to the Sunday-night meetings of the student religious group. He speculated about the possibility of dating girls from a nearby girls' college.

The counselor in the meantime had listened supportively to his cathartic outburst and had been somewhat reassuring. Harry ended the session by saying that he planned to have a stag party that very night for some of his friends. He thought it would be a good bull session and added, "I am just learning how to do this sort of thing." *

The following semester another episode occurred which again brought Harry in contact with the counselor. (Again, there had been relatively little interim contact between him and the counselor. He apparently had formed some friendships and contacts which allowed him to make a fairly satisfactory adjustment. Combined with his strong feeling of independence, these associations had helped him to handle his problems without assistance from the counselor.) A student had reported to the Dean of Students that he awakened in the night and found his roommate, Tom, standing over him with a long knife in his hand. He was greatly frightened. Tom had been discharged from military service after psychiatric hospitalization and had had several episodes on the campus which appeared to have psychiatric implications. He was hospitalized immediately in the student infirmary, and plans were made to transfer him to a VA hospital. Some of the students in the house were packing Tom's clothes and other belongings when Harry entered the room in a highly emotional state. He knew Tom and had heard that he was in the university hospital. He now demanded to know whether Tom was being moved out at his own request or at the instigation of the boys.

The counselor was called to the house. Harry approached and spoke to the counselor as he entered Tom's room, in which several students had gathered.

Harry said, "I knew Tom very well. In fact he is one of the few

* This kind of conference is not unusual to a counselor. A student comes in depressed and emotionally upset, and the counselor calmly encourages him to talk out his feelings. He in turn will reflect and clarify these feelings, while maintaining a supportive attitude. After a while the client begins to place himself and his environment in a wider perspective and often ends by deciding on a course of action.

fellows that really understands me. We have similar problems, I think. I have had spells like the ones he is having. He is a screwball; he won't admit it and he is putting up a front, but that is no reason to treat him like a baby. I saw him in one of these spells one day, when we were in a dive downtown. He saw a girl that reminded him of someone he had loved early in life who had been killed. He went wild. He took out a knife and began threatening everybody in the place. I took hold of him, walked him home, and put him to bed. He seemed to be out of his mind, but I knew that he wasn't going to do anything. I heard that story his roommate told, and apparently he was acting very similar to the way he behaved in that bar the night I took him home.

"Tom is a good student. He is working hard, but he just flunked a quiz, and that is what put him in this state. He really is very fond of his roommate and I think his roommate knows it. I think his roommate is just a coward and cannot face him." (Incidentally, Tom's roommate not only was afraid of Tom, but felt that Harry might want to avenge the injustice and pursue him with a shotgun.)

After Harry had given this story, he became uncontrollably tearful, turned away from the counselor, and sat on the bed. Before long he gained control of himself and turned around, with tears still streaming down his face, to join the conversation among the students in the room. When Tom was hospitalized, Harry became reconciled, and the issue was closed.

Another semester passed before the counselor had any further contact with Harry. Then he came in one day complaining about a teacher who, he reported, was making life unbearable for him. (Undoubtedly the teacher felt the same way about Harry.) In class Harry challenged the teacher, who was probably autocratic in his methods. The teacher maintained the dominant position, leaving Harry frustrated and unable to do anything but walk the streets for an hour or two. He said that during the interval he was in conflict with this professor he had often gone to the pool hall. He was so aggressive that he had knocked the pool balls almost off the table, but he had felt better when he finished the game.

He mentioned that he became irrational whenever he lost his temper. Several times when he was younger, he felt that he had come close to killing his father. As he talked about this, he admitted that with time he had gained more control. "What I fear most," said Harry, "is either getting out of control and fighting madly or else bursting into tears. Either reaction would put me back in the same position that I was in as a child in school, puzzling my fellow students and disgracing myself." (This explains why Harry had such a strong need to control his behavior.)

He talked about several incidents that occurred on the campus when he had taken the part of another student who was an "underdog," or when he had been *defeated by someone in authority*; he either became violently angry or turned to the wall, sobbing. Harry had left this conference without indicating what he was going to do about the situation, but with greater calmness and more perspective.

About a week later he stopped the counselor on the street and said that he had gone into the autocratic professor's office and had a long talk with him. He had gotten a better grade than he thought he would on one of the quizzes, and this may have mended the relationship to some extent. He said he was beginning to *feel differently* about the professor and the course; until this time he had not imagined that he could possibly pass it or even continue going to class. Now he thought he could earn a passing grade.

Psychiatric evaluation

Again, a long period ensued between the last interview and the next contact with Harry. The counselor was out of town, but in his absence referred Harry by mail to a psychiatrist in the Student Health Service. The following is a full report of the psychiatrist's examination of Harry, including an evaluation of his present emotional status and prognosis for the future. It gives us another assessment of Harry.

> Presenting problem: *inability to complete Certified Public Accountants' examination because of the tension and panic-like reaction which he develops.*
>
> Present illness: *In June of this year the student had gone to take the state CPA examination. However, before he could complete it, he became extremely tense and panicky and returned to his home without having completed it. At that time he wrote to the clinical psychologist who counseled him, asking about a drug which his father had read about in the newspapers. This drug was myanesin. It was suggested that he come to talk to the psychologist when he came back to school. The student returned to school and went to see him about this drug and also about his inability to complete the examination. It was quite evident that he had had a great deal of emotional disturbance for a number of years.*

Personal history: The patient was the oldest of a family of two sons and one daughter in an upper-class Protestant family of British descent. His father was a self-made man who had a college education, was in real estate, and had many financial connections. The patient described the father as being extremely domineering and very tyrannical, while the mother was more passive and meek and attempted to shield the children. The other two children were in good health, but although the patient described them as having difficulty with the father, the counseling psychologist felt they were much more mature than the patient. The younger brother was in college; the sister was married and attended a university in a big city. The patient said that as a child he was rather clumsy and had difficulty in learning how to walk and run. He was overweight, so that when he was in high school they placed him on thyroid extract. He began having epileptic seizures when he was about fourteen or fifteen and was taken to a neurological specialist in Los Angeles. Apparently he had both petit mal and grand mal attacks, and there was some evidence of localization in his left upper extremity. A craniotomy was performed, and it was found that there was considerable scarring in the right occipital cortex. Nothing was done except to close the operating wound. At this time it was discovered that he had a complete left homonymous hemianopsia. There was a hearing defect bilaterally, which was apparently more severe on the right. He continued to have epileptic seizures and was placed on dilantin and phenobarbital. For three years he was on phenobarbital alone. At about this time he had the emotional upset in which he attempted suicide. He was placed in a sanatorium in Los Angeles and put back on dilantin. He has continued to take the dilantin.

After finishing high school the student went to a university and apparently made very excellent grades in his undergraduate work. He always led a very isolated and schizoid existence. He planned to take the CPA examination again in two states. After that, he apparently wished to join his father's office and handle the accounting phase of the business. However, he stated that he did not want to do this, but there was no evidence that he would attempt anything else. He apparently has never had any strong heterosexual attachments. He has led a rather isolated existence throughout his college career.

Self-concept as seen in an autobiographical story

In the latter part of his freshman year, after he had had several interviews with the counselor, Harry brought in a story which was obviously autobiographical. He had written it as an English assignment. It was entitled "The Outcome." When the counselor read it, he was somewhat surprised at how openly Harry could discuss feelings which he had been unable to deal with directly in the interviews. Much was learned about Harry's view of himself and of those around him through this story. The story, which was long in the original, is paraphrased below:

The story is told by a person viewing Henry, the central character. The narrator says that he sees Henry standing on a fire escape with one foot on the railing as though he were about to jump. He observes a fine-looking, well-dressed, attractive young man who is nineteen, but who has the appearance of a man in his middle twenties. Henry seems calm and composed, but this front is misleading, the narrator tells us. Henry tells him that he has tried and tried to get along in the world and now he is tired of fighting. Everywhere he has turned he has been rebuffed. Moreover, he feels that his emotions have nearly licked him; the many blows and their effects have caused him to lose all will to fight.

The narrator readily understands that Henry has had a hard time; that there has been a sequence of events, each of which seemed small at the time; but that the cumulative effect was enough to break the will of even a strong person. Then various events in Henry's life were reviewed, especially those that occurred during the early years, when no one knew what was wrong with him. "Some thought he was crazy, others thought he was spoiled; yet despite these handicaps Henry continued to achieve. Even his father failed to understand him; he thought the boy was spoiled. Not only did his father fail to help, but he would not let Henry fight his battles alone." We get a picture of a domineering father who nagged and used severe physical punishment, tended to fly into rages, and prescribed unrealistic restrictions. "He thought Henry too young to date or drive a car. He insisted that he should be working, that there was little need for play or teen-age loafing. Why should a young person have a car when there was bus service throughout the city? Not only did he prohibit Henry from having a car, but in addition he even forbade him to ride in a car with another teenager. There were scenes in front of Henry's friends; Henry was forbidden to go out and was sent up to his room, while his friends stood waiting, embarrassed, in the front hall.

"With time his epilepsy-like seizures began to increase in number and intensity. The doctors his father consulted did not seem to know the cause of his difficulty, but did not readily refer him to a specialist. At last the seizures became so serious that Henry was taken to a specialist in another city. At the large city hospital he felt that he was treated more like an experimental animal than a person. This led him to raise questions with the nurses, but they merely referred him to the doctor. He had a brain operation at this time, and the post-operative examination led to a judgment that the operation had been a success.

"Instead of improving his relationship with his fellow students, his return from the hospital merely aroused curiosity on their part. He had to wear bandages, and he was teased about this. He was asked if someone had met him in a dark alley, whether this was the costume of a nut, and he was jeered in other ways. This rejection by his fellows merely caused him to work harder and make better grades, but before long he had another discouragement. The mild episodes began to recur. This was very disappointing to him as he had had the impression that the operation would cure him entirely. Still he did not give up; he was intelligent, and his school work would furnish an outlet for achievement."

The narrator at this point comments on what a truly fine fellow Henry is — a person who shows character and respectable traits despite his difficulties. Henry continues with the complaint that he cannot sleep at night, that his brothers and sisters make too much noise, that he is continuing to have seizures, that he is on edge, and that the people who come in contact with him almost universally misinterpret him as a person. Some think he is crazy, some think he is short-tempered, and others regard him as a braggart. Again he said he wondered whether the struggle was worth it. The friendly narrator tells us that he lets Henry talk, letting him get all of this off his chest.

Henry ended the recitation of his discouragement by adding, "Father took me to a psychiatrist, who treated me like I was on trial for murder. After the interview my father had a private conference with the psychiatrist. He came out saying that the psychiatrist had labeled me a neurotic and suggested I be put in an asylum."

Henry ended his soliloquy by saying very firmly, "I am going to commit suicide." At that time he had a gun which he kept in his drawer and he flashed it as he made the remark. The narrator in the story frantically assured him he was not at the end of his rope and urged him to continue to fight. He reminded Henry of his assets and previous achievements. Henry replied, "I have been trying right along and the dirty, soulless, self-centered beasts around here continue to kick me, even when I'm down they continue to kick me! Did anyone really try to understand that I had a brain tumor and was not insane or spoiled? No! they merely became hateful gossips! I can't win in this cock-eyed world and you know it. I can't fight and cheat and tear other people apart to succeed. You know how hard I've worked, and what do I get — snubs, sarcasm, scorn! I even have a reputation for a nasty disposition among the teachers."

His friend, the narrator of the story, continued to encourage him, pointing out that he had improved in all respects and that his effort had not been in vain. "No!" said Henry, "I'm not going to give those creatures another chance!" With this, both feet were on the rail of the fire escape and over he went.

The narrator concludes, ". . . and I saw a fine intelligent individual with the possibilities of a great future become the victim of a cruel, heartless world which was made not by the creative forces in nature but by the terrible forces in man."

What does this story tell us about Harry? How does Harry really see the world, his fellow human beings, and himself? Note the sympathy and affection of the narrator, an imaginative friend. To what extent does this story satisfy a need for a sympathetic listener and a warm friend? Does it also satisfy a need for self-punishment or for pity? You may want to come back to this story after you have finished the case and re-evaluate its meaning when you are acquainted with the way Harry's life turned out at middle age.

FOLLOW-UP

After a ten-year period, during which there was no contact between Harry and the counselor, Harry one day dropped into the counselor's office. This was the first of two hour-long visits, the second occurring after still another ten years had passed. These two sessions give a rough picture of the course of Harry's development from his college years into professional life, as followed by a single counselor.

On the first of these visits Harry was approximately twenty-eight years of age and unmarried. He had established himself as an accountant, working in part with his father, and had developed a highly lucrative practice. By his own admission he was a hard worker, doing little besides working a very full day in the office and sleeping ten hours every night, a habit he had developed in college. When tension mounted to a critical point, he left town and visited his former instructors and friends. He belonged to a lodge and stopped to meet his fellow members in the lodge headquarters whenever he went through a city. He engaged in whatever type of recreation was supplied in the clubrooms — card-playing, pool, etc. — and met some new people. He did all of this to keep from being lonely. The primary motivation for these visits was apparently to show his former teachers and friends that he had been successful. The theme of this session was not very different from those in the sessions ten years earlier. Although his relationship with his father was now more adult in character, he talked about his father's role in the life of the younger siblings in the family.

He was still taking medication for his epileptic condition. Every now and then he tried to reduce the medication, but soon found himself going back to it again. He measured success not only by his daily accomplishments, but by the money he was able to accumulate and invest. He realized that the kind of life he was living was highly stressful and emotionally unhygienic. He saw the life of a university professor as more suited to what he would like. He felt, however, that he had worked out certain ways of living. He had certain rules which he followed in handling his relationship with his father: he stayed away from him as much as possible, and when they became too emotionally excited, he left.

Harry volunteered some factual information about significant events since his last visit. He said, "I flunked out of one professional school, but entered another and succeeded quite well. I have had a few minor accidents which occurred during epileptic episodes." On the whole the counselor thought he could be regarded as financially and vocationally successful, if not happy.

On the second of the visits, 20 years after the initial counseling period, he appeared a little heavier, not as well groomed, and slightly more overbearing, almost arrogant, with more firmly established opinions. The pattern of life he reported was similar to the one he had established in college and described on the previous visit. He required of himself a long day's work followed by a long night of sleep. Thrift, diligence, and sound investments had enabled him to accumulate several hundred thousand dollars. But he hoped to reach an even higher financial goal before retiring to do the kind of work that he liked better.

He had married and had two small boys toward whom he seemed to have a very warm attitude. At the time of this visit he was separated from his wife. He said she had a persecution complex. "She says that her parents dominated her and that she has exchanged their domination for mine. She left me and was awarded custody of the children in the settlement. Eventually her incompetence will force her to give up the children, and I will have to care for them completely." He seemed to be looking forward to this, almost wishing for it. He said, "She was a poor housekeeper and left me and the children for long periods of time. She would just take the car and drive around. I have been liberal with her, but there are certain right and wrong ways to live. There are certain correct and incorrect ways to handle one's finances. You have to have a schedule and live up to it. She failed in all of these respects!"

This session was longer than the others. Harry did most of the talking. He talked about his political position, very much to the "right." He felt that most of the national legislation was not good for the people. He was critical of his secretaries; even though he paid them well he was unable to keep one for very long. He said, "I just work too hard for them and they can't take it." After reciting his accomplishments and his standards and rules of life, he became more confidential and slightly more submissive and said that it had not been all rosy. However, he had triumphed over a number of people who had predicted he would never finish college or be able to enter a profession.

He said his health was not good. His blood pressure was too high and his physician had warned him about the possibility of a circulatory accident. He was unable to control his epilepsy, and he enumerated once again all of his physical handicaps which, though real, emphatically did not deter him from his daily activity. He said he had learned to live with his handicaps but that there were times when he thought it would be wiser, now that he was independent financially, to live a little more easily, perhaps to take a tramp steamer and see some of the world. He realized that this was easier to say than do. He admitted being lonely when he was away from the office and that he spent more than the average period in sleep, but he seemed to accept this as part of the kind of life he had to live.

Interpretive remarks

As the counselor listened to him, Harry became less depressive and less aggressive. His manner in the latter part of the interview became mild, and the counselor detected certain potential insights. Harry seemed to be aware that the life he was living was destructive and self-defeating, that there was a more satisfying way to live; but never did he relinquish his fixed moralistic attitude about hard work, economy, and puritanical righteousness. He believed that his wife and most other people were wrong; that they lived for their impulses and were governed by their feelings. It was as though he could not give up his attitudes, and saw no way to accept an easier, more satisfying life.

A great deal of research has been done concerning the "authoritarian personality," * although some aspects of it are controversial. An authoritarian individual is described as insecure, distrustful of himself, feeling threatened by life, and tending to have a corresponding cognitive style, or manner of perceiving and thinking, which is rigid, specific, and acquiescent. Such individuals show more prejudices against minority groups. They usually have experienced severe punishment in the form of parental aggression and withdrawal of love. To what extent does Harry fit the pattern of an authoritarian personality? To what extent might he be classified as autonomous and free to think openly and creatively about his problems and the people he confronts in life?

HARRY: Life Trends and Influences

What do you see in the life of Harry that is most significant? Give your spontaneous responses before turning to the questions which follow.

Distinctive personal characteristics

    a. Do you recognize a few personal characteristics which are outstanding?

* See Christie and Jahoda (24), McKinney (73), and Ruch (96).

    b. How do you think Harry's view of himself differs from what he would like to be ideally?

    c. If Harry seems highly egocentric, aggressive, and self-punishing, what might be considered the causes of this?

Significant relationships in life history

    a. What are the processes which operated in the relationship between Harry and his father that made the latter so important in his life?

      1. Do you see paradoxes in this interaction?

      2. What information would you seek if you could meet Harry's father?

    b. What role did Harry's big and energetic but defective physical equipment play in his relationship with various people, even in grade school?

      1. With his father?

      2. With males of his own age?

      3. With girls of his own age?

    c. What is the meaning of Harry's protective attitude toward certain people?

    d. What common factor in relationships with other people arouses Harry's aggressive or hostile tendencies?

Concepts helpful in understanding Harry

    a. Adler's concept of compensation (7, 48)

    b. Authoritarian personality (24, 73)

    c. Self-destructive tendencies; suicidal personality (12)

    d. Frustration-aggression hypotheses (12)

HARRY: Comments by a Graduate Student

At one point it is noted that Harry would give his life to protect his father, yet vicious battles are described. Part of his problem seems to involve an *inability* to be *accepting of angry impulses.* He overcontrols, and his anger comes out only as *passive-aggressive* or *explosive* bursts. It is unfortunate that this was not developed in therapy.

What significance can we attach to Harry's defense of Tom, the psychotic boy? Two possibilities come to mind: 1) He needed a "cause." By taking up some great cause he could better experience his own existence. The cause became a *raison d'être*, an attempt at finding self-identity. 2) He seems to have "struck out" in normal young society. No one really needed or wanted him. Here was a person who did need him.

Harry works all day, sleeps all night. Although he has made a very poor (even schizoid) interpersonal adjustment, he has somehow managed to preserve his personal integrity. He has the good sense to take a vacation before he explodes. He is in effect giving himself "milieu therapy."

Milieu therapy represents a divergence from the traditional doctor-patient relationship, typified by one or two hours per week spent in personal confrontation. Milieu therapy is an attempt to utilize the therapeutic potential of the individual's entire environment (or at times, the creation of a therapeutic immunity), to maintain an orientation toward personal growth twenty-four hours a day.

Sleep can sometimes be a way of withdrawing from conflict. In this case it is very important in helping him to use his need for achievement to compensate for failure in other spheres. Throwing oneself into work often serves as an ego defense.

The autobiography has much of the flavor of an "ultimate manifesto" to the world. It is a statement of how he would like to be treated by the world; the whole, unedited version probably contains hints about how he would like to be treated by the therapist. The story seems to indicate suicidal tendencies. What kept him from taking his own life? Ego strengths?

HENRY

The Athletic-Looking Writer

The case of Henry depicts a more or less normal individual, troubled but not incapacitated by emotional problems. His development is followed from his post-Army college days to a follow-up fifteen years later, when he is
married and has a family, and is established in a vocation.
A report of his subjective concerns while in college is included. Writing and dramatics, in addition to a few non-
directive counseling sessions, were among the expressive
outlets he used in seeking adjustment. All of these he
evaluates briefly in his follow-up letters. The presentation
here includes one of the short stories he wrote, which is
thought to reveal his attitudes and feelings as a student.

IDENTIFICATION

Anyone who met Henry on the campus might have been surprised
to learn that he was interested in writing. He had the physique of an
athlete — tall, heavy-set, and broad-shouldered. His posture was
slightly stooped. He was strikingly handsome in a strong, masculine
way, with a dark complexion and clean-cut, even features. He carried
himself with a becoming modesty. When approaching another person, he lifted his head, looked at him directly, and in a deep voice
but quiet manner addressed his listener. Probably it was this combination of well-proportioned physique and handsome countenance, with
a quiet but masculine manner, that made him attractive to others.

This attractiveness was not something that Henry seemed to culti-
vate or even appreciate. In fact he was usually seen coming into
classes alone. Even when he was in military service, he rarely went out
with the other fellows in a group. He was most embarrassed when

48

people assumed that he was active and successful as an athlete. Athletics were among the least of his interests; however, with the encouragement of his father, teachers, and coaches, he had participated in athletics during the elementary grades and in high school. His performance was only average at best; his heart was not in it. In high school he had the same coach his father had had, and the coach's tendency to contrast his abilities with his father's helped to reinforce Henry's ambivalence toward his father. He idealized his father, even though he had very infrequent contact with him (his father and mother were separated). He described the relationship between him and his father as more like that of two brothers. Despite his pleasure at being compared with his father, it was embarrassing that this comparison was always unfavorable, particularly with respect to athletics and social initiative.

OCCASION FOR INTERVIEW

Henry had asked for the interview in a time of "crisis," and doubtless it was such to him: he did not know whether he should stay in school. He was tired of it all; he was perplexed, and he wanted to leave. "This is not the first time I've felt this way," Henry went on to say. "It has occurred every now and then in my life. At times I have handled it by getting drunk alone. I was brought up as a Christian Scientist, and I have never really faced any personal problems before. My technique was to *repress* them. Now I am trying to face my problems because I know I have to. I tried once before to come to a decision, but when I began thinking about making a serious choice, I seemed to go to pieces. Once I did *make a choice*, while I was overseas, and I was quite disturbed about it for several days."

The counselor's first impressions of Henry, as he had seen him sitting in class and as he talked with him briefly a few times after class, were changed when Henry came in for his first interview. In this situation Henry was not as unemotional as he usually appeared. Although he maintained a somewhat impassive expression on his face, he seemed quite tense and jittery, had difficulty sitting still, and wrung his hands as he haltingly tried to talk. He was so nervous that he seemed to jerk. His usually calm voice faltered, and he had difficulty finding ways to express himself.

FAMILY BACKGROUND

Henry saw that one of the important factors in his life was his mother's constant criticism of him for being like his father. He had learned to feel *guilty* about the many similarities of temperament and attitude that others observed in him and his father. Apparently, from his mother's standpoint, his father had turned out badly. Henry at no point supplied the details and did not encourage direct questioning about them. The counselor assumed that Henry's father had been financially irresponsible, had tended to evade difficult situations, and was not as mature as his mother had thought he was when she married him. By seeing shortcomings in his father, whom he respected, Henry experienced conflict, and by recognizing himself as similar to his father he became anxious and unsure of himself and of his decisions. At this point in the counseling, however, this perspective was not clear to Henry.

The counselor encouraged Henry to continue to come in for appointments. Henry used the sessions to clarify his thinking so that he could make decisions with more confidence.

COUNSELING EVENTS

Nature of early interviews

For most of the early interviews Henry entered the office with an air of composure, but before long he became tense, restless, and tremulous. Things were not going well; he couldn't get down to work; he was wasting good time. He felt that he was shiftless and that he continually disappointed people. He had started the semester with good intentions and even with enthusiasm, but before many days had passed, he began failing to meet his daily responsibilities. "Everything is different," he said, "when I sit down and write. The words just seem to pour out. That is one aspect of life that is not drudgery." One of his courses that term was a creative writing class, which he enjoyed very much.

During the first several interviews, which usually occupied at least half an hour, the counselor learned relatively little directly from Henry. His comments were terse, often in the form of single sentences, and he would look to the counselor for response and for help in dealing with the issues he presented. It was very difficult to use the non-directive approach with him.* Henry was so responsive to the counselor's remarks that even when the counselor knew that he should be encouraging Henry to express his feelings, he frequently found himself talking instead.

Conflicts and "unwise decisions"

One of Henry's goals was to be a good student. He greatly enjoyed reading and had read widely in contemporary literature. He occasionally received superior grades, but these were interspersed with periods when he didn't study at all and was not conscientious about his assignments, causing his grades to drop. Then followed great struggles between his ideals with respect to studying and his actual behavior. Apparently the reality of systematic study was not satisfying. He enjoyed writing and valued it highly, but he used it as an escape from study. He spent hours at the typewriter writing and rewriting short stories. Although he received gratification from this and developed his skill, he did so at the expense of inferior grades.

Another matter that concerned Henry was his relationships with friends. "I have no difficulty meeting people; in fact, they accept me too readily. I am never able to uphold my end of the relationship or live up to the impression I think they have of me. This was true the year I was in the Air Force. There are times when I don't want to see people, and I actually make an effort to stay away from them. I can meet people in stories, and my relationships with them are good. I lack the courage to do the things I know I should do. I have to establish myself financially because I realize how important money is, and if I follow my inclination to be a bum, I won't have any money. This tendency not to meet obligations even shows up in my greatest love, writing. I have finished the first chapter of a novel, but I can't do the rest. I seem to be able to write when I don't have to construct; but I just let the typewriter do it for me. I realize that this is not writing in the creative sense, but realizing this doesn't help."

Henry experienced constant conflict between his impulses and what he felt was the wise thing to do. He told about anticipating a trip to one of the large eastern universities. He was going to look over the campus and investigate the possibilities of matriculating there. When he returned from the trip he confessed that his underlying motive

* This is a client-centered form of counseling during which the client is urged to take the initiative. The counselor merely reflects feelings and helps clarify them (Rogers and Dymond, 94).

was not to get facts about the school, but to visit a girl with whom he had been corresponding and who was "upsetting him." After he made this comment, he added, "I am glad to get that confession off my chest." He talked about his relationship with this girl. She was five years older than Henry, and was working for her Ph.D. He thought they had much in common, since they read the same books. He realized later that this was not an adequate basis for a lasting relationship. The girl was too far ahead of him educationally as well as in other ways, and there were little things about the girl that he didn't like. For example, she seemed obsessed with her own ill health, and took extreme precautions against catching cold or becoming fatigued.

Short-story writing

The counselor encouraged Henry to bring in some of his short stories. He also suggested to Henry that he write out some of his feelings in a free manner. Henry brought in some of the stories that he had written during this period, with the remark that writing them had helped him a great deal and that he was free of tension, both while he wrote and for a time after he had finished. He was apparently conscious of the fact that the counseling sessions were not productive because of his difficulty in being frank; he said he had never been frank with anyone. Because there seemed to be a marked contrast between Henry's lack of openness in the interview and his relative freedom of expression of inner life in his short stories, one of these stories is reproduced below.

Young Man of New York

by HENRY VANCE

He stared at the skyscrapers that fringed the south end of Central Park. The Plaza, Park Central, and the Tudor Arms reared their square, clean-cut heads into the cloudless blue. The mighty mountains of stone and their myriad windows, sparkling in the noon-day sun that girdled the park, thrilled the man with their magnificence. He couldn't help wondering why these huge bulwarks of civilization and wealth had not completely obliterated the park, the last stronghold of nature on Manhattan Island. To the left he saw the old hack stands near the Plaza, and that sophisticated lady of New York, Fifth Avenue. To his right was Columbus Circle, the hub of many streets, including Broadway. Behind him sat the girl.

This was the third day she had been sitting there. He might not have noticed her at all if it had not been for the book that she brought every day. He had recognized it as Proust's colossal work as soon as he had seen the binding, for he had a similar copy in his room. The mere fact that she read Proust convinced him that she was a girl whom he would like to know. The way she crossed her tanned, well-tapered legs, and the color of her dark blonde hair were also good arguments. Each day he had found her on the same bench and in the same position with all her attention bolted to the pages before her. Her only movements were to turn a fluttering page now and then.

His lunch hour was only forty-five minutes long, but he was more than willing to sacrifice eating for a stroll in the park. When a bench was free he would sit and meditate. If the only vacant spot was next to her, he would remain standing with his hands behind his back and his face turned upward, striking a pose of nonchalant absorption. After a while he would stroll around inside the little circle of benches, with his hands thrust deep into his pockets and kicking his legs out at the knee, hoping that she would look up and regard him as cutting a romantic figure. Only occasionally did he deign to cast her a glance; but always she remained the same, concentrated on Proust.

Once she had smiled absently at him while getting up to leave. Yes, that had been on the second day. By now he knew the exact minute when she would have to leave. His heart, breath, and whole being seemed to dissolve with time as that minute drew nearer. He coolly turned his back to her when she got up. Let her go! Then he'd watch her as she slowly walked away with her purse and book tucked under her arm. He tried not to look at her legs, but his eyes were uncontrollable; a little thin, perhaps, but not too bad.

Back at the office he was definitely not happy. He expected love to lift him from reality into a realm of indescribable happiness. When he thought of her, sitting on that bench in the park, a dull, painful ache crushed his heart. The longing to be with her plagued him persistently. He couldn't concentrate, nor could he enjoy the little that he ate whenever he did eat. Her image always monopolized his mind. What was she really like? Would she like him? Had she ever been out much before? If so, never to the point — he told himself he didn't care. He loved her for what she was. He only wanted her in a beautiful present and in a more promising future. He couldn't help being jealous of every move he imagined her to be making. If she went shopping, he wanted to go with her. If she went to a hairdresser, he would wait for her. He wanted to be wherever she was. What was more, he wanted her to want him to be everywhere with her.

At night, after going to bed, he would lie awake and think of her. He made up stories, tangled and interwoven, in which both of them were inexorably drawn to each other. At times he cast himself in the role of a conquering hero — boxer, great actor, budding politician, great writer — any role that would awe her friends and bring her rushing to his bosom. At other times he cast himself in the meanest of roles — a hack driver, who would win her with his latent charm and intellect, a man with whom she could settle down in a quiet little apartment and start a family. At times he even tortured himself with the thought of being turned down by her. Then he would disappear, to return after many years as a famous figure. Then she would bemoan her sad, obvious mistake. These martyr dreams were the only ones that pursued him into his sleep. He had had two dreams in which something or someone had come between them. Fortunately, these dreams were soon forgotten.

He thrust these memories from him and faced the present. Now was the time to sit down next to her and start a conversation. He turned his back to the Tudor Arms and stared at her for a moment. He felt helpless, unable to carry out his plan. He had known that he would break down at the crucial moment. Slowly he turned again. His body was sweaty and sticky all over. His heart was ready to explode and his breath was short and clipped. He decided to plunge.

He was next to her. This was the moment he had planned, the culmination of his dreams. She didn't look up from her book. He was tense and strained like a kid at his first dance. What the hell, he told himself and tried to relax. He tried to quiet the unruly rumblings in his breast by turning his attention to the Park Towers, those beautiful towers. Funny that he had never noticed them before.

"Isn't it a beautiful day?" Surprised, he jumped a little at her question and looked into her eyes. She was staring off through the trees as if mesmerized.

"It certainly is," he replied in a high, squeaky voice, cracked by emotion. She had spoken to him! She had broken the ice!

"I see you're reading Proust," he pursued, afraid of losing this advantage. She turned to him with a smile as if seeing him for the first time. "I'm drowning in him," she murmured ecstatically. "Have you read him?"

He was on firm ground now.

"I staggered through the first two."

"He puts everything in an entirely different light, as if they never really had any meaning before he discovered them."

"Yes — yes, you're right. But don't you think that he's a little prolix?"

She smiled and laughed a little. "That's the price we have to pay." She stared into space. "Good lord! Do you know what time it is?"

He tugged out the family heirloom. "Twelve-thirty on the head," he said, giving her a view of his teeth.

"Oh, I've got to run," she cried, picking up her things. "Goodbye."

He watched her hurry down the walk. He felt suddenly despondent, cheated by her hasty departure. And yet — hadn't he finally broken the ice?

The days became shorter. Instead of measuring them from midnight to midnight, he used noon as his yardstick. She was his dawn, noon, and evening rolled into one. Rapidly his whole life began to revolve around that little bench in Central Park. All morning he looked forward to his lunch hour. All afternoon he mulled over the short conversation with her. At night he lay awake in his bed, dreaming, hoping, wishing. He didn't dream of her any more. For some reason his nightly phantasies had ceased.

It had been three days since the eventful meeting. Three wonderful days full of meaning and purpose. The approach of Sunday frightened him. She wouldn't be there on Sunday unless. . . . The thought of a noon without talking to her was unbearable. He might never see her again. He had blown such a beautiful bubble of illusions and dreams, that a pin would not only explode the harmony of his life, but might ruin it completely.

She was wearing a green suit. A crazy feathered arrangement sat on top of her head. He came in on the beam of her smile.

"How are you today?" she asked.

"Fine, and you?"

"Wonderful. Say, when do you eat? You must have a very important position to be able to take so long for lunch."

He couldn't tear his eyes away from hers. Deep blue, like water, they laughed with his.

"Food doesn't interest me too much. I'd just as soon not eat if I can't eat all I want."

"Dining out is rotten, isn't it?"

"I'll say."

The warmth and harmony of the park spoke for them. Neither felt ill at ease when the conversation lagged. Such a lapse seemed more like a design to fit into the glorious pattern that their acquaintance was forming.

She broke the silence. "Isn't this a wonderful place to have in the middle of so much frustration?"

"It's my personal paradise."

"Along with seven million others," she chided with a smile.

"They don't spoil it at all."

She shifted her position so that she could look at him. Perfectly relaxed, he watched a group of frolicking youngsters coming down one of the walks.

"New York is such a wonderful place," she said, watching every movement of his head, his lips, his eyes.

"There's so much to do. Never a dull moment."

"That's the truth. Theaters, concerts, dances, everything under the sun."

"And three major-league ball teams," he suggested. She smiled and clasped her purse to her.

"I only wish that I could live long enough to see everything that this city has to offer," she exclaimed.

"I'm devoting my life to the pursuit of New York and its many facets."

"It should be an interesting chase, but I don't think you'll ever tree the game."

"I guess you're right. It's the game that's treed me."

"Oh, don't let it," she cried entreatingly, "so many people are swallowed every day by this great monster. Don't let it get you. Use it but don't become its slave."

"What do you mean?"

"Oh, it's easy to be a New Yorker. Coney in the summer, theaters and movies in the fall and winter, Times Square on New Year's Eve — but don't let this routine chain you, mold you into the same likeness as the seven million others. You've got a light. Realize it and let it show."

"You're pulling my leg."

"You told me that you wanted to be a writer. The only way to be one is to write. Don't become enmeshed in one job. Try them all, but, above all, write about them. Write about the people you meet, the thoughts you have. You can never do this if you become a New Yorker. You can't be a native of any city or country and be a great writer."

"I think maybe I get it. But a guy's got to live. He's got to have a little security."

"The only security you need is your writing. If you can put down man's experience in words, you've served your purpose. You're secure for eternity."

He was stunned by her words. They kept revolving in his mind. What does she mean? But he knew. He recognized the rut he had fallen into.

"I'm sorry, but I have to leave," she said, breaking in on his thoughts.

"Tomorrow?"

"Tomorrow!"

"Goodbye." He stood up, holding onto her hand.

"Goodbye." He watched her fade into the shadows of noon and for a moment he felt a surge of great savage happiness.

He had solved the problem of Sunday. By chance, he had been able to get two tickets to an afternoon concert at Carnegie Hall. This afternoon he'd ask her and he knew that she wouldn't refuse. This was his chance to start the ball rolling. These afternoon talks had been wonderful, but he had seen enough of the girl to realize that a half an hour a day would never do. Ultimately, he wanted to marry this girl. Mold or no mold, he wanted her to be the Mother of his children.

The clock near his desk must have stopped. He looked at his watch. No, the clock was right, a quarter to twelve. Good lord, but the minutes were taking their time. Slowly he put away the papers on his desk. He got up and walked over to the water cooler for a drink. It was only ten of when he returned to his desk. He looked out of the window to the building across the street. People just like him were waiting for the fateful hour. His mind drifted to thoughts of home, business, and finally gave up the pretense and hurtled down to that bench in the park.

Noon! He was off. There had never been so many people in his way before. The elevators had never run so slowly. All the traffic lights were against him. Certainly all of New York must be plotting against him.

He had trouble trying to keep from running down the walk. He stretched his legs to the utmost, constantly feeling the breast of his coat to see if his wallet was still there — the wallet with the tickets in it. They were right next to the picture of his mother.

The bench was empty! A cold gust chilled his heart. She is probably late, he thought. He sat down to wait for her, trying to quiet his throbbing heart. Surely, he thought, these people around me will think I'm crazy if I don't quiet my nerves. She'll be here soon.

Restlessly he shifted from one position to another, looking at his watch every few minutes. Maybe she's at another bench. Did she mention another bench? Certainly that must be it. He had forgotten. He leaped from the bench and plunged down a walk. Frantically he searched the face of every woman he saw. He covered every inch of the south end of the park trying to quiet the horrible doubt within him. Soon that doubt changed to a dull awful pain of certainty.

Every noon for two weeks he returned to the bench. He always kept a lookout for her, hoping to see her face among the millions of New York. Often he had followed a familiar pair of legs for blocks, only to be disappointed. Finally he stopped going to the park altogether. After three torturing months of searching, he left New York for a vacation. He went home. It didn't last. After a week at home, he hopped a train for the city hoping to find her again. Someday, somewhere, somehow, he felt sure that he'd find her.

THE END

Henry was somewhat ambivalent about submitting the five or six short stories that he presented to the counselor in the early phase of counseling. He had not shown these stories to anyone, partly because they revealed so much of a side of his life that he had difficulty showing to other people. On the other hand, he did want to have the stories read. Doubtless, his fear that his inner life was not acceptable to others had until now overshadowed his desire to have others read his stories.

To the counselor there seemed to be more consistency in the personality of the central figures in the stories than in the personality Henry showed in the interviews. The central characters in most of the stories were similar to the one in "Young Man of New York."

The counselor found the stories engaging and commented on them to Henry, showing his acceptance and enthusiasm. After Henry had brought in several stories it seemed that the interviews began to change, to become more open and productive. It is difficult to know how much of this change was due to the reduction of tension over a period of time during counseling and how much was due to Henry's acceptance of a submerged aspect of his personality, as a result of having someone else read his stories.

Concern over "failure"

Henry felt disturbed because he thought he was regarded as a failure not only by his parents, but also by his contemporaries. He said, "I am sure the fellows I went to high school with look at me as a nonentity. I never really accomplished anything in my studies or in athletics, and I failed to get into any extracurricular activities. I spent my time daydreaming about achieving greatness on the outside and in later life.

"There was one bright spot in high school. My English teacher praised a short story I wrote once and from then on encouraged me. That is happening again this semester in English, but now I am not doing anything. I have always had difficulty accepting myself as I really am. Instead I spend a great deal of time thinking about the success that I will achieve later, but not doing anything to achieve it. Now I am tempted to use the same method that I have used in the past when I have felt like a failure and disliked the place where I was — I want to leave and go someplace else.

"It is like the visit to this girl I mentioned. Sitting here in my room thinking about it, I was very hopeful about our relationship; and when I met her in the flesh, talked with her, and went out with her, I saw how different we were, and I saw that anything meaningful between us was not something I could anticipate in the near future."

Change in content of interviews

In the earlier interviews Henry had been preoccupied with the nature of his problem and his feelings about it. In later interviews he discussed some basic attitudes that had brought about his problem. He was beginning to gain some perspectives on himself and to show some capacity to verbalize them. There was an inkling of understanding about daydreams and the cathartic stories that he was writing.

In the ninth interview, four months after the first, he talked more freely than he ever had before. He said, "I am beginning to see trends in myself. I think I took on my father's attitudes without being able to really be like him. There is a conflict between the extroverted, aggressive success my parents expect of me and what I really am and want to be. My stories are a way to relieve myself of some of the feelings I have and to live my own conflicts through somebody else. My parents are very conventional. They are the typical, suburban type of people. They want money, they want success, and they are very sensitive about our status in the community. I don't want any of this; I just want to be myself."

Another indication that things were changing in his life was a statement he volunteered, "I am living in an apartment with several other fellows, and I seem to be getting something out of this." This was a mild statement, but contrasted with his previous retreat from his contemporaries while in high school and during the year in the Air Force, it indicated some progress toward the kind of socialization he could accept.

Later counseling perspectives

Henry continued to show less tension and nervousness. He spent more of the counseling period talking and less time waiting for the counselor to comment about what he had said.

"I read a book the other day," Henry began one interview. "It was about the relationship between a father and son, and I couldn't get that off my mind. I guess I was never worthy of my father, and I think I noticed that he felt that way about me. Once he took me out to dinner and I began stacking the dishes and pushing off the crumbs. He frowned and said in an irritated manner, 'Leave those alone. That is something for the waiter to do.' Despite some of the faults my mother thought my father had, these little conventional matters were very important to him, and I seemed to be constantly embarrassing him. He was critical of the clothes that my mother had bought for me. I was always trying to make my father proud of me and yet continually failing." Henry hinted that he may have had some deep hostility towards his father that he had not been able to face.

It was interesting for the counselor to notice the contrast between his impression of Henry, particularly at the beginning, and Henry's view of himself. This handsome, well-built, attractive young man apparently regarded himself as an awkward sap, constantly appearing stupid, and being deeply cut by the embarrassment.

Most of the other sessions contained reports of improvement. In one interview about this time Henry stated that he had been drinking most of the weekend — a period he had set aside for work. This occurred during the time when he was thinking through the relationship with his father. He began wondering whether in a way he wasn't trying to compete with his father. He said, "I have the strange feeling that I seem to be making trouble for myself — making myself appear inferior and perpetuating below-par behavior so my father will remain superior. I know that my father always wanted to be more successful than he was. I wanted him to have this success but did not want him to be shown up. My father is my greatest ideal, and I long to be around him; but when I do visit him, there is constant embarrassment. We seem so incompatible, and that spoils everything. My father wanted to write when he was my age, but he was never successful, so how can I become a successful writer? My father acted out his feelings and impulses much more than I ever did. He went to extremes in drinking, in his relations with women, and in his social life.

"I am beginning to realize that I have to find my own way out of the mess I am in. My father cannot help me. I will always love him; he will always be my ideal; but being close to him shows me things in reality, and that produces a conflict. I just don't have the courage to do the things I want to do. Maybe I can find my own way of living and still please my parents. I realize now that I couldn't please them in the way they want me to please them. I want to be the kind of person they want me to be, yet I don't accept their way of life. They expect me to fit into the mold of the standard youth, and I just don't fit. They are typical narrow-minded, prejudiced, suburban people, and I can't idealize the kind of people that they worship and who seem to me to be shallow."

At this time Henry was having greater success in his English courses and impressing his teachers more with his writing. He said, "I am thinking about going out for football next year. This might give me confidence. Perhaps journalism is the field I should plan to enter. This would afford me an opportunity to write. I am beginning to think that maybe the kind of people around the newspaper, with their tendencies to look objectively on contemporary life, are the kind of people I would enjoy. I think they would accept me for what I am." Before leaving the interview, he said with some satisfaction, "I let my roommate read one of my stories yesterday." This again was a step forward — a growth experience for him. He was allowing others to participate in his life; his world was expanding.

Henry reached another possible insight several interviews later when he said, "I have decided that I have come as far as I should in examining the relationship between my father and me. There are many things I understand about this now. I understand that going to pieces in front of people is related to displeasing him on my

visits. My relationship here with you is colored by this role of expecting to be awkward around other people, at least in my father's
eyes. I realize now that I got along better with the men in the Air
Force than I thought I had. I also realize that I have tended to follow implicitly the people I idealize just as I tried to follow my
father. The trouble was that all too often these were the wrong
kinds of people."

One day when he was feeling particularly good, he admitted that
when he first came to see the counselor, he had been almost on the
verge of suicide. "I was completely disgusted with myself. Failure
was all I could see in the past or in the future.

"I have a new girl I met the last time I was home. She knows my
parents, and she is very bright and understanding. I think she had
some kind of nervous breakdown some time ago. She comes from a
very good family, and I have known her for several years but my
feeling for her just developed in this last visit. I am beginning to
see my mother a little differently than I did before. She is more
than the conventional person preoccupied with things that money
can buy. She reads good books." (Again a change in perspective, an
expansion, for Henry.)

Something he said during this interview indicated that Henry had
been a very sensitive child — awkward and backward, never quite in
step with the other children in his class, feeling alone and different.
During his worst moments, the little boy within him seemed to
predominate, and there he stood, a mature-appearing man, feeling
as inadequate as a small boy. The factors or conditions which caused
this childhood sensitivity were not explored.

One year after Henry began the interviews, he withdrew from
school saying that he had decided to take a trip to Europe. He would
attempt to earn his way over. He thought this would be good for
him; he would be on his own and away from the pressure that had
troubled him so much. He felt that he had made great progress in
understanding himself, in dealing with his feelings, and in learning
to control his actions.

FOLLOW-UP

Two follow-up letters are quoted below, one written several months
after the counseling sessions stopped and a second written fifteen
years later, when the counselor wrote Henry asking permission to

use his short story in this case write-up. Before reading these letters, it might be interesting for you to review what you have gleaned from the preceding pages and to note what additional information you would need to predict the direction of Henry's future development. Then speculate as to what kind of adjustment Henry will make. Will he become independent, marry, find a career? Will he continue to experience the same kind of problems?

Several months after the last interview the counselor sent out a questionnaire to all of his clients, suggesting that they complete it, using additional space to express freely any attitudes they had and wished to voice. The major emphasis in the questionnaire was on what counseling had done for them, what aspects had been most helpful, and what aspects least useful. The substance of Henry's completed questionnaire, together with his own unstructured comments about what he was doing at that time, are presented here.

Henry indicated that during the year in which he had received counseling he had grown in social grace and in tolerance of himself and other people. He stated that he had stopped hating himself and other people and at last seemed to have more ambition. He had visited his father and for several months had been living with him. His father seemed to understand, more than he ever had before, what Henry was going through, and what was wrong. Henry felt that the counselor was very helpful in encouraging him to write out his "gripes" and thus get them off his chest. However, he felt that much of what he had written was not true about himself. He thought that if he had been urged during the interviews to take part in a community project, and thereby ease himself into society, it would have been helpful. He stated that during his year at school he had lost himself in a "dark corridor" that led only to himself.

The grades he reported on the questionnaire were average, on the whole, with one superior and one inferior mark. He stated that he had few friends but an average number of acquaintances. On a rating scale he indicated that he was much more enthusiastic about his future adjustment than ever before, that he thought he was average in his integration and stability, but that he was still definitely below average in his adjustment to his environment and to other people.

He was given a long list of adjectives and asked to underline the ones that he thought characterized him. He underlined: over-conscientious, restless, friendly, lazy, lacking in initiative, individualistic, idealistic, weak-willed, imaginative, egocentric, pessimistic, anxious, unhappy, and tolerant.

It is interesting that even though he reported himself greatly improved, more accepting, and happier than he was before, he seemed to point to many of the same personality traits that he had shown during the interviews. His manner of underlining was highly individualistic, with some traits partially underlined and others fully underlined. Henry explained this in the following way:

"I realize that my playful mood in underlining the above adjectives requires a little explanation. You psychologists give importance to the term 'roles.' Many people try to maintain some role and when that role is threatened, they collapse, or are at least unhappy about it. I may be wrong, but I think that this has been my trouble. This difficulty has been somewhat exaggerated in me. I tend to dramatize myself in everything. This accounts for my making such a colossal ass of myself on so many occasions. Unfortunately I have never been able to accept and play a role enough to do something in it or to be overwhelmed if it were challenged. I have been like a butterfly flitting through the ether; the slightest damage to my wings has rendered me completely helpless and unhappy. Just about everything I have done — talking myself into being in love, quitting school and taking out across country, deliberately hurting my family, etc., etc., ad infinitum — has been an *attempt to dramatize myself.* I can see it pretty clearly now. I'd have to write a book in order to explain to you how everything seems to fit into this theory. At any rate I think that I have found some answers.

"Every summer that I have been home I have had the chance to vacation at a spot on a lake. I haven't always taken advantage of these opportunities, but every time I have, the place has been the same for me. Since I was a child, I could live in this place and be perfectly happy and be myself. It is truly amazing, but its magic has never diminished. This has been the only place in the world for me where I could be myself and enjoy life wholeheartedly.

"For the past two months I have been working in a community theater, and I have discovered that this theater has the same effect as the beach. No matter how miserable I am during the day, I seem to drift out of myself at night. It might be that I am working for a common purpose rather than for my own, but there is something about it. At first I was afraid to think about it, afraid to hope, but every night it's the same. And then there is the added excitement of being on the stage before an audience.

"In one week I was fired from my job for incompetence, accused of being an unresponsive lover by the girl in college (toward whom

I now feel as cold as a fish), and rejected by Yale for not measuring up to their standards. I mention these things to illustrate this power of the theater. The theater hasn't made me forget; it has given me something more important to strive for. For the first time in my life, I know what I want to do; and I'm going to do it.

"My plans now are to return to college this summer with the intention of trying to graduate next June. I hope to see you next fall and perhaps talk to you about all this." (He did not come back to the University, nor did he write to the counselor again.)

Henry sent a personal letter along with the questionnaire; the letter shows the Henry Vance that is seen better in his stories than in the psychologist's office. Here we see the open, uncensored, somewhat insightful Vance after an experience with the Air Force, a first try at college, counseling, writing, travels, and life at home with his father. The letter follows:

Doctor,

Time passes, scenes change, and new ideas are formed, but basically there is no change in the individual. This awful truth has been made most clear to me since I left the hallowed environs of college. But the fact that I was trying to run away from myself is one that I've been conscious of for a long time. This time I had put an unusually thick coating of candy on my motives and I felt pretty good about things as long as that coating lasted . . .

I spent a few days in New Orleans, one of which included a very introspective afternoon in some French Quarter dives. During that afternoon I plied the bastard that always is with me with liquor. He drew the effects of the evil brew over his head like a concealing cape. Unfortunately I was watching him all the time and telling him what a fool he was. He wanted to get me drunk too, but I was too smart for him. I told him that we'd have to get out of town before he drank up all our money. I had to drag him out of the bar by the ear but we got out of town. I had to literally hold him up all the way across the West. He was always on the point of breaking down. I never realized quite what a hopeless rascal he was until I observed him on this trip West. At every opportunity he tried to crawl off to a stifling hole where he could die in his own puke. Perhaps I should have let him, but I'm convinced that that is not the way to do things. Now that I've got him out here in sunny Arizona, I'm going to try to rehabilitate him. It's a lot tougher job than I had anticipated. Every once in a while he entices me into a program of what he calls "innocent merriment." It's never until I wake up with the unholy effects of that merriment that I realize he has tricked me again. With the help of a very understanding father, I have been able to get us both a small part in a play at the community theater here. I'm sure that you will agree that this is a step in the right direction. I pity the character that we are to portray if we should ever come to blows in the middle of the performance. We are also trying to get into a university, as you may have guessed from the recommendation form enclosed. This may or may not be a step in the right direction.

Staying here and living with my father may be the very thing I need. I talked with you about him and I'm afraid my description of him was sketchy at best. We are so much alike that the resemblance is regarded as something of a phenomenon by the locals. The difference is, perhaps, that he represents everything I like about myself, and I represent everything that we both dislike about ourselves — if that makes sense. Of course, I am being hard on myself, but I counterbalance that by placing the sky as the limit on what I could do (and what I plan to do).

In other words I'm through running away and I'm through being dissatisfied with myself. I'm pulling myself up short. If I think I want to write for a living, I'm going to write. That goes for acting or anything else . . . I'll let you know how I make out. I've been writing one-act plays like mad. I've burned them up almost as fast as I've written them. However, I think I'm making some progress. Between writing, reading Shakespeare, and making occasional sojourns into the big city in search of a mistress (to keep my testicles from atrophying from disuse) I have kept rather busy.

I'll keep you posted on any breathtaking events — like my getting into a university. In the meantime I would appreciate it a great deal if you would take care of this "Personal Rating Blank" nonsense.

All this may seem a little odd. I have a feeling that this will help me find what I'm looking for. Not that I couldn't have found it in college . . . but things have worked out this way. . . . My recent actions have probably cast me in a most ridiculous light but I don't really care. As long as there are one or two people who know what I'm trying to do, I'll be okay. My father seems to know exactly what I'm looking for . . . or rather he knows why I'm looking. He's looked all his life and is still looking. As a matter of fact he is so much like me that he seems to understand all my quirks and shortcomings. It's wonderful and even strengthening.

I've got a few stories struggling along that I will send you as soon as possible. You will probably be the only person in the world that has a complete edition of Vance's works.

Love and kisses,

HENRY VANCE

Queries about Henry's development

What contrast do you see between the content of the interviews and the content of the questionnaire and letter which Henry wrote several months later? How would you evaluate his explanation for what he was then and what he is now? Did his father play a directing role in verbalizing for him what had gone on during this unpleasant year? Was his new attitude a result of changes that occurred during the counseling process, the emotional support his father eventually gave him, or the satisfaction of being useful that he got from participating in dramatics? Why did dramatics serve as a therapeutic avenue for him?

Second follow-up, after fifteen years

The counselor felt that Henry illustrated how one may use a creative avenue, writing in this case (as a certain small percentage of clients had done), as a cathartic outlet and as a means of personal growth, especially when a counselor plays the role of an appreciative audience. In addition, one of the short stories Henry wrote seemed to reveal much of his inner life before he was able to talk about it in the interview. Thus the counselor felt it would be valuable to include it in the case write-up. He wrote to Henry just prior to publication of this book, asking his permission to use the short story included in this case. He told Henry that he had been chosen as one of the cases to be reported because he felt the writings had played an important role in Henry's development. The letter was not answered, so the counselor sent another request in a registered letter. Below is Henry's reply. In this letter he does two things rather well: (1) He discusses critically the value of writing as a therapeutic influence; and (2) he gives a second follow-up, reporting what he has done during the fifteen-year interval.

He at first states that he cannot believe the stories really helped him. He had made a similar statement in the earlier follow-up when he contrasted the stories and the counseling with an adventure in dramatics. In the rest of his letter he indicates several times that the writing did help him.

You have my permission to use any of the stories of mine that you have. My only reservation is that they may not be an honest working-out of the theory you may be trying to illustrate. As I recall, the reason I started to write them was because you thought it might help me work out some of the problems bothering me at the time. I don't remember the stories, but I can't believe that they really helped.* I may be wrong, so use them if you wish.

The value of your suggestion that I start writing out my troubles has been demonstrated many times. I've been writing intermittently since undergraduate days. It's true that one of my motives has been to try to write something publishable, but the main importance of my writing has been its therapeutic effect. Although I've written a novel and much poetry in the last twelve years, my main interest has been playwriting. Since I've had some training and experience in the theater and since dialogue seems to be easy to write, I've tried to work out most of my devils in dramatic form. To a certain extent, such attempts have helped me very much. Thank you for the suggestion.

I'm not sure that I wrote to you after being finally accepted at ——— University (a large, well-known university of some prestige). I graduated in 1950 after two years of feverish activity spent in an attempt to become an actor. Acting, incidentally, turned out to be a much more effective release for me than writing. I achieved some success; I enjoyed taking on the personality of a character, the applause of audiences, and the bohemian life of the theater. After graduation, I worked for a few months in a city on the West Coast. In the fall of 1950, I married; my wife and I went to London for a honeymoon year; I studied at a university there and my wife, who is a consummate actress, studied too. It was a marvelous year. In 1951, we

---

* Emphasis mine.

returned to the States, where I did some work in off-Broadway theater and studied for a master's degree. In 1953, I worked as technical director and actor at a summer theater. After the season, my wife and I found ourselves in Detroit without enough money to get back to New York. I found a job teaching speech and drama at a small liberal arts college, where I directed plays during the regular school year and directed their summer theater project for two summers. For a number of reasons, we left there after three years and returned to New York, where I started to work toward a Ph.D. in literature. I started to work in the English Department in 1956 and have been there ever since. I am just now finishing my dissertation and will defend it this fall. In the meantime, we have begat three children and are buying a house and enjoying life.

It's odd that your letter should come just when I seem to be having the same difficulties I used to have at college. Earning a Ph.D. has been difficult for me; not only have I had to work to support a family while studying, but I have also been pursuing other interests, mainly the writing of plays, which has kept me from getting the work done. Possibly the main problem is that I am only occasionally a good scholar. My imagination has some dangerous as well as beneficial tendencies (let me hasten to state that the danger threatens only me). When I am able to control it, I can work well. At other times I can think of a thousand better things to do than revise my musty chapters.

Excuse these thoughts, but you asked me how things have been going. To sum up, I can say that as a family man, I am supremely happy; as an individual coping with making his mark, I am less blissful.

Naturally, I am very interested in your project. If you are trying to prove that writing helps, I can testify in behalf of your theory.

This letter will doubtless stimulate a number of questions from anyone who has read the entire case. In addition to any the reader may have, we raise these: How well did the facts elicited in the counseling sessions and in Henry's writings predict the later events that occurred in his life? Can we agree that Henry did become a forceful, resourceful, and achieving individual? How much of this did we see in the early interviews? If Henry was struggling against the various forces represented in his personality (for example, conventionality and individuality), did he resolve these? If so, in what ways? How well did he succeed in being true to himself and to those qualities within himself which he regarded as being strongest and most integral? How well did you predict the course that Henry's life would finally take before reading his final follow-up?

HENRY: Personality Patterns and Influential Persons

What do you see in the life of Henry that is most outstanding? Respond in your own way before turning to the following suggestions.

Outstanding personality trends

　　a. How much insight leading to action do you see?

　　b. Can some of his behavior be called regressive, that is, assuming childish ways in times of difficulty?

　　c. Are there examples of running away from problems and rationalizing the flight?

　　d. In what ways does he dramatize himself and his experiences?

　　e. Are his artistic accomplishments enhanced by personal conflict or are anxiety and conflict a hindrance to his creativity?

Relationships in personality development

　　a. With whom did he seem to identify in his development?

　　b. In what ways did he serve as a pawn in the battle between his parents?

　　c. How did influential persons affect his developing strengths and problems?

Concepts helpful in understanding Henry

　　a. Working through of insights (51)

　　b. Rationalization (80)

　　c. Expressive techniques: psychodrama, writing (72)

　　d. Nonconformity leading to creativity (66, 112)

　　e. Inadequate integration and personal unity (51, 59)

JOE

The Fantasy Suitor

In the case of Joe we see a college youth with emotional
conflicts, who seeks counseling in a mental hygiene clinic
at the time of an academic crisis. He is later counseled
more consistently, but superficially. After graduation he
maintains contact with the counselor at irregular intervals
for non-directive sessions and is followed in this way for
approximately fifteen years. Thus we are able to observe
the extent to which his self-defeating traits remain the
same and the degree to which he progresses toward vocational and emotional maturity. The case includes results
from a Wechsler-Bellevue Intelligence Test and the TAT
projective personality test.

IDENTIFICATION

Joe Browski has made a very good vocational adjustment at the
age of thirty-five. He has advanced steadily on a big-city newspaper
in the Great Lakes area — his home vicinity. He was elected president of a plant employees' organization, probably one of the best
elective offices he has held in his life. He has many acquaintances
and probably several warm friends. At present he is unmarried, has
no absorbing hobbies, and spends a certain amount of time in the
evenings with acquaintances at bars. He has occasional dates, frequently going to night clubs. Otherwise, he is quite thrifty. Recently, he rented a small apartment away from home.

During his college days Joe was thinner, but otherwise, the same
tall, energetic person with light complexion and short blond hair.
He tried to be friendly, informal, and humorous, but his humor was
not always effective. Apparently his model and ego ideal * was mascu-

* The ideal the individual strives to attain.

71

line; one would have speculated from his behavior that he definitely wanted to be thought of as a typical man. He conversed readily about current events and sports, and he seemed to prefer the company of men, with whom he was a little more at ease than with girls. He was not socially naive, but his *rapport* with others was not as effective as he apparently desired. He tended to dress in sporty clothes, reflecting his lower middle-class background. His grooming and clothing resembled less the typical college student than the military veteran found on campus at that time. Let us see him through the eyes of the counselor fifteen years ago, when Joe was a college student.

OCCASION FOR INTERVIEW

Joe first visited a college mental hygiene clinic voluntarily when he was a sophomore. He complained of being jittery and nervous and having a tight feeling in his stomach. He said he couldn't study and was irritable and restless most of the time.

In response to the *counselor's questions* about himself, he indicated that he was a veteran of World War II, had served in the infantry, and had been wounded in the left leg. He noticed when he was discharged and returned home that he was more irritable and had more arguments with his parents and younger brother and sister than he did before he was drafted into the service. He stated that he was also drinking more.

He had liked the service and made many close friends. He didn't object to being told what to do, but felt that he could assume more responsibility than he was given. He said that he had always worried about "how things would turn out." The questioning and free expression during the counseling session seemed to relieve much of Joe's tension for the moment, and he was encouraged to come in again when he felt tension was mounting.

The next time Joe came to the counselor was just before an examination, about a month after the first interview. He had experienced an anxiety attack during an examination in physics and this made him dread taking another examination. It was easier for him to talk this time, and he calmed down rather quickly. During this interview he discussed his interest in writing, and the counselor encouraged him to bring in some of his writings. He never did.

The counselor did not see Joe again until just before examination time the following semester, except for a brief visit after the semester was over, when he announced that he had finally passed the course that worried him. Again, he was tense and anxious and concerned that he might not make the grades he needed to graduate on schedule. The counselor was reassuring and attempted to give Joe some *perspective* by pointing out that he was creating certain pressures for himself, that he had not *set up alternate goals*. It is doubtful whether these statements were helpful to Joe, but his *relationship* with the counselor seemed to help, because as he talked, he became less anxious. The counselor felt that Joe respected him and that he enjoyed the interviews. While it had a man-to-man character, their relationship seemed to pivot on the psychological first-aid Joe received when he was anxious — a relationship of *dependency*.

It may be noted that Joe *waited* until tension mounted and anxiety became overwhelming before he sought professional help. He did not follow the counselor's suggestion that he try to find the basis for his tensions through regular conferences.

PERSONAL HISTORY

Joe described his mother as a nervous woman who had suffered a breakdown when he was around five years of age. His brother was about four years younger than Joe. He evaluated the family atmosphere as congenial on the whole, except that his parents seemed to be over-solicitous of his welfare and too concerned over the hours he kept.

This is all the information we have about the Browski family or about Joe's early environment. We know little about the conditions in his home and neighborhood or about his attitudes and activities early in life. We know nothing about the effect of his mother's breakdown upon Joe or how long she was away from the home. The reader may speculate about these matters as he gains more information about Joe. Joe talked very little about his childhood and his family. He answered rather nervously and briefly the questions put to him about his early life in the first few interviews, but he rarely volunteered information on the subject.

From comments made by Joe's childhood friends, whom the counselor knew, and from his observation of Joe's behavior with his college friends, the counselor hypothesized that Joe had wanted very much to be a part of the neighborhood gang as a child, but had remained on the periphery. There is no evidence that he had participated in any team achievement in sports. He did, however, have some good friends that he had known for a number of years, who came from the neighborhood in which he grew up. His father was a semi-skilled laborer, and it is possible that either his parents or his grandparents were immigrants. He was probably *sensitive* about the socio-economic status of his parents. He showed an interest in *police work* throughout the years the counselor knew him; in fact, he said that several times he had thought seriously about going into this vocation. We shall see this interest later in some of the fantasy themes.

The counselor noticed on several occasions that Joe had a barely perceptible *speech block*. At times he stopped talking very briefly and had difficulty articulating a word or phrase, but immediately regained composure and resumed his rapid speech. This tendency may have been more apparent in earlier years or it may have been symptomatic of earlier conflicts. The speech block was not mentioned or explored in any of the sessions.

We have almost no direct information about Joe's high school years. We do not know the extent to which he participated in sports, hobbies, or extracurricular activities; his grades; the extent to which he dated; his aspirations to attend college; his relationship to teachers and fellow students; or his attitude toward himself. We can speculate about these on the basis of the TAT fantasies presented below and information about his college life. We may wonder what would have occurred if he had had the advantage of contact with a sensitive and understanding counselor in junior or senior high school. After reading his test scores below, the reader might conjecture as to the role a counselor having access to his TAT stories might have played. The kind of spread seen in these test patterns often suggests emotional difficulties.

COUNSELING EVENTS

Test results

After several interviews Joe was referred to the psychometrist, and he was given the *Wechsler-Bellevue Intelligence Test*. His verbal score was 141, performance score 91, and full-scale I.Q. 123. These scores indicate that his verbal intelligence was definitely superior, even when compared with his student peers. The disparity between the two scores is striking. His verbal superiority is manifest in much of his behavior. This verbal skill, or effective use of words, represents achievement as well as being a means of defense. The psychometrist reported that he was much slower on the performance items.

His profile on the *Minnesota Multiphasic Personality Inventory** showed scores within the normal range. However, his scores on the *depression, psychasthenia,* and *schizophrenia* scales were outside the normal range, suggesting he might have some problems in these areas. His scores on the following three scales were near the upper limit of the normal range, bordering on the abnormal: *hypomania, masculine-feminine* (tending toward femininity), and *psychopathic deviate.* These findings are compatible with his description of swings in mood and with some unrealistic attitudes that appeared throughout the interviews.

Despite his high intelligence, Joe did relatively little reading, and most of what he did read was popular in nature. He seemed to have poorer than average acquaintance with world affairs. This might be expected of a bright student coming from a low socio-economic background, where books and intellectual magazines are absent, and where there is neither adult support nor encouragement to develop his natural capacities. He apparently talked with a few of his intimate friends about his own superficial problems. Although he dated very little in college, his dating practices were not unlike those of his closest friends. One suspects that he may have wanted to date, but that he felt inferior to most of the girls on the campus. The dynamics of his sexual development are not clear. He seemed somewhat *narcissistic,* and some of his attitudes towards himself support this hypothesis.

TAT fantasies

The psychometrist gave Joe the *Thematic Apperception Test* (TAT). He was presented with the pictures described below and asked to make up a story, telling what the persons in the picture are thinking and feeling, what led up to the situation pictured, and what will be the outcome. Below is his response to Card 3. (It is a picture of an apparently young but ambiguous individual — that is, it might be a girl with short hair or a boy with long hair — sitting on the floor with back to view, head on arm, resting against a divan.

* See pages 6 and 232 for descriptions.

There is an object that might be a toy pistol on the floor beside the figure.)

> The boy has been playing with his friends. They were playing with all the heart and spirit that youth can put into something. Then he returned home and searched the house for something to do. Failing in this, he sat down on the floor and found the nearness of the couch too great a temptation. He leaned against it and then found that he was very tired.
>
> Now he huddles up against the cushions. His thoughts stray, and from a tired little boy, he becomes a great businessman with plants and offices all over the country. But the business world becomes tiresome and he becomes a detective, known as a shrewd investigator that can outshoot and outfight any criminal. Catching a desperate criminal, he returns home to the little boy huddled against the couch and wonders what the rest of the day will bring and if he'll be able to get a couple of hits in the baseball game against the Tigers tomorrow.
>
> In later years he'll look back to the days of his youth and think of the life he led as a child, when his only worries were getting a hit in a ball game. Now he has other problems; but he has a job and a wife and children, and problems can be solved as they come up. Sometimes when he sees his oldest son lying on the floor after a day at play, he secretly steals along on the trip his son takes. But his son never knows that his dad is always there when he makes an arrest or closes a deal.

What trends seem to appear in Joe's fantasy? One can see here the suggestion of achievement motivation, the fantasy of an unusually successful businessman, with some ambivalence about such success. His orientation is essentially masculine and conventional. One also sees his interest in the detective field and some inclination to regress toward the simplicity of youth.

Let us now look at Joe's response to Card 4. (It is a picture of an attractive man and woman in a partial embrace. The man seems to be turning away, and the woman seems to be pleading with him. The background is ambiguous. There is a vague picture on the wall of a scantily-clad woman.)

> When Bill was in high school he never paid too much attention to girls. He was too busy playing on the team and working. But his last year in high school he started dating Jean. Then

he went in the Army and they wrote letters to each other. Then the letters stopped, and Bill always wondered why. He never knew; but it didn't matter, because there were others, although not the right one yet.

Then he was discharged and he again began dating Jean. She was a nice kid; after he'd taken her out a few times he found out that she wasn't the sweet kid he thought she was. He wasn't happy about that. She had been going with his buddy, Chuck, but that was over. He thought she should have told him about it. He thought he loved her, but he wasn't sure. She was in love with him, she said. He compared her with all the things he wanted in a girl and the more he thought, the less he was sure. He decided he wanted to look around and wait. He told her he'd call her up later, but he never did.

Six months later Jean was married. Bill had dated four other girls in the meantime. He was looking, but he hadn't found what he wanted yet. He's still looking.

A certain amount of insight into Joe's attitudes and feelings can be gained from these projective tests. Joe invented fantasies about experiences and events that could well be related to his own concerns, but which he could not discuss frankly, even with a counselor whom he respected.

In the second story above one can see Joe's concern about dating and his apparent block in heterosexual satisfaction. Both of these stories suggest a lack of relationship between the real life Joe was living and the fantasies in which he indulged.

In two other TAT stories the theme involved serious misfortune occurring to someone emotionally associated with the writer, and he seemed to blame himself partially for the mishap. Another recurrent theme was the return to childhood and enjoyable play with other fellows. The "big-deal" fantasy seemed to recur frequently; reading through the nine stories, one gets the impression that the narrator felt that the world was a difficult place to live, and that he was not as lucky as others.

Counseling after college graduation

Joe graduated from college on schedule and immediately got a fairly good job with a newspaper in the city where he grew up. He continued to keep in contact with the counselor concerning his personal problems through long letters, unannounced visits, and occasional interviews scheduled by appointment. After Joe left college, he had a tendency to drop in unannounced and expect to talk for several hours about his anxieties. The counselor was successful in indicating to him that it would be necessary to schedule these appointments ahead of time.

Working as a newspaper reporter for several years did not seem to change Joe very much in terms of his internal organization. He bought a handsome new car, began dating more often and saving his money. He handled his job with at least average competence and continued to get moderate raises and advancements. He occasionally dated girls he met in bars; but they failed to satisfy his standards, and he did not date them seriously or often.

Then he met May. She was a good Catholic, as he was, but she came from a middle-class suburban family, a higher socio-economic background than his. She was a graduate nurse and lived with her mother and sister. Although she was in all respects "what he had been waiting for," she, apparently, had been waiting for something different. They dated for many months, and she became the central concern of several long letters and long visits to the counselor. While he was dating her, he had, on numerous occasions, what he called "a bad case of nerves." At these times he had difficulty sleeping for three or four days at a time, woke up during the night or early in the morning, and tossed in bed until it was time to get up.

It seemed to the counselor that although Joe was dating May quite seriously and had a very strong feeling for her, he realized from her behavior that she was not as receptive of him as he had hoped she would be. After one long interview, the counselor attempted to encourage Joe toward some perspective about his relationship with May. He suggested that, because of May's family status, emotional calmness, religious orientation, attractiveness, and neatness, Joe had been reluctant to be frank with her for fear she would not be as receptive as he might wish. Instead of discussing their differences openly, he had been sending her roses, giving her presents, making use of his prestige as a newspaperman, and taking her to glamorous and interesting places. Although this had taken place over a rather long period of time, they had not learned very much about each other. He had previously told the counselor that May had once said, "We are worlds apart." This had been a traumatic experience, because in his fantasy she had become the girl of his life.

She told him he ought to date other girls, and although she rewarded him occasionally with a good-night kiss and perhaps some casual caressing, she was probably in conflict about him. Apparently her mother thought him a nice young man. She may have been impressed with him as a man of the "right" religion, who had some economic security, and who would not take advantage of her daughter. Sometimes they merely sat in the living room and talked with her mother or with family friends that happened to be there, but Joe often took her to the top events in the city, for which he could obtain tickets through the newspaper office. Undoubtedly the girl appreciated having an escort with a press badge and also recognized the same qualities her mother saw in Joe; but she gave no indication that she loved him or felt that she would be able to live with him as his wife.

Joe sensed May's doubts, and his work began to lose some of its appeal. He looked forward to talking with her on the telephone or their weekly dates; he reminisced about a birthday present she had given him, his reception by her mother, or any kind thing May had said. Now and then he wrote her a note giving her just an inkling of his feelings. He noticed that there were some nights when she said good-night affectionately and other nights when she left him abruptly on the porch. He showed no enthusiasm for any of the other girls he met. He spoke of May as being in "the big league," as being better than the others.

During the three years that he was dating May, dimly aware that he was making no progress, he took a couple of vacation trips to such glamorous places as Miami and Reno, partly in the hope of meeting someone as attractive as May. These trips always ended in disappointment.

During the summer they went swimming together. May was a good swimmer and enjoyed the pool and the sunbathing. Joe was very self-conscious about his physical appearance in a bathing suit and about his inferior swimming in contrast to hers. Their divergent attitudes toward the pool became a point of contention. At times she would wander off and talk with other friends, producing in him a feeling of rejection.

Instead of discussing their disagreements, Joe wrote letters to May hinting at the trouble. One of these letters prompted a frank statement from May, telling Joe that he was emotionally immature and that she did not appreciate his futile attempts to be humorous. All of this caused him to "suffer inwardly," as he put it.

When he had disagreements with her or when she could not see him because she was "busy," he "found himself" driving toward her neighborhood and circling her block several times. He realized that this was senseless, because he could not have justified his presence there if she had happened along, but he felt an "irresistible pull" toward her.

Most of his college friends were getting married, and he was becoming more and more restless and depressed. He bought a tennis racket, and also began working out in a gymnasium. He referred to the need for "more cold showers," which the counselor interpreted as a euphemism for his struggle with the urge to masturbate — a matter that he never discussed frankly.

Joe felt that May was not being frank with him, but this may have been a projection of his own feelings. He began to realize that during the three years of dating there had been no progress toward marriage with May. After a long conference, in which he recited many of the above details, the counselor suggested that he seek more intensive counseling in the city where he lived, and strongly suggested psychiatric consultation. This came as a shock to Joe. He did not take the advice but apparently had several conferences with a priest instead.

His adventure with May came to an abrupt end when she phoned one day, to tell him that she was engaged. She said that he had been a good friend and she did not want to hurt him; that she wanted him to know before she gave the news to the paper. To him, this was merely sugar-coating a bitter pill. He felt that this "romance" represented three wasted years in his life; however, for the last few months he had felt this climax coming. He had bought himself a hi-fi set and had begun collecting art books, drinking good Scotch, and smoking cigars.

Joe's concept of himself and his relationship to May can be seen in part in his habit of avoiding personal references in letters and in conferences with the counselor. He referred to May not by name but by phrases such as "the sweet thing" and "the little doll." Even in referring to himself, he used "this fellow" instead of "I," and he called his letters to the counselor "reports" and "parole check-ups." These circumlocutions illustrated his inability to come to grips with his identity and, possibly, with the reality of his situation. Apparently he had some friends with whom he could talk between interviews, and this may have helped him, over time, to gain a better perspective on reality. However, it remains doubtful whether Joe ever evaluated objectively the possible consequences of a marriage between May and himself.

FOLLOW-UP

First interview

After breaking his ties with May, Joe became a little more frank in his interviews with the counselor. He talked about his parents and about his decision to get a small apartment away from home. He described his mother as a harsh disciplinarian who still attempted to control his behavior. He and his father "drifted" in and out of the house. If he ever introduced May to his parents, he gave no indication of it to the counselor.

By the time the last interview took place, about fifteen years after the counselor's first contact with him, Joe had shown considerable progress in his ability to talk frankly about himself and to refer realistically to May. He could now admit that he had always felt shy and inferior in the eyes of girls, that he probably was emotionally immature for his age, and that his ties with his family had been stronger than they probably should have been. He hinted at a strong fear of rejection by others and had some perspective into his self-centeredness. At this time he was also less defensive in his outward behavior; he put forth less effort in an attempt to appear jovial, well-adjusted, and successful, and seemed to behave more naturally and spontaneously.

The reason for this final interview was a conviction on his part that he ought to change jobs and move to another city. He had even considered leaving the newspaper field and going into the field of private investigation or police detective work. The counselor, although doubtful that Joe would make such a drastic change, reassured and encouraged him, reminding him of his assets — superior intelligence, the progress he had made in his field, vocational security, development toward a more realistic understanding of himself, and his high energy and social skills.

This interview had more of the characteristics of effective counseling than any of the others: (1) the relationship was one in which Joe showed less resistance and more security; (2) he showed a greater tendency to come to grips with a personal problem and less tendency to talk about a superficial difficulty; (3) he showed greater release of inner tensions, discussed personal matters more freely; and (4) he seemed to see himself in a broader perspective. How long these perspectives would be retained and whether they would be applied to new situations could not have been predicted with any certainty. A later interview, described below, shows that these insights turned out to be largely verbalizations, too weak to withstand the pressure of strong personal needs buttressed by past habits.

Second interview

Joe called from his newspaper office about a year after the follow-up interview described above. He was in a cheerful mood and asked for an appointment on his day off. He planned to drive down and talk over a matter with the counselor. For the first time, Joe showed some awareness of his obligation to the counselor by bringing him a small gift that he had bought when he was on the West Coast looking into the possibilities of going into detective work. He reminded the counselor that at the time of the last interview he had thought about leaving home and establishing himself in a city on the West Coast. He had had a trial job on a newspaper out there, but had never become fully involved in it. Before leaving home, he had become emotionally involved with a Protestant girl twelve years younger than himself who, like May, was from a social class higher than his own. He even phoned her from the West Coast and arranged to see her when he returned, and immediately proceeded to close out his contacts there. For three or four weeks after he arrived home, he showered her with attention in the form of flowers, candy, gifts, and phone calls. She responded with appreciation and some tangible evidence of affection.

Joe sought advice from a priest that he had known and respected. Despite the priest's advice against marrying Anne, he proposed to her. She was very frank, saying tearfully, "This is hard for me to say because I do like you. But I am not in love with you. You live a unique life. For example, you seem to be attracted to certain kinds of people and places that are new to me (underworld characters and dubious nightspots), and there are two big differences between us — religion and age." She added that he seemed to be greatly absorbed in himself and that most of the things he did were things he thought she would like rather than trying to discover what she really wanted.

Joe then said to the counselor that he planned to see Anne that very night and sought the counselor's advice as to whether he should pursue the matter further. He felt that she had some feeling for him and that there was hope that more might develop. The counselor suggested that Joe re-evaluate the facts he had presented — the differences between him and Anne, the advice he had gotten from the priest, and the fact that Anne had said she did not love him — and then ask himself, "Is there anything encouraging in the relationship that should make me hopeful? Am I not engaging in wishful thinking on the basis of Anne's response to me as a man who has been very good to her?" The counselor continued in this direct manner, breaking somewhat the precedent of earlier counseling with Joe, and said, "Joe, aren't you repeating the same procedure that you went through in your relationship with May? Are you being realistic? Don't you see some very strong similarities between this girl and May, with the possible difference that this girl is more responsive to you as a male?"

This approach by the counselor was very effective. Joe seemed a little stunned, but very soon began to make insightful statements such as, "I guess I am egocentric" and gave some examples. He remarked how much more comfortable he had felt when he was talking than when he was listening to the girl, and the many times he was bored when she was exploring her interests. He also said, with a smile, "I guess I ought to have more confidence in myself at this age. It does seem a little ridiculous for me to drive hundreds of miles to get your advice about whether I should continue to date this girl. I guess what you are trying to show me is that here I am, a boy from the edge of the slums, who is trying to get into the society crowd." All the time he was talking, he continued to use his uniquely evasive expressions, referring to the girl as the "present talent," and to his amorous relationships as being in the "kissy-lip department."

The counselor again pointed out to Joe his many assets, strengths, and achievements. At the end of the interview he suggested that Joe tell him what he had gotten out of the session and told him to be sure to include the positive aspects of his personality. Joe did this rather effectively. He said, "Well, you have shown me that this is not going to work out. It will just get me more shaken up and make me 'couch bait.' I guess I see that I have to look within myself more. As you have said, I am intelligent, I have established myself in a vocation, I have a sense of humor, and I guess I'm a good catch for a girl. I definitely lack confidence in the 'girlie department.' I have known lots of girls and I guess very few of them appeal to me, for different reasons. There are those that have very shady reputations that I meet in the places I go. I did get a real scare once. I almost got serious with one, and I found out she was sleeping with another fellow. But she certainly sprouted wings in my presence."

The counselor added at this point, "You might add that you tend to forget there are two people involved in a marriage; that you are mainly thinking about your needs and the personal benefits of a relationship with a *certain kind* of girl. You seem to need a physically attractive girl, from the right side of town. Your relationships with these special girls are rarely the kind that will test the compatability of the deeper interests and attitudes of both of you."

Joe left, apparently a sadder but wiser man. This interview occurred about a year after the first follow-up, and at this writing still another year has elapsed, with no word from Joe. A question may be raised at this point about the role of the counselor in Joe's life. It might be added that on several occasions Joe mentioned talking with older men about some of his intimate problems, and apparently he spent a good deal of time talking with the priest mentioned earlier. What do we see of Joe's attitude toward his *father*, in either the TAT stories or the comments that he made in some of the interviews? Was his father the kind of man he could respect and with whom he could identify? Was he looking for a stronger personality who could give him advice and could help him to trust his own decisions? What role was played by the "underworld characters" in the borderline nightclubs to which Joe seemed irresistibly drawn? Did they represent a *masculinity* that Joe unconsciously felt he lacked? Could the counselor have been more effective if he had been more directive early in his relationship with Joe? (We have at this writing no evidence that the direct approach to Joe's deeper traits and motives taken in the last interview was effective or ineffective.)

SUMMARY OF TRENDS

We have followed a young man approximately fifteen years in his development toward maturity. We have dipped into his past, using his reports, and obtained fragments of his early life and his relationships with his family and peers. The counselor knew some of Joe's pre-college friends and was able, in part, to reconstruct his earlier environment from this. What information was not obtained about his early family life which might have shed light on his development?

The counselor, by and large, used a supportive and somewhat nondirective method rather than an interrogative and analytical approach in dealing with him. This was done in part because the counselor recognized Joe's sensitivity and thought it best to provide a counseling atmosphere in which Joe could come to grips with his conflicts and sensitivities at his own rate. We might speculate at this point as to Joe's status in respect to various aspects of his self-development when he first saw the counselor.* Was he looking toward May to bolster his self-esteem, to give him a sense of self-extension, and to improve his self-image? Had he been secure in all of these aspects of self, would he have gone through the storm and stress that he experienced while dating May?

What can we hypothesize about Joe's growth in the future? Is he now more realistic than he was earlier?

JOE: Trends in Development

What do you see in the case of Joe? Give your spontaneous reactions to Joe before turning to the questions below.

What kind of person was Joe, in respect to:

    a. strong and persistent psychological needs?

    b. attitude toward himself?

    c. areas of anxiety and defensiveness?

What people in his life might have influenced the development of these traits? What role would you speculate was played by:

    a. Joe's father?

    b. Joe's mother?

    c. his early associates and social background?

    d. other significant persons and experiences about whom we have little or no information?

What additional information is needed to evaluate hypotheses about the role of early personal influences?

Concepts helpful in understanding Joe

    a. Self-image, identity, esteem, and the experiences that shaped them (3, 28)

    b. Immaturity in the development of a male role (32, 89)

---

* G. W. Allport (3) analyzes the proprium, or self, as having the following aspects: 1) sense of bodily self; 2) continuing self-identity; 3) self-esteem; 4) self-extension; 5) self-image; 6) self as rational coper; and 7) self as propriate striving.

c. Preoccupation with insecurity and inability to participate in interpersonal relations (33, 76)

JOE: Comments by a Graduate Student

Joe courted the girl for three years, with no apparent sex contact and very little gratification. We can wonder what Joe was looking for in this relationship. Could it be that Joe would prefer a permanent, asexual courtship with a nice girl — i.e., just like a man — to avoid the threat of marriage and sex? We know that he was more at ease with bad girls — the barflies. Some men are addicted to prostitutes but have notoriously poor marital relationships.

KEN

The Lonely Delinquent

Ken's situation is that of an emotionally disturbed youth who was eventually sentenced to the penitentiary. The case includes a written opinion from a state hospital physician of the "old school" as well as a report from a psychiatrist well trained in newer techniques. This report contains the results of psychiatric and psychological examinations with diagnosis and prognosis, at a private mental hospital of outstanding repute. The several counseling interviews were supportive and not deeply therapeutic. Some understanding of the dynamics of a juvenile delinquent is furnished by Ken's comments about his relationship with his parents and contemporaries and with an "ideal" personality whom he admires.

IDENTIFICATION

The young fellow I saw coming into the warden's office was quite a contrast to the Ken I had seen in counseling conferences a year earlier. There stood a tense, pale, almost tearful youth, unable to carry on much of a conversation but obviously pleased to see someone he knew and to get a glimpse of the outside world through the warden's window. The few letters he wrote while in the penitentiary also showed a withdrawn, subdued individual, able to write only about inconsequentials.

Ken's hand trembled as he extended it to meet mine. There were many lapses in the rather unproductive conversation. After mentioning friends and relatives who had written or visited him, he added, as he stared out the window at the street and buildings, "This is the first time I've seen the sky." The interview was brief; but as I drove back to my office I was preoccupied with how much this young man's human responsiveness and potentiality had been reduced, or suppressed, as a result of this prison experience. No significant effort had been made by anyone at the penitentiary to understand Ken or to explore the cause of his conflict with the law. The result could be seen in this depressed, subdued individual.

The above statement is taken from the notes of a clinical psychologist who had seen Ken several times during the year preceding this visit at the prison. The counseling and other events leading up to the time of Ken's imprisonment constitute the major part of this case.

OCCASION FOR INTERVIEW

The counselor had first seen Ken at the request of a physician whom Ken's mother had consulted. This physician, having only a superficial knowledge of psychiatry, was making arrangements to commit Ken to a state hospital. He may have been motivated by an attempt to save Ken's mother from even greater disgrace by explaining Ken's behavior in terms of mental illness rather than criminality. The incident which precipitated this action was Ken's arrest for holding up a small grocery store with a real-looking toy gun. Ken was accompanied by another fellow, his own age, who had been in trouble previously and had been in a reform school. In view of the physician's action, the prosecuting attorney delayed the trial until a more complete psychiatric examination could be made.

Appearance

Ken was average in height, slight in build, and meticulous about his grooming. His aggressive, tough-appearing mien was a sharp contrast to his thin serious face, small wrists, narrow shoulders, and slender body. When he first came into the office, he was tense and nervous and had some difficulty in starting to talk. In fact, his face twitched a little when he first sat and faced the counselor. When he saw that the counselor was accepting in his attitude and understanding of anything he might say, he began to talk in a serious but slightly defensive manner. Before the interview was over, he had managed to smile a few times.

Ken's carriage, mannerisms, and walk gave the impression that he was not going to be pushed around by anyone. One would conjecture that his ideal for himself was masculinity. He admired men who were tough and able to defend themselves. However, he did not exhibit the unselfconscious kind of masculinity that one often finds, for example, in an athlete who has been in the rough-and-tumble of competitive sports and has had predominantly male companionship all his life; rather, he seemed to dread not being masculine and was consciously striving to cover up this fear — he seemed *defensively* ✓ *masculine.*

Initial part of an interview

Ken apparently appreciated the fact that the counselor, who was affiliated with the university, gave freely of his own time, even though Ken was not attending the university. Furthermore, he seemed to realize that the counselor understood his difficulties and accepted them simply as events that had occurred in his life, without passing judgment on them.

After this initial defensiveness had dropped away, Ken began discussing his problems frankly and openly when the counselor suggested he talk about recent events in his own way. The range of topics touched upon was wide: his girl; the solicitous way his parents had treated him recently; his own feelings of guilt; his attitudes toward himself; his relationship with his father; and brief allusions to events in his history which showed his behavioral instability.

One of the crucial matters discussed was Ken's disappointment that his police record prevented him from getting into any of the military services (the country was engaged in World War II at the time). Ken at no time during the interview excused himself for what he had done. He said, "I have done wrong. To put it crudely, I have served time, and I probably ought to serve it again for what I've just done. That is the biggest blow of all — to realize that I am 'in this category.' I have let my parents down, and I've disappointed the people who have put their trust and faith in me. I don't feel necessarily that I've ruined my life; I think I can come out of this. I wouldn't call myself emotionally unstable. In many respects, I'm just an average fellow. I am restless."

After Ken had made these statements, he went on to talk frankly about a problem that was of great concern to him. "There is something inside me that makes me do these things. I am easily led, particularly under certain circumstances. When I am in a certain mood, I don't think things through, and without knowing how it happened, I find myself involved in a serious matter — a matter that will cause me a good deal of grief later. This last episode was like that. A boy invited me up to his room. He reminded me of Bruce. (Bruce, who is discussed later, was one of Ken's greatest ideals.) When I went to his room, I didn't realize what he wanted; I didn't know that he had a criminal background, or that he wanted me to go in with him in doing 'a job.' But after I got into it, I just didn't seem to care. This sort of thing has happened before. You may have heard that I ran away from home a number of times, and got into various kinds of trouble whenever I did this. I just don't seem to realize the consequences of my acts when I get in a certain mood. Right now I have a girl; she's a fine girl. I respect her, and my behavior with her has been honorable. But I don't think of her at such moments. Now the whole affair is off. I have a feeling that if I were happily married 'this thing' wouldn't have happened."

It is interesting that he associated his involvement in this antisocial activity with marriage. He seemed to feel intuitively that his antisocial behavior occurred because he didn't have a well-ordered love life.

He went on to say, "I wish I could put my finger on just what the difficulty is. If I could, it might help me. Right now I'm not sure that I wouldn't do this again. Sometimes I'm very much afraid of this tendency within me. I've done something wrong, and I've just got to take the rap." He talked about a time when he was paroled as a juvenile and described his cooperation with his parole officers. They had respected him and thought that he had gotten something out of the relationships.

PERSONAL HISTORY

Relationships with parents

The interviews included a discussion of many events that occurred early in Ken's life. They are described as he reported them. At first he simply pointed out that he did not get along very well with his father, that they were too much alike. Later in the interview he complained that he had never been able to confide in his father; that his father was the last person he would ever go to for advice or to discuss matters. He felt much closer to his mother.

Ken was an only child. He described his father as very opinionated and highly irritable. "He has made a point of telling me whenever I've done something wrong. He acts as though he has never made a mistake and I am always in error. My father is close to my mother;

he loves her very much and needs her. I am in the same situation. My mother loves me very much and shows it. I think my father is jealous of me, and I'm somewhat jealous of him. I think, however, if my mother had to choose between my father and me, it would be in my favor.* [This kind of attitude is referred to technically as an *Oedipus complex*.]

"Right now, because of what I did, my lawyer urges me to stay off the streets. Since I am not working, I spend a lot of time at home. I'm around my father much more than I should be. He is trying to be on his good behavior, but we irritate each other greatly. My father has never tried to win my companionship, so it's very difficult now. We seem to have a truce for a few days, but then we both begin to show irritation.

"There is another way that my father is like me. He has very few friends or contacts with other people; I think his being a lone wolf has made it very difficult for me to meet other boys. If my father had friends, I could meet their sons. At no time has my father encouraged me to have friends. When I talked about going to college, he opposed my joining a fraternity. I think if I had gotten into a group in high school, or could look forward to one in college, it might have made a big difference. I didn't feel free to bring friends home. As you know, my family has very little social status or prestige, but they have a great deal of pride. [Ken's father was a clerk in a hardware store. He had held this job a long time, but had none of the traits of a modern salesman.] I realize I cannot blame all of this on my family. I have never developed the traits that would enable me to make friends."

We might offer the hypothesis that this unresolved conflict in the family was a source of much of Ken's later emotional disturbance. It undoubtedly was one of the bases for his aggression, anxiety, and guilt. Furthermore, his relationship with his mother, and possibly his grandmother (who was also over-protecting), greatly influenced his role with the opposite sex. He did not have, in his early life, a strong male figure to emulate.

Feelings prior to episode of antisocial behavior

Ken talked during several interviews about his attitudes and feelings prior to the times he left home and got into trouble. "Just before

* The quotations in the interview are not a transcript of what Ken actually said, but are rather an attempt by the writer to reconstruct the flavor of the conversation from notes dictated later.

I get into trouble, I am very moody; I have a 'don't-care' attitude. Also at that time I seem to hate myself and hate the people around me. I even hate the people I love and who love me. This is not because of frustrations. For example, the last time I got into trouble everything in my external environment seemed to be quite normal, but for some reason or other I seemed to be highly critical of myself. I know I'm a sensitive person. I'm not as sensitive as I was earlier, when I was in grade school. I have very high standards — I wish they weren't so high. Whenever I fall short of my standards, I hate myself and I seem to act blindly. I don't care what people think. Of course, underneath I care very deeply what people think. I've never been entirely satisfied with myself. I've never had the kind of recognition that I would like to have, and now I'm beginning to wonder whether I'll ever be able to work hard enough to earn it."

One can see here the number and depth of Ken's conflicts. They involve his whole concept of himself. He has high standards and aspirations that he has not been able to reach, perhaps because he lacks the emotional stability to make the effort. His daily accomplishments seem meager when measured in terms of his strong need for self-esteem.

Feelings of inadequacy

Occasionally Ken talked about his feelings of inadequacy and inferiority. He regarded himself as a failure and thought that others did too. This feeling led to depression and to hostility and aggression, expressed in the form of antisocial behavior.

Ken mentioned feeling inferior early in life because he was not a good athlete and also because he was poor in mechanical ability. He had to learn how to fight during grade school because, being a little fellow, he was frequently challenged by bigger boys. Perhaps one of the greatest frustrations in his life was his feeling of exclusion from boys' groups. This may have been the result of his own unavailability when the groups gathered. He felt he lacked the ability to become a part of the many male groups that existed, either teams or informal groups. Although he never admitted that he felt rejected by his age mates, he acted as though this were true.

Attitudes toward girls

Ken talked very readily and in some detail about his relationships with girls. These apparently were among the most satisfying relationships he had, in contrast with his typically frustrated relationships with boys and men. "For some reason, I am the kind of fellow that girls like, even though I don't seem to be too aggressive toward them. I am not the kind of fellow that tries to make time with a girl. Yet, I've had many physical intimacies with girls. It just seems to happen. I don't take advantage of them, and I don't lead them astray. However, my relationships with girls do not seem to be backed by very strong feelings on my part — not nearly as strong as one would think, considering the number of girls I've known and how intimate we have been."

Work experience

Ken's mother seemed to fight some of his major battles for him. After he graduated from high school, she obtained a job for him with the dry goods store where she worked. He seemed to have regular habits, and he saved his money until summer, at which time he visited his cousins. While there, he became sick and accumulated debts. His mother came down, paid his bills, and agreed that he could continue with his job there until fall. In the fall, he returned to his home town, resumed his old job, began dating a girl of whom his family approved, and started saving money. He continued his attempts to get in the military service, including the merchant marine. Finally, he decided to enter the university, with the hope of studying dentistry.

Interview with Ken's mother

When Ken first came to the counselor, a psychiatric nurse arranged a supplementary interview with Ken's mother at the suggestion of the counselor. Here we get a professional person's observations of Ken's mother as she gives her view of Ken's development. The nurse described Ken's mother as a "very sweet woman," relaxed, conventionally groomed, youthful in appearance for a middle-aged woman. She was employed as a receptionist in the office of a small department store. She had many social contacts in the town, was very well liked and respected, and had been successful in interesting a number of adults in Ken's problems.

She described Ken as having been an ideal child, easily disciplined, and healthy except for typical childhood diseases. There were no problems during early toilet training. At about nine years of age he struck his head in a fall and "was unconscious for some time." When he was about twelve years of age he began to show nervousness and cried in bed at night. At this time he complained about sensitivity in gym classes. He had difficulty dressing in time or remembering his locker combination. Ken's mother gave no evidence to indicate that he had any hobbies or interests which might have satisfied his needs and led to the development of strong adult interests or skills. He seemed to spend much time alone, possibly daydreaming.

His mother visited the school when he was in junior high and had conferences with his principal. The principal considered Ken to be quite bright; and at his suggestion Ken was given extra work and music lessons. In addition, he was put on the school safety squad. His mother also asked the family physician to "talk to him about his nervousness." Despite these measures, he continued to have periods of despondency. Neither Ken nor his mother had any interviews during his grade-school or junior high school years with anyone professionally qualified to treat his emotional difficulties.

Ken spent the summer before he entered senior high school visiting his mother's cousin. It had been a happy experience. He reported in one interview that this cousin was his favorite relative. She had been extremely popular as a girl. She was pretty, was fond of him, and he admired her about as much as he did his mother. (She and his mother had grown up together and were like sisters.) Moreover, her husband became Ken's masculine ideal. He taught Ken to swim and was a constant companion during that summer. Ken remarked that his father should have been like his cousin's husband. However, at about this time, Ken learned that this beloved relative was an alcoholic, and he was greatly disillusioned. The disillusionment was not mentioned during the early interviews, but he related it later as one of the most disturbing things that had happened in his life.

Bruce, an "ideal"

Bruce, a boy that Ken met and idealized in high school, played a major role in his adolescent life. He said, "Bruce in many ways represented all of the many traits that I didn't have and wanted so much. I enjoyed him. He was handsome, had a good personality, he seemed to like me, and spent more time with me than most of my other acquaintances. I didn't see him as having any bad traits. He couldn't! I was a little frail in grade school and not an athlete, and Bruce was an athlete. I could talk to Bruce. I had never been able to talk to anybody before, least of all my father. Now I can't quite understand why Bruce meant so much to me. All I know is that he did, and whenever he suggested something, I was right with him. It wasn't until later that I realized he had a 'record' and many bad traits. I got into trouble for the first time with him [arrested as a juvenile offender]. It was with him that I began cutting classes."

We might speculate as to what Bruce meant to Ken. Ken was looking for a masculine ideal who would be responsive to him. He viewed his father as a good man, but a colorless and cold person with whom he was competing for his mother's love. His cousin's husband had been an ideal, but that lasted only for a summer. In Bruce, Ken had the friend he had been looking for — one who was brave and who was willing to defy the rules of the school and, perhaps inferentially, the rules of his parents.

They ran away from home together several times. Ken never mentioned what the episodes of running away from his parents meant to him. They certainly got him away temporarily from the emotional triangle of the home; they allowed him to have the full attention of his friend, to satisfy many needs of a quiet boy who had always felt inferior. He felt included, perhaps for the first time. He could now feel he belonged to a male group, even if the group was only two persons. His behavior now included acts of aggression against all that his father, in his conservative way, stood for.

When Ken became restless and ran away, he rarely thought of the consequences of his acts. Up to this time, his behavior had not gotten him into any trouble that his mother couldn't get him out of. However, when Bruce and Ken were arrested, the realities of the situation could not be overlooked, and Ken was quite disturbed. The one person and way of life that had meant so much to him were wrong in the eyes of his mother and of people he accepted as good people.

Much of the above information on Ken's early history came out of several counseling sessions. In fact, much of what occurred during the sessions gave Ken an opportunity to relate the events which led to his delinquency in an understanding and accepting environment. The section that follows, therefore, is largely a continuation of what went before, including two psychiatric reports from two different institutions.

COUNSELING EVENTS

Attitudes toward society's standards

What was right and wrong, good and bad, was for Ken an area of confusion and conflict. During most of the interviews, Ken indicated how much he was at odds with society. He referred to the chicken thief who gets caught and punished while the embezzler is allowed to buy his way out. He mentioned the "big boys" that got away with crooked schemes. He showed a strong antagonism toward social standards. In reality, he was *ambivalent* in his attitude toward the standards of society. He often admitted that he had done wrong and would have to pay for it. He remarked that he didn't care what people thought, but then corrected this to say that underneath he did care. He viewed himself as a stubborn individual. He suggested that possibly he was too impulsive.

Once when he was discussing his own character, he said, "I have a bad reputation, and my father has a very good one." Without verbalizing it, one got the impression that he would like to add, "And look at him; look what kind of a person he really is." There was the suggestion that his father was the kind of person that many people would respect, but that underneath he was cold and colorless. Furthermore, his father was not, in his eyes, a success — socially, economically, or vocationally.

Ken's relationships with girls also had some ambivalent elements, as suggested in his previous remarks. He referred to them at one time as a chase. "Going after girls," he said, "is like a fox hunt. That's the most important thing about it."

"What might have been"

On numerous occasions Ken stated that if he had been included in a group, if he were happily married, and (he suggested, but never clearly stated), if he were not in his family situation, things would have been different for him. Apparently Ken was looking for a male ideal with whom he could *identify* — a model, as it were, whom he could imitate and in whom he could see his own identity reflected. It was not clear to him what kind of person he really was and where he belonged. He wanted response from his fellows, to be accepted by them. For reasons that lay largely within himself, he did not get this acceptance. This isolation from others was related to the sensitivity he had experienced in junior high school, his alleged failure as an athlete and as a "regular fellow," and the consequent hostility, which may have alienated potential friends. Personal identity as an acceptable member of his peer group was something he had never experienced. He thought that if he had experienced it, life would have been different.

Ken's relationship with most adult males was not good. He admitted that his lawyer knew very little about him and would have a hard time defending him. This may have been projection. He said, "The psychiatrist spent only half an hour with me and yet came up with a long report. At no time did he look me straight in the eye." Ken's parole officers and male teachers all tried to befriend him. Possibly they seemed to Ken to take a paternalistic role. Whatever the reason, Ken never developed a warm, clearly positive relationship with any of them.

Psychiatric opinions

Ken was sent to a state hospital for three weeks, between the time of his arrest and his trial, while he was still on bail. It was during this time that he spent half an hour with the hospital superintendent who wrote the "psychiatric report" quoted below:*

> We have diagnosed Ken as a case of psychopathic personality with asocial and amoral trends. It is true that he displays some schizoid symptoms, but one cannot say that he is legally insane. It is very definite that he does know right from wrong, but he goes ahead and does these abnormal acts as he has in the past. It is impossible to state the cause of this abnormal condition; but heredity might play a part, though his environment has not been very conducive to learning proper conduct. There is little we can do for him in a mental institution. We can attempt to use psychotherapy, and try to show him his abnormal acts; but there is no type of therapy that would cause an improvement in such a condition.**
>
> I doubt if we will be able to give him very much of value in psychotherapy, because he is so supercilious and refuses to accept any advice. Electric shock treatments might scare him into trying to do better; but this is unpredictable, as we have not had good results with psychopaths in the past. He is a trying patient to care for — resenting any authority, picking fights with other patients, and being very superior in his attitudes. He attempts to explain his foolish escapades with the law by stating he was drunk at the time; I doubt this very much, judging by his mother's description of his criminalistic tendencies. I would

---

* As explained later, this is not the kind of report that a well-trained psychiatrist from a modern institution would submit. It is an informal opinion from a medical officer in a state hospital.
** The emphasis is mine, indicating attitudes of the physician that are questionable.

have more hope for him as a schizophrenic than as a psychopath.

This report was written about fifteen years ago and does not reflect
the kind of statement we might expect from a well-trained psychiatrist at that time. It was written by a hospital superintendent in a
poorly-equipped institution with a very low budget. Frequently physicians in such institutions had very little formal, supervised, and
specialized psychiatric training. The letter contains many questionable attitudes toward diagnosis and therapy.

In contrast to this "report," the one which follows was written by
a competent psychiatrist at a well-known, well-staffed psychiatric institution. Ken was sent to this private psychiatric institution for
evaluation after he had been discharged from the state hospital. This
report by the psychiatrist summarizes the findings on Ken after several days of complete physical, neurological, laboratory, and psychological examinations in a modern, well-equipped psychiatric hospital:

> Physical, neurological, and laboratory studies were essentially
> negative.
> Clinical psychiatric examination revealed a very intelligent
> young man. The psychological test showed the same natural en-
> dowment of the boy, but also revealed the presence of intense
> anxiety and an underlying depressive trend. Although he is at
> times slightly incoherent, there is no evidence, either clinically
> or on the psychological test, of the presence of psychosis.
> At the staff conference we agreed that we were dealing here
> with a very severe neurotic character-structure, which has al-
> ready led to three episodes of antisocial behavior, and which
> very likely will, unless checked, lead to further recurrences.
> Treatment in such cases is extremely difficult. Psychoanalysis
> has sometimes been undertaken; but it has usually been diffi-
> cult, expensive, and prolonged. The results have not been very
> satisfactory.
> We feel quite pessimistic about the ultimate prognosis. But
> in view of the many fine qualities the boy possesses, it might be
> possible, with treatment, to help him to make at least a more
> satisfying adjustment, if not a more complete solution of all of
> his underlying problems.

In contrasting these two reports, one notices that the two writers
saw Ken very differently. One saw him as a "trying patient," the

other as "a boy with many fine qualities." They agreed in their relative pessimism about his prognosis. The hospital superintendent was preoccupied with the legal aspect, while the psychiatrist gave a broader picture of Ken as a person.

In view of the psychiatric reports and in spite of numerous character witnesses whom Ken's mother obtained for the trial, Ken was sentenced to five years' imprisonment in the state penitentiary. His family visited him. The psychological counselor made one visit to the prison, which was mentioned at the beginning of this case report. Another older person, a newspaperwoman and writer who had a son Ken's age, made several trips to see him, taking him gifts, and encouraging him to write.

FOLLOW-UP

The reader's prediction

It should be interesting to pause here and speculate as to how you think Ken develops from this point. Will he continue the kind of life he led prior to his encounter with the law? Will he complete his parole without incident? Would you predict that he will settle down, get a permanent job, marry, and live a conventional life in a community where his past is not known?

To what extent do you think he will show the influences the newspaperwoman had upon him, follow up his impulses to write, and keep in touch with her? What are your conjectures about his vocational aspirations? Do you think he will attempt to get more education and enter a profession, as his mother hoped he would; or will he settle in a less prestigious vocation similar to the kind he previously had? It might be valuable to attempt to support your speculations with pertinent facts from the information presented here.

Outcome

During the counseling period, Ken had expressed the wish to write a book about some of his experiences. No writing of any kind ever materialized; in fact, the two letters the counselor received were very meager and uninspired.

Ken remained in the penitentiary four years and learned a trade. When he was released, he moved to another city and lived away from his parents. He obtained a somewhat routine job, and met his parole requirements without incident. Within a short time after his prison experience, Ken married and had a family. Although no details are available about his life after his parole, second- and third-hand information indicates that he is making at least a satisfactory adjustment.

There is no doubt that the penitentiary was a distressing and possibly inhibiting experience for Ken. Apparently he made very few friends there. Just before and during the trial Ken seemed to be developing deeper insights and more realistic perspectives into his behavior. He had more conviction about his ability to control his behavior than he had shown earlier. What effects imprisonment had on these perspectives is not known. He apparently did not seek further education nor aspire to positions of leadership or outstanding achievement.

KEN: Interpretive Trends and Relationships

How would you describe Ken as a person? Keep in mind:

    a. his realism, adaptive potentialities, and integrity.

    b. his identity. Did he see his role in life clearly?

    c. his need for status and friendship among other young people.

Did his problems begin at twelve or thirteen years of age, or did they only then become apparent, because of adolescent pressures?

What relationships were most influential? Describe Ken's relationship with:

    a. his father.

    b. his mother, describing her complex and paradoxical role.

    c. Bruce.

    d. others mentioned in the case.

Concepts helpful in understanding Ken

    a. Oedipus complex (44, 96)

    b. Adolescent identity (25, 89)

    c. Psychopath or sociopath (25, 91)

Other concepts which may have some relevance to this case are: delinquency; psychiatric report; psychopath.

KEN: Comments by a Graduate Student

I would entitle this case "A Cry for Help — But No One Answered." The mother's intrusiveness in Ken's life was extraordinary.

She was manipulative and demanding — in what seemed a very "nice" way to most of the townspeople and presumably to Ken too.

One can see illustrated here defensive masculinity, the Oedipus complex, and susceptibility to interpersonal influence. He was easily swayed. He had an ineffectual father — a barrier to appropriate sex-role modeling. His mother was socially aggressive and personable, but she placed considerable emphasis on facade. This characteristic is frequently cited as influential in character disorders similar to Ken's.

A mood of loneliness and desperation precedes some of his anti-social behavior and suggests a need to call attention to his unhappy position in life — in effect, a cry for help. He is anxious, and his antisocial behavior seems *reactive*, in other words, he is in process. This may help explain why he was finally able to "make the grade."

He showed inability to make contact with age-mates as a young boy. Sullivan calls the development of contacts with age-mates the *isophilic experience*.

Ken seems to be a desperate, lonely person, kicking and thrashing around, hoping for something, anything, to happen. It does: he lands in prison. Immediately after his release he plunges into marriage. The magnitude of his loneliness seems to have hit him hard and made him realize the importance of a stable relationship.

LEWIS

The Severely Neurotic

Lewis is a youth with acute psychoneurotic symptoms who
was observed and treated over a period of several years.
Some exploration of his family's behavior is included.
Since his counselor was absent from the university for a
period of about a year, we see the effects of the termination of therapy, which was both supportive and directive.
In the counselor's absence, Lewis was referred to a physician who was less understanding and accepting of his
symptoms. An unsolicited letter a year after his graduation
indicates how such an individual continues to function in
most areas of life, and the degree to which distressing
symptoms continue. A critical discussion of the dynamics
of the case written by a graduate clinical student follows
the presentation, demonstrating how such cases may be
used for sophisticated critiques.

IDENTIFICATION

Lewis was first seen while he was a freshman in the College of
Arts and Sciences. He was eighteen years old at that time. He had
come from a town of three hundred population. He had the appearance of an untidy, self-conscious, submissive, and quiet student. He
was slightly below average in height and weight, and was poorly
groomed.

Complaint

He was first admitted to the university hospital because he had
inhaled fumes of benzene, which had been put in his pipe as a practical joke. As the result of this, he complained that he could not get
his breath. This feeling of breathlessness had recurred periodically

since that occasion, together with complaints of weakness and nervousness. Five times during the school year he was brought into the hospital by fellow students. At first he complained of difficulty in breathing, and later his symptoms extended to nervousness, weakness, and gas in the abdomen. During these periods he became anxious and hyperventilated;* he stated that he swallowed air.

PERSONAL HISTORY

Lewis was an only child. His father had had "spells" similar to those Lewis was experiencing when he was a young man, and his mother was also somewhat nervous. Lewis entered school at six years of age. He had had no playmates to speak of until that time, but had stayed close to his home. He was greatly frightened by other children when he entered school. He complained that the town hoodlums "beat up on him." His parents over-protected him. He felt awkward and inferior when he first entered school. He remembered himself as a normal, vivacious child before that time. He described a childhood accident in which he cut his hand badly, lost a considerable amount of blood, and fainted.

His record in school was good. He had a superior grade-point average in high school. His college aptitude percentile score was 97 in terms of national norms, placing him in the top 3 per cent in ability, despite a relatively poor college record.

His mother was a serious, conscientious, and very religious person. He remembers that she frightened him greatly when he misbehaved as a child, telling him he would be punished for his sins. He attended services in a country church; and he had associated religion and religious beliefs with fear and punishment.

He remembered his grandfather (his mother's father) as being "very nervous." He attended many movies with an uncle, most of them exciting adventure stories which frightened him. He masturbated as a child. When his mother discovered him doing this, she told him he could be punished for this "sin" by becoming insane. *It seems likely that his biological and social background contained a strong potentiality for anxiety and emotional insecurity.*

* Hyperventilation is the process of breathing more deeply and rapidly than is normal and necessary to maintain the oxygen-dioxygen balance. When there is an excess of oxygen in the blood, breathing automatically slows down until the oxygen-dioxygen balance of the blood is restored.

In his later development he tended toward introversion. His mother prevented him from playing with most children. His experiences on the playground at school were very unpleasant. He shunned other students, daydreamed at frequent intervals, and spent much time in the woods alone, hunting and fishing. He felt inferior to most of the children in the town (his clothes were, in fact, inferior). He learned to play a musical instrument, but always felt self-conscious when he played before others.

COUNSELING EVENTS

When Lewis first came to the counselor's attention, he was living in a large cooperative house on campus. He had relatively few friends, made few contacts with the other students, and did not date or participate in any extracurricular activities. He spent his extra time practicing his music, which had come to be a great source of satisfaction to him.

When questioned, he admitted that he was quite unhappy, was very poorly adjusted to his environment, and had such vivid daydreams that at times he found it difficult to distinguish between what he had daydreamed and what he had actually experienced. He said that his "nervousness" had increased greatly over the past two years and had reached its peak during the periods he was in college. After the students put benzene in his pipe as a prank, his "nervousness" took the form of inability to get his breath. He was *highly suggestible* and revised his symptoms readily to fit any illness suggested to him. This suggestibility is further illustrated by the acute phobia of rabies which he developed later.

He was fairly well oriented in general information compared with other freshmen. He seemed ambitious and had some insight outside the area of his disability. He spent much more time studying than the average student, but his concentration was very poor. He had broad interests. His philosophy of life was not very clear, although he was trying to formulate it.

He was quite interested in girls, but never could summon enough nerve to ask a girl for a date. He daydreamed quite a bit about them. His daydreams were so vivid that when he came face to face with a girl about whom he had daydreamed, he was too embarrassed to talk to her.

Diagnosis and therapy

What kind of behavior disorder is represented by Lewis's symptoms? His persistent panic suggests a type of psychoneurosis known as anxiety reaction.* However, he had many schizoid symptoms, particularly the vivid daydreams. Once or twice he reported feelings of strangeness and unreality. However, after some months his personality seemed to focus more consistently on the anxiety syndrome. He became progressively more involved in the activities of typical college students. Various diagnoses in his hospital records were: poisoning, general; cardiovascular neurosis; anxiety neurosis; hysteria; and nervous fatigue.

In the early stages *psychotherapy was both directive and non-directive.* The directive aspects consisted of suggestions which emphasized more contacts with other students, improved grooming, substitution of activity for daydreams, spending more time with his music, careful selection of motion pictures (many fear-provoking movies threw him into a highly emotional state), and encouragement to write out disturbing thoughts or ideas (this had a good effect at first but later tended to make him introspective). The non-directive aspects of therapy consisted of allowing him to talk freely about his problems, daydreams, and previously repressed sexual fantasies and impulses.

In addition, some of his behavior was interpreted to him in terms of its physiological basis so that he might understand it better. He was shown that he became acutely conscious of normal physiological responses to what he interpreted as danger; awareness of these augmented his fear and prolonged the physiological reactions.

He seemed to show an irregular but noticeable improvement for about two months. At that time he was accidentally exposed to some rabid dogs and urged to take preventive shots. Lewis then developed a phobia for rabies, in addition to his previously established pattern of anxiety symptoms.

By the end of the school year, when he was preparing to return home, he had definitely improved. He had started to play in one of the campus dance orchestras and had gained success and satisfaction from this. He made a list of suggestions for himself which he intended to follow when he went home. The suggestions emphasized facing his problems, being more aggressive, having more contacts with people, and talking over his difficulties.

* This is one form of psychoneurosis in which the most predominant symptom is a marked degree of morbid and objectively unfounded dread.

Second year in school

When Lewis returned to the university in the fall, he reported that he had not been well at home. He seemed much more tense and uneasy during his first visit to the office. He said that toward the end of the summer he had had "spells" almost every day. He had seen a doctor at home, who diagnosed his difficulty as a neurocirculatory disturbance and told him that he would not be able to help him very much.* He had looked forward to his return to the university and to an active program of school work, social contacts, dates, and work with the orchestra.

In the first month of the semester he had another of his "spells." He came to the clinic in a taxi. He looked ill, was unsteady on his feet, his complexion was pale, and he seemed terrified. In order to demonstrate to Lewis that the symptoms he was experiencing were an exaggeration of the normal physiological concomitants of emotion, the counselor suggested that they leave the office and *take a walk, to talk about his difficulties.* His reply was, "I can't walk now, not in this condition." The counselor took him firmly but gently by the arm and they went for a walk. Within six or eight minutes Lewis was feeling well and reacting quite normally. At the end of fifteen minutes he was able to walk home by himself. During the walk he belched air frequently, and then began breathing much more normally. This kind of treatment, together with the rather broad combination of directive and non-directive therapy mentioned above, brought about considerable improvement, in contrast to his condition when he arrived, nearly disabled by his "spells." The semester as a whole was one of the best he had had.

He went home for Christmas vacation and came back greatly improved. He seemed better mentally and physically than he had been in a long time. He commented that he was surprised at how well he had felt while he was at home. His parents were pleased and commented on his improvement. He seemed to become conscious for the first time of the progress he had made during the school year. Probably his adjustment to being at home, in the old familiar atmosphere, was easier after the year he had spent away from it.

During this year his social habits changed greatly. In the early part of the year he had feared girls intensely; later he began dating them.

---

* From this comment it seems the physician regarded his condition as a disturbance of the circulatory system — especially heart action — which was not organic but related to psychological factors.

He continued to improve and gained confidence in his work with the orchestra; but throughout the semester he had periodic "spells" of anxiety. His stays in the hospital as a bed-patient dropped from five in the first year to two visits in the second year; he came into the clinic only three times during the year, each time complaining of pain in his abdomen.

The counselor's absence

At this time the counselor who was seeing him left the university for ten months. During his absence Lewis had no psychotherapy. Since he was a part-time student, he could enter the hospital only as a private patient. During this period he visited the hospital or clinic ten times — the greatest frequency of visits during any period that he was in school.

When the counselor returned to the campus, he made the following notes:

> I saw Lewis in early February and realized that during the ten-month period of my absence he had developed many more symptoms. He had a marked facial tic* that had not been apparent before, and he was much more nervous and anxious. He had had another experience with a dog he believed to be rabid, and this intensified his fear. During February and March he had visited the hospital or clinic five times. His phobia for rabies became extremely acute at times, and he began phoning me at night in a terrified state. He was sure he had rabies. He felt he "couldn't go on." All sorts of disturbing thoughts came to him, including the fear of suicide. I realized that immediate and drastic treatment was called for and seriously considered persuading him to commit himself to a state hospital. Investigation indicated that he probably would not be accepted there, so I decided upon an intensive period of directive therapy as an alternative.

This young man, it seems, had developed a dependence on therapy and on this therapist in particular. He had improved under the therapeutic program, but when the therapist left the university for an academic year, Lewis became worse. His symptoms returned, and he seemed to be more disturbed than ever. Inquiries indicated that the physicians in the clinic were somewhat annoyed by his continual re-

---

* A spasmodic twitching of certain facial muscles.

appearance with symptoms which had a psychological or functional
rather than organic basis. The treatment they gave him — scolding,
in contrast to the acceptance by the counselor — was partially responsible for his worsened condition. After a period of renewed acceptance and understanding, he was able to see that his symptoms were
bringing about rejection.

More intensive treatment

After the psychologist had returned and brought himself up to
date on Lewis's activities, he decided that Lewis would need intensive
therapy. Several sessions a week were planned, at first on consecutive
days. These sessions were a combination of directive and non-directive procedures, with initial emphasis on relaxation and waking suggestion. Perhaps if Lewis were being treated by a physician today,
tranquilizing drugs would have been administered; but this program
of therapy antedated the use of such drugs.

The clinic psychologist helped Lewis to review the nature of his
condition. He reminded Lewis of his assets and accomplishments, and
of the fact that his symptoms disappeared whenever he was accepted
and actively engaged in talking or walking with the counselor. Little
emphasis was placed on analysis or interpretation beyond this. When
Lewis began to feel better in the interview, he was encouraged to assume more responsibility and to talk about his problems and activities
as he saw them.

Some of the suggestions given by the counselor were recorded on
tape, and Lewis took this with him, using it together with his own
suggestions in daily periods of relaxation. As time went on, the suggestion and autosuggestion phase of the therapy diminished and the
non-directive phase increased. Another therapist might have placed
more emphasis on analysis and interpretation than this counselor did.

The results of these sessions were surprisingly good. Lewis soon
began to improve, showing gains in insight, confidence, and self-
control. When he left the university in the latter part of May, he
wrote the following:

> By the use of this method of suggestion I am now able to
> take advantage of many facts about my physical condition. This
> gives me a feeling of security concerning it. Once this was not
> at all possible. I could go over this reasoning in my mind, but it
> had little effect on my body. Taking these suggestions in a re-
> laxed condition, I am more able to use this logic to guide my
> behavior and feelings and to calm myself.

FOLLOW-UP

Here are excerpts from a letter Lewis wrote to the counselor one year after his last visit:

Yes, I'm really a family man now-a-days — I have a wife and a ten-month-old girl. We are intensely proud of the little doll. She is exceptionally healthy and, if you'll forgive my prejudice, very beautiful. I'm enclosing a photo of her.

After leaving school a year ago, I went home and played in dance bands. It wasn't the thing for a married man; so I decided to try teaching. I am in a high school of 350 in a small town — just about the right size. This has been a valuable experience for me. I teach a little of everything, but not music, which would be more my line. It keeps me busy — and that has been very good. Since I've been married and settled down somewhat, I find it much easier to get my work done. My mental health has improved in many respects, although I am still bothered with my heart. I do not have severe attacks nearly as often as I once did: I am aware of the extremely irregular rhythm I have, as you no doubt suspect, but I have been unable to convince any physicians that I am near death. I still have symptoms of sufficient severity to convince me of ominous consequences, but I have no worries about rabid dogs or moods of depression. If I could ever get the better of my heart disturbance, I think I should be much more successful and happy. Teaching is quite a nervous strain for me and I would prefer to try something else later on, but I am glad I have done it and hope to continue with it for a year or so.

LEWIS: Patterns, Development, Adjustments

What did you see as you read the case of Lewis? Give your own spontaneous reactions to Lewis before turning to the questions below.

Unique, enduring characteristics

    a. What needs do you think Lewis's rather striking symptoms served?

    b. Do you see several persistent dispositions or traits that were dominant in his life and related to his unique behavior?

   c. Do you know anyone who has patterns of behavior and experience similar to Lewis's?

Development of personality

   a. You might find it interesting to review the factors, including his basic physical constitution, which contributed to his adult personality.

   b. What influences during his life might conceivably have changed the course of his development?

   c. To what extent does this case furnish you with some illustrations of neurotic symptoms and different counseling procedures?

   d. What kinds of relationships and life meanings do you think were important to Lewis, even though he was not conscious of them?

Concepts helpful in understanding Lewis

   a. Strong dependency needs (9, 88)

   b. A constitutional predisposition (26, 86)

   c. Early anxiety conditioning (6, 26)

   d. Inadequate masculine identity; sex-typing (67, 88)

   e. Childhood isolation from peer culture; social isolate (52, 88)

   f. Sense of identity with work, marriage, and fatherhood (32, 54)

   g. Need satisfaction through neurotic symptoms (115, 117)

Other concepts which may have some relevance to this case: neurosis; psychosis; secondary gains; hysteria; symptom choice; self-conscious reaction; phobia; psychosexual development.

LEWIS: Comments by a Graduate Student*

The Oedipal conflict

Lewis's case is interesting from several points of view. One of the most striking features is that the psychiatric symptomatology and underlying psychodynamics present almost a "classical" case of psychoneurosis. Many of the psychiatric formulations, particularly psychoanalytic elaborations, which have been developed attempt to

---

* The author asked Mr. Shahe Zenian to give his impressions of the meaning of this case in terms of his clinical training. His evaluation is included here as an example of how these cases may be used with advanced students in clinical and counseling psychology as a point of departure for critical discussion.

explain various mental and emotional illnesses by hypothesizing "model" situations. The well-known Oedipus complex is such a model, implying that under certain conditions a child will be cast into a relatively protracted conflict between affectional demands upon his mother and competitive struggle with his father. This has sometimes been characterized as a "family romance." The Oedipal conflict is resolved when the child finally introjects* the father image — that is, when he identifies with the father rather than competing with him. As a result, what was once a threatening, punitive figure then becomes incorporated within oneself and provides the basis for super-ego formation. Thus the external father image becomes internalized.

Although this is a very brief summary of the Oedipal situation and hardly does it justice, it should be noted that the classical analytic point of view maintains that all children go through more or less the same situation at a certain period in early childhood (usually between the ages of four and seven). It should also be stressed that the Oedipal relationship, taken as it is from mythology, is for the child a symbolic relationship, heavily laden with infantile, unconscious material, and rich in fantasy. It is erroneous to attempt to translate these notions (they are not "theories," strictly speaking) into the prosaic language of our reality-oriented adult world. It is far better, and far more correct, to think of these formulations as symbolic, or even "poetic" models. Frequent reference has been made to the "metaphorical" language of Freud; let us try to keep this in mind. As we examine Lewis's case a little more closely, we should also bear in mind that since this is a symbolic model, we cannot possibly expect one-to-one relationships on every point. Sometimes the model does not apply at all, or at least does not seem to, because what is manifest (observable) has been filtered through so many distinct individualistic aspects of one's personality. When the symptoms are more obvious and the psychiatric pattern more clearly delineated, the underlying dynamics seem to fit the analytic model much better. Lewis's symptoms seem to lend themselves readily to such an interpretation. Here, then, is a clinical evaluation of the case from the standpoint of an eclectic analytic orientation.

Clinical picture and dynamic diagnosis

A brief overview of Lewis's case reveals the following salient features. He was an only child, with a strong-willed, over-protective

---

* Introjection is the process by which the individual tends to absorb the personality of another into his own experience.

mother and a weak father. He was alienated and intimidated by his peer group in early childhood. He seems to have taken active recourse to fantasy (personal dream life), both as a retreat from what he perceived to be a hostile social environment and also to compensate for the meagerness of his interpersonal relationships. This seems to have been a long-standing and characteristic disposition on his part. Not having experienced the proper affectional (love) relationship with his parents, which would have provided the basis for all future relationships with others, he simultaneously distrusts close ties with others, yet is prone to becoming over-attached in a passive, dependent manner. One aspect of his infantile attempt at seeking affection is his suggestibility and the development of an essentially hysteroid personality. His sexual experiences and outlook were of a restrictive nature. In his therapeutic relationship with the counselor he develops a strong transference and exhibits a marked regression during the counselor's ten-month absence. His diagnosis reveals a variety of psychophysiologic reactions, predominantly cardiovascular and respiratory types, and psychoneurotic disorders, which include anxiety, phobic, and depressive reactions.

Hysteria: conversion and psychosomatic

If a single term were to be employed that would best describe Lewis, it would be "hysteroid." The term is derived from "hysteria" and the suffix "-oid" means "like" or "similar to." It is a generic term and should not be construed as equivalent to saying that Lewis was "hysterical" (a special psychiatric diagnostic term). Many of his reactions are similar to a conversion reaction (psychiatric diagnosis) while others are similar to psychophysiologic reactions (better known as "psychosomatic"). On the basis of symptomatology alone, perhaps Lewis might best fit the diagnosis "psychoneurotic disorder, anxiety reaction," since most of the time his anxiety is diffuse. However, at other times it is more specific, as in his phobic reaction to rabies.

Technically there is quite a difference between symptoms of conversion hysteria and those of a psychosomatic type. In conversion hysteria, the psychic energy which is blocked, or not permitted to express itself, is said to be due to a repressed impulse. The energy which is dammed up is expressed in the form of a physical symptom; that is, it is "converted," hence the name "conversion hysteria." However, psychologically speaking, this is an "expensive" symptom to maintain. It requires many additional conscious reactions on the part of the patient to "explain" why he has the symptom. These of course must be "invented." Often they are quite shallow, and sometimes the patient does not even bother consciously to account for his symptoms. His rationale may be obviously phony, even to the inexperienced observer, or he may be totally unconcerned about it. This latter reaction has been characterized as "la belle indifference." In short, hysterical reactions are not very "sophisticated"; in fact, conversion hysteria is more likely to occur in people who are not noted for their mental brilliance. Lewis himself could not be characterized as having utilized his potentially high intelligence. A conversion reaction is a fairly blatant form of neurotic symptom, but it does cause a certain amount of pain and inconvenience. Consciously the patient is not as concerned as he might be, but he is punishing himself and his superego is placated. Moreover, this seems to involve "denial" (a specific defense mechanism), again quite an expensive mechanism to maintain.

Secondary gains

Lewis is not unaware of his symptoms, therefore does not fit the picture exactly in terms of his symptomatology. But it seems clear enough that he was highly suggestible, which is a definite "hysteroid" characteristic and that he received considerable "secondary gain" from his symptoms. That is, the pity and concern of others toward his illness were in themselves reinforcing agents. Counseling itself might have inadvertently provided some secondary gain. Lewis was "getting attention" by having an "illness." Recall that his interpersonal relations at school were not the best. He was relatively withdrawn from the other students in the dorm, and openly admitted to the counselor that he was unhappy. Getting attention by developing a physical ailment is quite characteristic of children. One need only recall the dramatic manner in which a young child exhibits a tiny scratch to his mother. Aside from the very real sensitivity to bodily assault, the child is quite obviously seeking parental affection. He usually gets it and quite often it is of the sort where "you kiss it and it will go away." This sort of "miraculous" cure is condescending child's play, but it also characterizes rather well the hysteroid reaction to pain and physical illness. In later life the specific manifestations might assume more "adult" forms, but the underlying dynamics remain the same. Note how readily Lewis responded to directive therapy. Recall now, if you will, our brief discussion of "symbolic" representation in the Oedipus complex. Isn't the counseling situation symbolically similar to "kiss it and it will go away"?

Symptom choice

Psychoanalysis proposes a firm psychic determinism. Often this is mistaken for "fatalism." Fatalism is teleological, for it states that what will happen must happen, in order to support what has gone on before. Determinism states simply that what has happened is due to something that happened before, that "there must be a reason." There is no inevitability associated with it; it merely states that psychological reactions are not fortuitous. Consequently "symptom choice" is not capricious, but must have meaning. Lewis's predominant symptoms, aside from generalized anxiety, were respiratory ailments, phobic reactions, and cardiovascular reactions. The last of these seems to fit better into a psychosomatic category, so it will be dismissed for the moment. But the other two occupy our attention, for we are confronted with the puzzle — why breathing difficulties? In both the respiratory and phobic reactions the onset was due to high suggestibility. But why should Lewis respond to these and not to other ailments that undoubtedly "suggested" themselves? From our knowledge of conversion hysteria we know that the particular symptom itself is a symbolization or a caricature of some underlying conflict. Lewis's predominant symptoms have already been stated, with a brief overview of his psychiatric profile. Among other things we have described him as being "passive dependent." *

Some analysts have described all of maturation and personal growth as a process of repeated "separations" — first from the womb, then from the mother, then from the family constellation. Adulthood has been equated with autonomy, personal independence, and ability to take care of oneself.

Symbolically the most dependent condition is represented by intrauterine life. The extreme regression of the catatonic schizophrenic is dramatized by his assumption of a fetal position. We might say the infant survives by oral preoccupation. This is the mode par excellence of its existence — oral dependency. If development does not progress satisfactorily, an infantile stage might very well characterize the rest of one's existence. Independence is hampered. According to Freudian interpretation the Oedipal stage is the stepping-stone to all

---

* The infant is breast-fed by the mother and this has an aspect of passive pleasure. It represents the extreme in human dependency — a dependency that is associated with eating — oral dependency. If the individual retains a dependent attitude toward the world during his later development instead of learning to satisfy his needs through his own efforts, he is said to be an oral dependent or passive dependent individual.

future autonomous development. An unsuccessful resolution of this stage leaves the child incapable of achieving the requisite balance between infantile impulse (the beast) and adult control (civilization). Introjection of the father-image is tantamount to relinquishing unconscious impulses and immediate libidinal gratification in favor of greater ego control and socialization. Successful resolution of the Oedipal stage symbolizes acceptance of external restrictions — in short, becoming more concerned with the outside world. A lack of Oedipal resolution would mean an earlier dependency relationship might be stressed out of all proportion to its actual meaning.

Breathing is intimately related to eating in the actual process of ingesting food. Breathing is momentarily disrupted as food is swallowed. Breathing is also disrupted by heavy sobbing and crying. Breathing is one of the few physical activities necessary to life which has both autonomic and central innervation. Thus, from the standpoint of physiological control, "voluntary" cessation of breathing, even if unconscious, represents a denial of life itself. Respiratory symptoms are therefore intermediate between hysterical conversion reactions (which affect, for the most part, striated musculature) and psychophysiological reactions (which affect smooth musculature). Ailments of the respiratory tract thus bridge these two main types of disorders.

It is interesting to note that Lewis thought of himself as a "normal" child until he entered school. This suggests that "everything was all right" until he had to leave his mother. We know that his mother over-protected but at the same time frightened him. We might assume she was quite ambivalent about her own motherhood. As a child Lewis provided an easy target for his mother's doubts about herself. She was a very religious person and from the brief description given we might surmise she was quite fundamentalistic in her beliefs. She no doubt forbade excessive enjoyment of carefree libidinous gratification. Lewis's own early strivings to express himself were probably restricted. Recall that we assumed individual autonomy to be an index of maturity. We might surmise further that Lewis's own attempts at autonomy, however miniscule, were fraught with discouragement and reproof. Masturbation during childhood is such an attempt at a form of "self-reliance." In a crude way the child is demonstrating that he can provide pleasure for himself. But his mother identified this with insanity, and dealt the double blow of discouraging his strivings towards independence and thwarting his sexual expression. Other "outside" activities were also discouraged so that eventually all Lewis had to relate to was his mother and this in a very passive manner. A mother is perceived by the child as providing the primary food source. Getting love via the mouth is still his main form of receiving affection as he grows up.

So we would hypothesize that Lewis was frustrated in his search for maternal affection; he probably wanted far more from his mother than she was willing to give, particularly a free, warm, spontaneous love. Not receiving love and affection in reality, he retreated to fantasy. His mother, on the other hand, was domineering and hostile, but felt guilty about this. Her consequent over-protection of Lewis may have been a reaction-formation of her own rejection. Lewis's father was passive; he seemed to have had the same type of symptoms as a young man that Lewis had. It is doubtful whether Lewis successfully incorporated the father-image provided by such a weak person; there is no doubt that he remained dependent upon his mother. We might suspect that he cried a lot as an infant and child and was given to heavy sobbing. Investigations have frequently associated other respiratory ailments (asthma for example) with separation anxiety.

From the above information, liberally interspersed with suppositions, we can see why a breathing ailment fits in with Lewis's personality dynamics. It is no accident that it originally occurred with a pipe. His current source of oral gratification (symbolic mother-love) had been poisoned. The associated loss of breath is interpreted as a direct symbolic representation of a cry for help and a threat to die. Hyperventilation, with its cessation of breathing, served both these purposes. As a result of his attack, he was brought to the counselor instead of being returned to "mother." The transference of affection from a symbolic source to a psychologist is quickly effected. The phobia for rabies may have a similar explanation. There may have been childhood associations to events that we know nothing about. But Lewis's high suggestibility may have generated a ready-made symptom from these. Usually a phobia is related to some traumatic incident and the resulting "fear" is an exaggerated defense against a recurrence of the trauma. Lewis made considerable improvement in therapy. The counselor drew upon and enhanced Lewis's own strength, while setting an example of independence by his own behavior. Many others have remarked that a direct interpretation is the best recourse in such cases.

When the counselor left for ten months, Lewis regressed considerably and developed a facial tic. It could be hypothesized that this was of a "sad" or "angry" expression rather than a happy one. Tics usually caricature the underlying situation. Frequently they are associated with superego development and inconsistency on the part of the parents. Lewis had meager opportunities for superego development with a harsh, severe mother. It is possible that when the surrogate-mother (the counselor) left, Lewis, having developed too great a dependence on him, unconsciously felt deserted and rejected. It was as if someone were saying, "See, he left you. Go back to your old mother." But the "old mother" was frightening and Lewis symbolized his ambivalence in a facial expression.

Lewis's suggestibility made a more direct therapeutic approach highly effective. He needed structuring and direct examples. His walk with the therapist provided the vivid demonstration that he *could* walk himself. It was characteristic of Lewis that things had to be demonstrated by actions, not only verbally. However, Lewis's basic character was really not modified. Years later he developed more pronounced symptoms of an entirely different nature. We might speculate that his hysteroid reactions and symptoms had been "exposed" by therapy, so that he had to resort to the far more complex, even more submerged, cardiovascular ailment.

MARY

The Slow Learner

Mary's case presents the development of a young woman
of borderline intelligence from a family of high achievers.
The presentation includes her view and her parents' views
of her life. Several years after completing the high school
special curriculum, during which she worked and lived at
home, she entered a school for special education. The
case indicates the influence on her of accepting friends
and engaging activities, as well as reporting some changes
in her own perspective and that of her parents after intensive educational and supportive activities during the
period of special education. The results of psychological
tests given at the school for special education are included.

IDENTIFICATION

Mary was a 23-year-old woman when the counselor first knew her.
She was petite and blonde, with a very clear complexion and average
physical attractiveness. She wore clothes well and was about average
in stylishness. Mary was the third child in a family of four. Her
parents were employed in professions and lived in an above-average-
income neighborhood. Her initial problem was inability to keep up
academically with her age-mates — low school achievement. This in
turn led to other social and emotional problems which she handled
with varying degrees of success.

PERSONAL HISTORY

Mary's story

The following autobiographical sketch is a result of an interview
with Mary prompted by an earlier interview with her father. The
instructions were: "Mary, won't you give the story of your life as you

118

saw it, emphasizing the most important things that happened?" As you read Mary's somewhat fragmentary story, observe what she has recalled and what she has omitted. It might be helpful to speculate about the motives she may have had in selecting the incidents and experiences that she describes or omits. What are the predominant themes in the story?

"I was born in 1938 in the _____ Hospital, in a city of about 25,000 people. I went to nursery school, but I don't remember very much about it, or about kindergarten or the early years in the laboratory school I attended. When I was in first grade, we lived for a year in Florida, and my older sister and brother and I rode a school bus every morning. I remember that once I sat on the boys' side and everyone scolded me, and I was *ashamed*. In the second school I attended in Florida, there was a real strict teacher. She made me sit near the window once. I didn't know what I did, but she scolded me and this *frightened* me very much. While we were down there, there was a hurricane and we didn't have lights for a day. I got up once in the middle of the night and I couldn't find the bathroom because it was so dark, and I was *scared*. My brother collected shells from the seashore, and I joined him. The shells that I collected *weren't any good*. I remember once my father wanted to take a picture of me, and I didn't want it taken. I don't know why now.

"The next year we returned to the city in which I was born, and I was in the first grade again. I remember the teacher whispered to me one day that I was going to flunk. I don't remember my reaction. Another time she sent me to the nurse. I came back and told her the nurse was gone. She took me upstairs and led me to the nurse. The real reason why I didn't go to the nurse was that there were certain rooms that I didn't want to pass. I was afraid of the children in these rooms.

"In the third grade I had a student teacher who helped me with my reading. I liked her very much and I remember that I sent her a Christmas card, but I got the wrong address on it and had to take it to her after Christmas. She was an important teacher to me. In the fifth grade I remember that I didn't have a student teacher to help me with my reading. I had at this time the first man teacher that I ever had, and I was kept after school several times as *punishment*. I was supposed to go with a group of girls to a Camp Fire Girls' meeting, and I remember they had to wait for me and this was *embarrassing*. It seems to me I didn't want to work when I was in school.

"In the fifth grade I met one of the best *friends* I ever had, Helen, and we spent a lot of time together. I would go over to her house almost every day. We were always together. Once she persuaded me to be in an opera that was given at one of the colleges. I was late to practice for it; I had missed my ride, and then I wanted to *drop out*. She tried to talk me into it but she couldn't. Her family belonged to a country club on a lake, and she used to take me with her. I always acted like I was one of the family because she would have to pay for me if I were a guest. My own family spent one summer at a place we had near the Gulf, and I wanted to take this friend with me, but we didn't have enough room for her. When I got down there, I found the whole summer very *boring*. Once when my family went down there for a few weeks, *I didn't want to go*, and finally the girl next door invited me to stay with her. I remembered we went sledding and I spent some of the time with my good friend Helen.

"When I was ten years old, I was playing with a group of children in a pile of leaves. A neighbor's big dog ran after another dog and he stepped on my face while I was lying in the leaves. I had to be taken to the hospital and have my face stitched. This was just an experience. I don't remember it as being unpleasant.

"In my neighborhood we played games such as circus, carnival, and cops and robbers. We thought we had the best gang in town. I remember I hated a girl that lived on the next street. When she came over, we would hide. I don't know why I disliked her; it was because everyone else did. My friend next door, who was younger than I, used to play dress-up. We would go into the yard and when a car came up, we would hide behind a tree. I knew that they saw us, but I pretended they didn't see us. This girl taught me how to play cards. She was *better than I was* even though she was younger. She beat me in almost every game we played together — including hopscotch. I worked with a group of girls in school about this time on posters for our candidate for school princess." (Apparently Mary liked working as a team for a common loyalty.)

Mary was asked about the various lessons her parents had given her — music, dancing, and horseback riding. She was *not too much impressed* with these and had no memories to report. She did say she remembered having to take voice lessons once after school, and she hated it because she had no one to walk home with and the lessons took her away from her friends. "We worked on the same song over and over again. The teacher gave me candy every day, but even so, *I quit going.*" (Mary's father had hired a college student to teach her, hoping he could work into tutoring her. Mary's attitude indicates the failure of this and other similar projects.)

When asked about her reaction to the birth of her sister, when Mary was seven years old, she replied, "I remember she was brought home in a neighbor's green car, but I don't remember how I felt toward her." She also could not give any clear memories of reaction to her older brother and sister.

"During junior high school I remember going around with a girl who dressed in sloppy clothes. She had been brought up having an easy life, and she didn't keep herself clean. She was a 'drip.' Once I remember she accused me of losing some of her golf balls. I went around with another girl who stole, lied, and cheated." She intimated that neither of these girls impressed her. They were just girls with whom she could do things.

In senior high school she transferred from the laboratory school to the large city high school. She described it as something new and different. She was glad to get away from the laboratory school because she was disgusted with it. No one there seemed to be interested in her. In senior high school she made friends with a girl named Estelle. They spent hours talking to each other on the telephone. "Estelle decided after a while that she *didn't like me,* and she sent me notes telling me mean things. I couldn't remember what was in them. She even got some of her friends to write me notes. This was a time when I needed friends because I didn't know how to handle Estelle's attitude toward me. I tried to get her to come and spend the night with me, but she always made excuses. At this age I didn't understand as I do now that she just didn't want to be with me. *I didn't make many friends* the next year. I wanted only the best kind of friends or none. My good friend Helen of several years ago had moved away. She was still a good friend, and we used to write a great deal."

The interviewer prompted, "What about camp?"

Her parents had planned the camping experience with the hope that it might lead to experiences of success and acceptance. "Camp — this was something new and different. I got away from the routine. It was a *good* experience, but I wouldn't do it again for a million dollars. One of the girls in my cabin was a Negro. She was a nice girl, but I couldn't understand her attitude toward me. Sometimes she seemed to like me, and other times she seemed to resent that I had so much and she had so little. She used to tell me about her financial difficulties, and I just didn't know how to handle this. I didn't know what to say. She *hurt my feelings* a few times. She seemed to like me when she first met me, and then she seemed to hate me. This has happened often. I guess I'm hard to live with. Maybe I don't do enough of the work. I did make a few friends at camp. They are all married now.

"At camp they picked certain students to be in a leadership village. I was picked, but I never did get the certificate that some of the other girls got. They didn't tell me that they had changed the rules. It seems I would have to go another year, and I doubt whether I would have been a counselor anyhow. There were some good things about the camp. I worked in the office and I worked in the crafts shop. This experience helped.

"After high school I took some non-credit courses in the University, and I enjoyed that. I met Louise, and she and I used to go together with a group of girls to the mental hospital every week to help entertain the patients. The patients needed friends. Louise made friends with me on the bus going over. She was one of the first girls who approached me and started a friendship. Except for my very good friend Helen who left town a few years ago, she was one of the very few friends who kept the friendship going. I was beginning to come out of the shell that I was in in high school. In high school I didn't do anything; I just went to school and came home. Louise tended to bring me out. She liked me, but not as much as I thought she did. I realize now I wasn't important to her. She had so many friends. When she got married, there were some girls who turned up in her wedding party that I didn't even know. She did correspond with me after she left the University.

"I met another girl in the University, and I learned something about friendship from her. She hadn't had a close friend before. She had the idea that making close friends produced difficulties. I had to start this friendship and I kept it going. She had a boyfriend, and of course love is more important than friendship; but I was important to her. She treated me like a younger sister. She arranged a couple of double dates that didn't pan out. I had very few dates in high school. Boys didn't like me then. Once in junior high I took a boy to a Sadie Hawkins dance, and we were selected the couple with the best costumes.

"I spent a year in another country with my parents, and I got a job in a nursery school there. I found this fun but very wearing. I dated a boy who was a native of that country. We never really became serious, but I figured he was the kind of person I could live my life with. I liked him very much, but I didn't love him. I could do without him, although I did miss him. We never had any difficulties. He said when we first began going together, 'I like you a lot, and I hope we part as good friends as we are now.' I think he had seen too many American movies, and he tried to talk me into going to his apartment. He thought all American girls did this.

"Now I am going with a boy who is in the service, and he is trying the same sort of thing. First I didn't know what he was talking about when he said, 'I want you.' When I realized what he wanted, *I was shocked.* Then I told him that we wanted different things and suggested we not meet again. He said he would not talk with me about this again, but he continued. He and I are so different, and he seems to want different things than I do."

As you read Mary's story, as given in an interview, and written up by the interviewer, what impressed you about it? What are some of the themes that she saw running through the twenty-three years of her life? What memories stood out? What might you expect a girl to discuss in telling the story of her life that Mary omits? To what extent does *failure* and *rejection* seem to dominate this story? What are some of the major *positive experiences* which enabled her to grow as a person?

Life history as seen by parents

Much of the information about Mary's development was furnished by her father during an interview with the counselor. He seems to have had some insight into her adjustment, although he admitted after reading Mary's story that he and her mother at times during her development failed to realize how unhappy she was. They regarded Mary as having certain problems which were rather difficult to solve, and they attempted to solve them by supplying her with a private tutor, lessons in music, dancing, and horseback riding, and later, camping experiences.

Mary was very small and thin at birth and was less attractive physically than the two older children during the first two weeks of life. Apparently she had not only the best of care from her mother, who greatly enjoyed bathing and caring for babies, but there was also a childless negro servant in the home at that time who loved Mary dearly. In fact, she had said on numerous occasions that the only reason she continued to work for the family, who resided in an inconvenient location, was because of Mary.

Mary was definitely behind the other children in all aspects of development. She was *slow in walking and talking.* She was, however, treated very much like the others at home. She was taken to nursery school at a very early age and was accepted eagerly because this particular laboratory school was interested in training students in the care of a child who had not yet attained bowel and bladder control. Mary was *slower in gaining control* than the other children of the family.

She apparently received considerable *affection and attention* from the college students working in the nursery school. At kindergarten age Mary entered school with several other children her own age from the same neighborhood. She seemed to enjoy it. She was given a Stanford-Binet Intelligence Test by the teacher, who seemed somewhat disturbed at her inability to get a valid I.Q. for Mary. The teacher said that she had a hard time giving the test and obtained an I.Q. around 100, which was *quite low* for that school. It may well be that since Mary's brother and sister had had I.Q. scores approximately 30 points above this, the teacher may have been lenient in administering the test.

Up until the early grades Mary had seemed to be a part of a rather large neighborhood group. She played readily with her brother two years older and his friends, and with the girls of her own age in the neighborhood. They usually played as a group. She remained a thin child, but one who seemed to be a personality in her own right. She played enthusiastically with the other children, singing and playing her own solitary games when she was alone.

Temperamentally, Mary was a somewhat stoic, poker-faced child, but exuberant in play. She seemed basically happy and interested in the world around her. She played the role of a *junior partner* of the gang, a role she was willing to play most of her life if she could be included in the group. When ill at home, she demanded attention, moaned and groaned, and was very verbally disagreeable. This irritated the other members of the family, and they all scolded her — even her brother, whom she greatly admired. She was more negativistic than the other children after four or five years of age.

Mary's older brother took her out on the street with him and seemed to accept her thoroughly as a younger member of the family, although from the very beginning Mary did not show the promise, either physically or mentally, that the other children had shown. Her parents stated that they had tried to accept her as an individual. This was probably harder for them to do after she began having difficulty in the first grade and finally was not promoted to the second grade.

Academic difficulties

During the year of her first-grade school experience, the family lived away from home, and Mary attended three different schools that year. She continued to drop behind the average children in the laboratory school. The teachers in the school arranged in almost every grade to have a special student teacher for Mary, although Mary seemed to profit very little from this. One reason Mary seemed to avoid the learning situation was that her sister seven years younger could read better at five years of age than she could at twelve.

It was in the pre-adolescent period that Mary's parents began to realize that she was *not included* as much as the other children had been in friendship and social groups at school. Even Mary later mentioned confidentially to her father that the boys seemed to dislike her because she was backward in classwork. One can understand the social problems Mary was having as a pre-adolescent and junior high-school student from the story that she herself related.

Social-emotional problems

Her parents first noticed her emotional reactions to the social problem when she transferred to the large high school and persisted in seeking the friendship of Estelle, the girl mentioned in Mary's story, who *rejected* her. She talked this over briefly with her father, on several occasions, and at one time was quite tearful, which was unusual for her.

Mary's parents also noted that she had been more obstinate than the other children. She seemed to resist the things they were trying to do for her, and was often negativistic when her mother tried to help her dress or do things for her. For example, when she was given riding lessons, after a few times she discontinued going without letting her parents know. It wasn't until after a month that her mother learned that she wasn't going to these lessons, even though they were being paid for. She said that the horses frightened her; the instructor was rather strict and apparently not very sympathetic.

Mary's mother indicated that during middle childhood Mary was a great source of concern to her and produced many conflicts. She had found Mary lovable as a small child, who needed and accepted her nurturance but who later, after she had been in school several years, was very *resistant*. Mary rejected suggestions which her mother knew were best for her. She rejected advice about clothes, diet, and activities. In fact, her mother felt that she was being rejected as a person by Mary. She also stated that for a period Mary was a source of conflict between her and her husband. Her husband intimated that she, rather than Mary, was the initial and major cause of Mary's rejection; this made it very difficult for them to deal with Mary and her problem.

In the early years of Mary's life, both her parents and teachers noticed that the other children in the class seemed to treat her like a younger child, including her in the group, but often sheltering her. It was only in the pre-adolescent years when these children began to pair off into groups that Mary seemed to be *left out*. An incident which Mary told her family one night at supper, with "a stiff upper lip," helped to alert them to the problem she was quietly, but painfully, facing. She had been nominated and elected secretary of her small class. These were children with whom she had grown up and had a good play relationship. After her election, the president of the class sent the candidates out again, explained that Mary's academic deficiencies would not allow her to perform the duties of the office, and suggested another vote. This time Mary lost. Mary was told about this later and it upset her. She felt that the president might have suggested her for another, less demanding office.

Her parents were pleased that the one staunch friend, Helen, seemed to be loyal and accepted Mary without reservation, despite her difficulties in school. Helen and Mary were really very different in intelligence level. Helen graduated from college and later went on to graduate school. They found in each other real friendship — basic understanding and acceptance. Helen may have been the most rejected of the three children in her family, and Mary's adulation may have been what she most needed at the time.

These two girls seemed to complement each other; according to the parents, Helen helped Mary through that difficult period. Helen's family eventually moved away from the community, and it was then that Mary began seeking other friendships, although she failed to find one until she had finished high school.

In high school her counselor realized that she would not be able to graduate with a diploma and placed her in a special program her last two years, which consisted of spending part of the afternoon as an assistant in a school for handicapped young children. This came at a time when Mary felt she had no friends, and the high school counselor paired Mary with a more severely retarded girl who was also socially obnoxious, from Mary's viewpoint. These two girls worked together in the small school for handicapped children. Mary never did develop a warm friendship with this girl but continued to associate with her, at least in the school situation. The girl constantly tried to be a friend, but Mary regarded the girl as "beneath" her and did not accept her. About this time, the employment counselor attempted to give Mary a series of tests and said it was almost impossible to get her to cooperate in a testing situation. It seemed as though her handicap in the school and testing situation was, in part, the result of her relative retardation in comparison with the other children that she knew. Mary had to work very hard for what little progress she made, when progress seemed to come naturally to the other children. The learning situation seemed to be a defeating one to her, so she partially solved the problem by not trying.

At this period in her development Mary's parents planned the summer camps. The first day at camp was always a traumatic one. Mary became nauseated and could not keep down her food; but she never gave the slightest hint that she didn't want to stay at camp when she told her parents good-bye. She seemed to gain a certain amount of confidence and satisfaction from the contacts she made during the camping period. She even visited several times during the year at the home of a girl she had met at camp, who lived 150 miles away.

Mary's father described an interview he had with the camp director after Mary had spent two summers there. She had told him that Mary usually praised the talents and achievements of the other members of her family. The camp director regarded Mary as a "Cinderella" of the family. She probably was not acquainted with some of the difficult realities in the family and community. Mary's father pointed out that he and her mother were aware of the disparity between Mary's general ability and that of her classmates and the other members of her family. Mary could have gone to another school, but that might have been considered a stigma against her and would have taken her from her play group. Moreover, her obstinacy (a reaction to her felt failure) further complicated relationships in the family.

Post high-school experiences

After Mary finished high school, she continued to work in the school for handicapped children. She liked the director of the school, with whom she worked closely, and apparently the director *accepted her with warmth.* She continued to dislike the close association she had to have with the retarded girl who worked with her. With this in mind and with the realization that Mary should develop some vocational skills, her parents contacted a friend of the family who was head nurse in a nearby hospital. The hospital was conducting at that time a training program for practical nurses. Mary quit her job to take this training. She was one of the younger trainees, and again, as in previous school situations, she fell behind the group. However, she was given a somewhat menial job working with older women in a supply room, mainly washing bottles and handling equipment. She received fairly good pay, and she saved most of the money she earned. She was punctual, but apparently not very efficient. Eventually she was discharged, and this was a traumatic experience for her.

Instead of returning home, she went to the home of a younger married woman, one of her father's former secretaries, who had been her confidante. This woman understood Mary because of her own childhood problems and was a source of emotional support, particularly during this period. She treated Mary as an equal. Mary did a certain amount of baby-sitting for her, and the woman did some tutoring for Mary. However, the tutoring usually gave way to conversation or "counseling" sessions in which Mary talked out her feelings and attitudes. This occurred over a period of almost a year and was very helpful.

After Mary lost her job at the hospital, she was readily re-employed, but at a much lower pay rate, in the school for the handicapped. She continued to work there for several years. This gave her something to do and some identity and satisfaction. She enjoyed it and was successful in working with the children.

As Mary tells in her story, she began to "come to life" again when she took non-credit college courses in her extra time and met some girls her own age who were similar in personality, intelligence, and background to her friend, Helen, who had moved away from town. She joined the YWCA and participated in a project on Saturdays entertaining patients in a nearby mental hospital. She enjoyed the girls who were working with her in this. They accepted her as an equal.

The year she spent abroad with her parents, she corresponded regularly with many of the friends that she had left at home. Despite her retardation in reading, spelling, and writing, she worked hard on these letters and apparently improved her basic communication skills greatly. She did her first steady dating while abroad and held her first unsupervised job as an assistant in a nursery school. She made several good friends with girls there. She met a European boy on the boat returning home, who later proposed to her by mail. She did not accept his proposal. After she returned and was taking the non-credit courses in the University, she dated steadily another boy, who was a veteran of World War II and who had spent about a year in a VA psychiatric hospital. He, too, had academic difficulties but showed a considerable amount of initiative and sporadic vocational success. He proposed to her and was very much disturbed when she did not accept his proposal. Both his family and her family thought it would be unwise for her to continue dating him. Because her friends thought little of this boy, she too was not very enthusiastic about continuing the relationship and initiated the break.

The present

At present Mary and her family are trying to discover a vocation that might suit her. There are certain jobs that she could hold that she definitely does not want. There are other jobs for which she knows she does not have the skills necessary. Her mother at present has a full-time job, and Mary is taking more responsibilities in the home. These are rather simple and consist of cleaning up the kitchen, tidying the house, preparing the daily meal every other week, and remaining at home to handle any phone calls or receive packages from delivery men. Mary also spends some time looking at television, writing letters to her friends, keeping a diary, caring for her clothes, and occasionally going downtown to shop for herself. She has a few dates and phone calls from friends. Through the YWCA she met a number of foreign students of both sexes, roughly her own age. There seems to be great mutual attraction between them and Mary. She has developed some warm friends and has dated several of the boys from various countries. She is under less stress than at any time in her life except early childhood, and can use her own initiative to a greater extent. Her parents were a little concerned that her being alone most of the time might cause her to regress rather than to develop. This, however, did not seem to happen. At present she sings more while working — something she did when she was a very small child — shows greater spontaneity and affection for her family, seems to be developing more confidence socially, has a better disposition, and is increasing her vocabulary and general knowledge of events. She reads more of the newspaper than she used to read; now she glances over the society page and reads captions under pictures.

Her trip to Europe and travels within the United States gave her a background to appreciate some of the things she sees on television and in magazines. She is gradually improving in conversational skills and social relations. She is now *seeking* social contacts with contemporaries and is taking a certain amount of initiative in meeting others in social groups.

For a period of three or four years she has belonged to a college club associated with her church. She attends this club almost every Sunday and plays a minor role in it. She is fairly realistic about her capacities, and seems capable in selecting friends. They represent well-balanced young women with idealistic values, and with her interest in people, she accepts them readily as persons.

She has, during this year, of her own accord, engaged a tutor — a girl her own age who was a graduate student in English. She arranged to assume financial responsibilities for their weekly meetings and spent some of her time at home working on basic exercises in spelling and simple written English. She was also inspired by the tutor to do a little painting with water colors and produced one or two rather satisfying products. At this point she is again desirous of getting a job that she can handle, preferably working with small children.

Mary's mother

Mary's mother read the above account after it was completed and then added the following:

"The accounts which Mary and her father have given are very complete, and I have little to add. One important factor which has not been mentioned is Mary's bed-wetting, which continued regularly until she was eight and a half years old. All methods of control were tried, without pressure being applied to Mary, and finally, for the last few years, no controls were tried. Suddenly, one night, the bed-wetting ceased, and never occurred again. This period coincided with the younger child's night training and her remaining dry during the night.

"Mary's small size and her shy manner were very appealing, so that she probably had more babying than the older children. In addition, the maid mentioned above was completely devoted to Mary and gave her unlimited attention, actually taking her from her mother on occasion.

"Mary's obstinacy and negativism developed most strongly during her early years at school. I found her a very frustrating person to deal with. After her father suggested that this had developed from an initial rejection by me, I found all my dealings with her fraught with difficulty and emotion. None of my actions toward her were clear reactions of the moment; I was always in a turmoil, questioning whether I was acting directly toward her or reacting through a complex interaction of rejection and immediate need. Further, I felt deeply *guilty* toward her and this has colored all my dealings with her.

"I have wondered if this guilt does not have a very real basis. When Mary was a year old, my extreme fatigue forced me to go to our physician for a thorough physical examination. I feared I was having a recurrence of the tuberculosis which I had had in late adolescence. Examination showed an extremely low metabolism and I began to take thyroid extract, which I have continued until the present. I ask myself, 'Is Mary a child who received too little oxygen in the fetal state, and is this lack the basis for her handicap? Why didn't I know of this and do something about it?'

"Mary's *attitude toward herself* has concerned both of us parents. The fact that she can't learn readily does not seem to us so important as her self-attitude. She has greater capacity than she has used in these areas. Because she sees her contemporaries and her older brother and sister accomplishing much more than she, she believes they do it easily. She does not see other people's efforts — they all seem to do well without strain. When her own efforts result in failure or poor work, she gives up. I notice this in household duties. Because I do things easily, she expects to do the same on the very first try. Again and again I've pointed out to her that my early efforts were also unsuccessful and fumbling, that my ease has come from long years of trial-and-error, but she does not accept this — not really. She wants and expects mastery immediately.

"Her *negativism* is frustrating to me both emotionally and in specific instances. A number of our plans for her — all of them, in fact — are the results of long and careful thought, weighing her abilities, her likes, and the possibilities for her future. To have the person for whom one has planned long and painfully reject the results of the plans — especially out of inexperience and lack of knowledge — is most frustrating. Add to this our natural anxiety for her, and you get a good deal of emotion.

"For the past four or five years, I have been very passive toward Mary, initiating no plans, suggesting nothing, simply cooperating on any request she makes. I recognized some time ago that a good deal of her negativism toward me was a simple result of trying to frustrate me. Since so much of her own experience was frustrating to her, I felt I was helping her to frustrate me by allowing her to get satisfaction from doing it. Whenever I thought she had a definite need which had to be filled, I would suggest to someone else (her brother or sister or a friend) that Mary should be doing this or that, and she cooperated with them. I was careful not to suggest anything to her that would be too serious a matter if she decided to thwart me by not doing it. She learned that she could be the center of an argument between us parents, and arranged matters to produce this result. For instance, several times when we went to buy her some article of clothing — a hat or something — she would come home to her father and say, 'I hate this hat. Mother made me get it.' Naturally, her father would say to me, 'Why do you dominate her so? Why don't you let her select her own hats?' The truth was, I had taken her to the shop, told the saleswoman that we wanted a hat for Mary, and then left the selection up to the two of them, simply giving the final approval after I had impressed upon Mary that it was her choice — not directly, but by asking her, 'Do you like the hat? Is this the one you want?' then complimenting her on it, and paying for it.

"Since I have become more passive in Mary's life, she is much more pleasant and affectionate toward me. Perhaps I should insert here the odd fact that while she seems to need and want affection, only recently has she accepted any caresses from us. She has, since about six years of age, made herself rigid when we embrace her, and seldom returns a kiss. It used to affect me very deeply when she was younger, when I would go into her room in the morning to waken her. As with the other children, I would lean over her and kiss her. Immediately she'd kick at me and strike me. This is something I've never understood. It grieves me to recall it now, as it grieved me then.

"I realized as Mary grew into the teens and had few friends that she would develop socially much later than the other children had and that dating boys would probably not be part of her life, at least not until she was a good deal older. So with Mary we planned parties for the girls, of the sort at which they wouldn't expect to meet boys — i.e., luncheons, etc. They were dismal *failures*. Except for one girl, the other guests had no compunction about declining the invitations or just not turning up for the party. I know this affected Mary very much, and so we gave up on that. I thought it would be a good way to keep her in touch with her contemporaries, but evidently it was not.

"I recall that one of Mary's early experiences was being very close, almost as a sister, to an extremely gifted girl who was just a few months older than she. We were neighbors, and it was assumed that the two little girls would grow up together. But as they developed, their differences showed more and more. The difficulty was that after I had arranged special lessons in dancing or music, invariably the other child would start lessons with the same teacher, immediately outshining Mary. And so immediately Mary would want to quit the lessons. Later on, when the girls grew toward their teens, they saw little of each other, and this source of pressure was removed from Mary." (It will be noted that Mary in her story made no reference at all to this girl, despite the fact that she was a close neighbor and Mary played with her daily in her early life.)

REMEDIAL EVENTS

Evaluation and special training

At the age of 23, after the period described above, Mary's parents decided she needed special attention of a formal kind. Her father communicated with the Institute* and made an appointment for an evaluative examination. When Mary first arrived at the Institute, she was somewhat quiet and unenthusiastic, but after the interviews with very accepting professional workers, she wanted very much to enroll and did so as soon as the Institute was able to arrange for housing. Below is a summary statement of the crucial findings growing out of the evaluation.

> Sentence structure was aberrantly lower than the mental-age level; reading, writing, and spelling performances were very poor. Spelling appeared to be at about first- or second-grade level. There appeared to be no concept of how to use phonics in reading or spelling. Reading was at about third- or fourth-grade level. It was noted that occasionally, while taking dictation, she substituted and for an. This girl was able to imitate all the phonemes but tended to omit many of them in final positions

---

* This Institute accepted any handicapped individual who had, among other difficulties, a speech problem.

and occasionally in initial positions in minor lapses in specificity of speech.

A psychological evaluation was done by the staff psychologist using the International Leiter Performance Scale.* The mental age was 10 years, 6 months. The attenuated adult I.Q. was 81. There was a scatter which ranged from 9 to 19 years. The high scores were in vocabulary and comprehension. The low scores were in reading, arithmetic, and high-order abstractions, giving a maximum probable I.Q. of 90+. It was further reported that this woman had functionally dull-normal mental ability. Verbal integration, both spoken and written, breaks down at the high integrative level. One is also impressed by the fact that her vocabulary comprehension is far above her spontaneous verbal output.

It was recommended that this girl receive speech training and special tutoring, to enable her to work in a situation suited to her level of development, so that she could know success and regain confidence in her own ability. Further details of the training program will be worked out and then discussed with the parents.

FOLLOW-UP

After five weeks at the Institute, Mary came home to attend a wedding of one of her friends and stayed with her parents for a week. Her parents and older sister had noticed her enthusiasm for the Institute in the frequent short letters they received from her. They seemed to notice an improvement in all of the written language skills in the letters.

After she had been home for a few days, her mother made the following statement: "The effect of this five weeks has been all positive. There has been a general maturation. She shows more thoughtfulness of others. She has always shown this for the people outside of the family, but now she seems to include the family. She seems much less hostile to us and more considerate. She more readily accepts our suggestions and seems much calmer, with fewer nervous habits. She also seems to have improved physically. She has gained weight, her complexion is clearer, and she looks better. I notice that

* This is an intelligence test of the performance variety, which puts greatest emphasis on non-verbal intelligence.

her vocabulary is larger. She attempts words she didn't use before and her speech has greatly improved."

Her father's comment was: "She shows much greater happiness and spontaneity. She is more of a real person reflecting confidence. She is more affectionate and treats us more like contemporaries than elders. Her perspective on her surroundings seems to be broader and much of this is due to being in a new environment and away from old memories of failure and inhibition. After three days at home she was ready to return to the Institute and I feel that if she'd stayed home longer, it would have been undesirable."

The family visited the Institute several times and had an opportunity to observe her in her relationships with the other students when she was not aware that they were present. They noticed her great enthusiasm and a tendency to show more initiative, an apparent feeling of being at home at the Institute. This trend was more evident with each visit. She had planned a program for them to meet her teachers and other professional workers at the Institute. She had arranged for them to take one of her teachers, who was a great source of inspiration for her, to luncheon. They noticed the easy relationship she had with her fellow students. She was very happy with the housemother in her cottage, an older, motherly woman who treated her as an adult, but who helped her with her assignments in the evenings.

Mary is now taking on certain responsibilities at the Institute as a volunteer worker. She has made contacts with a church group off the Institute grounds and has made a number of friends with the younger professional workers. She has been looking forward to getting an apartment with several other girls and living without a housemother as soon as the Institute approves this arrangement.

MARY: Trends and Personal Relationships

What do you see in the case of Mary? Give your spontaneous reactions to Mary before turning to the questions below.

Of all the information about Mary, what central patterns seem important? Note especially:

a. what patterns seem to be outstanding in Mary's report of her life.

b. the contrast between projects of her own selection and those initiated by her parents.

    c. her strongest needs, wishes, and strivings.

    d. the social roles she played.

In considering Mary's development, what was the role of relationships with other people?

    a. her parents, siblings (brother and sisters)

    b. friends; reasons for their importance

    c. family background; its conscious and unconscious demands upon her

    d. the kinds of rejection she experienced

    e. the Institute and the accepting climate there

Concepts helpful in understanding Mary

    a. Intelligence and aptitude (63, 112)

    b. Temperament and basic constitutional trends (30, 80)

    c. Social rejection and affiliation (25, 89)

    d. Acceptance and human relationships; early basic trust (25, 89)

Other concepts which may have some relevance to this case: role expectancy; role conception; role rejection.

MEHMET

The Troubled Middle-Easterner

While teaching in Turkey, an experienced counselor from
a mental hygiene clinic in the United States was approached by some of his students there for counseling.
Although Mehmet was seen for only a few interviews in
addition to contacts in a small class, the similarities and
differences between a Middle-Eastern collegian and an
American student can be noted and observations can be
made regarding the universality of basic psychodynamics.

IDENTIFICATION

Mehmet was a quiet, mature student in the College of Commerce
in a new, English-speaking university in the capital of Turkey. He
was tall and thin, good-looking and well-groomed in his only dark
suit, highly alert, very respectful of teachers, and cooperative, as is
the Turkish custom. Mehmet was twenty-seven years old and had
grown up in one of the smaller cities in Turkey. Although he talked
much about his father, he never mentioned his father's vocation.
From other facts it may be surmised that his father was a moderately
successful merchant with considerable initiative. However, his experiences were limited almost exclusively to the average-sized old city
in which he lived, and his perspective, therefore, was rather narrow.
Mehmet had been enrolled in an old-fashioned Turkish university
in the field of medicine, but had withdrawn and was pursuing the
curriculum in commerce. Outwardly, Mehmet looked very much
like the modern young Turk attending a university where English is
the prevailing language and where students are highly conscious of
the trend toward westernization. Inwardly, however, Mehmet represented a struggle between the past and the present, and he found it
very difficult, as his statements reveal, to be as easy-going as many
of his fellow students.

A Turkish youth feels it is his highest duty to please his parents — to carry out their plans for him and to submit to his father's wishes. The parents often think in terms of well-established vocations for their sons. This Westernized school offered training in fields not previously offered in the Turkish university curriculums. Here also, young men and women were permitted to arrange social affairs such as dances and parties. This was not the custom of their parents, who often had little contact with their prospective spouses before their own parents planned the marriage for them.

OCCASION FOR INTERVIEW

Mehmet's American teacher, a Fulbright lecturer spending a year teaching psychology in Turkey, had identified him as an intensely interested, well-prepared, and conscientious student; but he had never singled him out as differing from the twenty-five or thirty other young male Turks who were in the class. One day Mehmet waited until all the other students had left the room. He then came up to the lecturer deferentially and said, "Sir, may I talk with you some time in your office? It is very important." The instructor gave him an appointment for several hours hence.

PERSONAL HISTORY

Several weeks after the interview took place, Mehmet was given a *Pre-Interview Blank* to fill out. His responses shed some light on his background and development. Thus they are described here, before we turn to the interview in the next section.

In one item of the Blank, Mehmet was asked to write his history prior to college and to comment about his parents, their temperament, and their attitudes toward him. This is what he wrote: "I like my parents, but my father still considers me a child. I have to tell him everything I do. Sometimes I think that if I were alone I could find a better life. Because I had no independence from my father, I lost my self-confidence when I was only fifteen." His comment about other members of his family runs as follows: "I have two brothers and two sisters. My elder brother is somewhat good to me. My little brother is really pitiful. He has gone into military service.

(Every Turkish male serves his country for a period without pay.) My sisters are extremely good. I always pray for their happiness, but they don't understand this way of life. Their ship of dreams is always destroyed on the rocks of reality."

Grades and study habits

Mehmet's grades, on the whole, were good. He had many A's and B's, but he had made some grades below average. He studied more than the average student and showed much more initiative and creativity. He and another student had voluntarily made a very elaborate, multi-colored chart for the teacher. Whereas most Turkish students in this university do not study as hard as the average American, they are much more eager than the American student to do little chores for the teacher, such as erasing the board, carrying his briefcase, and opening the door for him. Mehmet was often ahead of the others in serving "his teacher," particularly if the others were not around.

In the *Pre-Interview Blank*, Mehmet had this to say about his health: "I never suffered from an illness, but I suffered from my outlook." Concerning social life-history, including early playmates, groups, camps, offices, friendships, Mehmet had little to say but commented, "I have no idea or I don't remember anything other than I have already mentioned."

On the subject of "school history," which included reactions to first attendance, best and poorest subjects, reactions to teachers, etc., his response was, "I shall never forget, when my father left me alone in the school, I burst into tears. Later I liked to be always in school instead of going home. My peer group was excellent. I was really a good student while I was at college."

The item on religious history brought this response: "My family is religious and conservative. I consider those who believe in God as brothers. I live for the future. I have some ideas to serve my country in a better way." In the section labeled "Summary," asking for important factors in development producing happiness or sadness, Mehmet quoted this poem:

> How happy is he shown and taught
> That serveth in another's will;
> Whose armor is his honest thought
> And simple truth his utmost skill.

COUNSELING EVENTS

When Mehmet entered the room for the conference, he was pale and tense, and more submissive than usual. He began the interview by pulling a letter out of his pocket, holding it with shaking hands, and saying, "Sir, I am very unhappy and distressed. My life has been torment for many months and I need your help very badly. I thought that if I could talk with you I would feel better."

Specific aspects of ambivalence toward his father

"This is a letter from my father. He is a good father and I love him, but he does not understand me. He treats me as though I am a young boy even at the age of twenty-seven, and I can do nothing but try to submit to his wishes. But, Sir, I cannot submit to his wishes. I have tried and tried, even though it is painful to me.

"Sir, my father writes me and when I see the letter, I begin to tremble. I take it from the mailman and put it in my pocket and am sad all day. Sometimes I carry it around for more than a day, then I tear it open and see what it says. Sir, it is like taking a beating to read his letter because he almost disowns me and accuses me of being a bad son. I do not want to be an unworthy son but I must do what is best for my country and for me.

"My father wants me to become either a doctor or a lawyer, and I entered the University with the sole idea of pleasing him, as do most Turkish youth. But I found that was not what I wanted, or at least that I could not study merely because he wanted me to. So I left school and got a job in a very small village in the East of Turkey teaching school."

A job and further education

"In this village where I was a teacher, I barely made enough to live on. I learned much, living with these poor, God-fearing people. Sir, you would not believe how poor these people are. Some live in caves. They have none of the things that we have in the city. They must eat anything that grows and they are entirely dependent upon their own produce. Even an onion, when it ripens and can be eaten, is a treat to these people. Sir, they taught me much about life, and I love these people and was glad to be their teacher.

"But then I felt I must leave and do something more for my

country. So here I am, back studying commerce. I have great ambitions to know how to deal with these people, and that is why I am in this faculty. ["Faculty" is synonymous with our word "college."] I spend most of my time reading in the social sciences. Recently I achieved much in learning to type. I would like to talk in class but my language difficulty hinders me. [His spoken English was well above the average of the class.] I like to write original writings; it is my hobby."

In the course of relating his conflicts with his father, the nature of his family, and his previous teaching experiences, Mehmet began to sob uncontrollably. He continued to try to talk. His teacher made it clear that these conflicts were understandable, that he was under tension, and that he should cry if he felt like it. Soon, he gained control and continued to talk. "Sir, there is so much unhappiness in the world. I love the members of my family but they seem unhappy. My father, in being a good, old-fashioned father and thinking that he must guide our lives, has almost ruined his children. My sister is married to a man of whom he approves but whom she does not love. She talks to me often because I am living with her, and tells me of her heartache. But what can I do for her, Sir? I have nothing but my own problems, and this makes me very sad too. My young brother is bright, but he too must live as my father wants him to live."

Attitude toward his peers and himself

"Most of my friends already have occupations. They have graduated from universities. They earn money and stand on their own feet. I have lost several years, which would have enabled me to be earning money today, but I still have no vocation and must still accept money from my parents for my education and living. This makes me very sorry, Sir.

"I like people but I am often afraid of losing their friendship. When I feel that people are too good for me, especially girls, I try to escape from them. I have never had a chance to invite a friend, a girl [Mehmet meant, I think, that he did not have a chance to date girls], and when invited, I try to find excuses. Most of the people around me are like bad watermelons. I think the inside is sweet and good, but when I cut into it, it is horrible. So I cannot adjust myself. I am a lost soul.

"I am suffering from an inferiority complex. I make a mirror of those who always criticize me. I need a girlfriend, but because of my ignorance of social activities and dancing, I am usually rejected from indoor meetings and pleasure." This is largely Mehmet's *perception*. There are many Turkish students who do not dance, because social dancing is a new, Western custom. There are many parties given by groups of young people in which dancing is rare and optional. The Turkish students very often give individual renditions at these parties. One will sing and another will recite a poem or a piece. Several of the men might dance a folk dance. Very often the girls sit on one side of the room and the boys on the other. It is true that the old Turkish kind of party was less frequent in the new university; but if Mehmet had not been bound up in his own problems, he might have found a more satisfying social life.

Mehmet, like many other youths in various parts of the world who suffer feelings of inferiority, gave the outward appearance of the opposite of inferiority. As one saw him coming into the classroom he observed an erect, alert, quite handsome young man. He was very hard-working, with good school achievement. The *feeling of inferiority* is a subjective matter and is not necessarily related to accomplishment. To be sure, a young person who is so disturbed is highly sensitive to mistakes and slights from others. He may have such a strong need for success and recognition that he is a perfectionist in attitude, sets his *level of aspiration* unreasonably high, and has more feelings of failure than he would if he were more realistic about himself.

Mehmet's comment about his friendlessness is a more serious matter in Turkey, it seemed to his teacher, than it would have been in the West, because a Turkish student is rarely without a friend. One of the most outstanding observations made by a Westerner living in the Middle East is the existence of these deep friendships among young people. Every youth finds a friend, and this friend is very important to him. The Turkish word for friend is *arkadash*, very similar to the word for brother, which is *kardash*. The typical Turkish student will refer many times during a conversation to "my friend." Mehmet was one of the few members of this class who was a loner. He said, "I had no friend while I was a child. My life is monotonous. I always think of it, and I am afraid nothing supports me or helps me in this. Some say you should learn dancing. Some say it is your nature; you were born so.* Well, I believe someday I will feel better. In our faculty [i.e., college] most of the students seem to be happy,

* These statements seem to indicate that Mehmet had talked over his emotional plight with someone, despite his claim of no confidants.

and I admire them. They never complain. Every small event makes them happy."

Mehmet's initiative and conflicts

Some of the above quotations came directly from the one conference Mehmet had with his teacher. Others were taken from the Pre-Interview Blank he filled out rather diligently when it was given to everyone in his class. Turkish students were reluctant to write about their personal lives to their teacher and hand it in, but Mehmet was one of the first to write out his feelings and bring it to the teacher. This occurred several weeks after the interview. In the interview he was more open and confidential about his inner life than some of his fellow students. He showed more of the kind of initiative and achievement motivation found in the Western world than would be found in his culture.

At the end of this single conference, he was told he could come in again at any time. He did not return for a personal conference but was very responsive to the counselor (who was also his teacher) on such matters as class assignments and came up after class for brief conferences on several occasions. However, he did not linger after a specific matter was discussed.

The cultural issue

One of Mehmet's conflicts could be traced to his living in two cultures — the old Turkey of his father and the newer, more Westernized Turkey, which allowed more individual choices. It should be added that in his present environment the older generation parents adhere to the Islamic custom of directing rather thoroughly the lives of their children, to the point of choosing their vocations and mates. Some Western-oriented Turks, on the other hand, see Turkey as developing industrially, with greater freedom for the individual, more specialized education, and greater opportunities for youth in directing their own destiny. Do you think Mehmet would have had the same sort of difficulties if his parents had migrated shortly after his birth to an American community?

FOLLOW-UP

After this rather long interview, in which Mehmet engaged in much self-disclosure, he was invited to return whenever he wanted to.

He did not ask for another interview. His relationship to the counselor remained very much as it had been previously. He continued to be very respectful, cooperative, and hard-working.

At the end of the year, Mehmet brought his teacher a brand-new notebook with hard-back covers and said, "Sir, would you write in this for me? You can write as much or as little as you want, but I shall cherish it always. I want this to remember you by because you have helped me a lot."

When the writer left Turkey at the end of the academic year, Mehmet said farewell along with the other students. From all indications he was planning to complete the educational plans under way.

MEHMET: Personality Patterns

Before trying to answer the questions below, what do you see in the life of this Middle-Eastern youth?

Distinctive characteristics

    a. Do you know an American young man who is very similar to Mehmet?

    b. What are three or four of his most outstanding personal dispositions?

    c. What other information about him would you need to understand him better?

    d. In reading Mehmet's story, what understanding do you get of the culture in which he lives in contrast to Western culture? Is this the basis of his problem?

Significant relationships and events

    a. Why is Mehmet having the conflicts he is experiencing, when many of his contemporaries seem not so troubled?

    b. What events and relationships may have produced the lack of personal unity seen in Mehmet?

    c. Why do you suppose Mehmet did not volunteer any information about his mother?

    d. Mehmet says he lost his self-confidence when he was only fifteen years of age. Why then?

Concepts helpful in understanding Mehmet

    a. Erikson's adolescent search for identity (3, 33)

b. Ambivalence; approach-avoidance conflict (*84, 101*)

c. The self-defeating nature of neurotic behavior (*61, 103*)

d. Cultural conflict (*61, 73*)

Other concepts which may have relevance to this case: personal disposition; self-confidence.

MEHMET: Comments by a Graduate Student

The father had goals for Mehmet from which Mehmet fled. But in looking over his shoulder to escape from his father, he is running smack into a professional career (commerce) which is almost a carbon copy of his father's. Mehmet may have some glimmering of awareness of this conflict — though he says he wants a career in commerce, he *actually* spends his time reading more abstract economic literature and writing poetry.

There were other boys in that classroom who were caught in a culture conflict — hanging on the brink of Westernization. Yet, they didn't approach the counselor after class, while Mehmet did. The culture conflict appears at best a necessary but not a sufficient cause. Mehmet seems better understood in terms of a more familiar neurotic paradigm, such as described above — escape from anxiety through self-defeating devices.

PHYLLIS

The Unhappy Perfectionist

Phyllis came from a close-knit family living in a small community. She was bright, high in academic achievement, and somewhat puritanical in attitude. The case traces her struggle with her affection for a boy and with a severe emotional crisis. Considerable detail is given in describing stormy counseling sessions as well as the outcome of this therapeutic relationship, which lasted over a year. The results of the Rorschach Inkblot Test and the TAT projective test are given. Brief follow-up information is included.

IDENTIFICATION

Phyllis, twenty-two years of age, was neatly groomed and conservatively dressed. She was about average in size and weight, and feminine in her mannerisms. Although she was not unattractive, she did nothing to enhance her appearance. When she was seen on the campus, she was usually alone, walking intently with quick steps, and with her head raised or turned to one side as though she were looking at something in the street. She rarely fixed her glance on any person or object that she passed. If someone happened to say hello to her, she either pretended not to hear or had a blank expression or seemed startled. On first encounter, she seemed gentle and sweet, but before very long, as one talked with her, a strong puritanical, purist streak appeared. At times she seemed affected, through her use of broad a's and careful, self-conscious diction. She took a prim, highly critical attitude toward differences in speech patterns, dress, or behavior.

146

OCCASION FOR INTERVIEW

A distant relative, a boy about her own age, was also on campus, pursuing a graduate course in psychiatric social work. John was a wholesome, rather calm, pleasant, bright, hard-working, and confident young fellow who came from a small town adjacent to the one where Phyllis grew up. She often phoned him, asking to talk with him if he had the time. Soon he began to see that she needed continued assistance of a professional nature. However, he knew she would resist any suggestion that she seek or accept such help. He probably saw not only that she would have difficulty talking to an older man, who was also a potential father-surrogate, but that she might also be forced to minimize a relationship with John that she had come to enjoy. She had always been fond of him, but he was a little concerned now that this fondness might become an emotional involvement.

Phyllis had begun discussing her personal problems with John originally when a mutual friend of theirs, with whom she was in love, had stopped writing to her. This was a boy who ate at the boarding house where they had taken meals the year before. John had been somewhat pleased when the boy had left school, because he thought this boy might take advantage of her strong infatuation. He intimated that undoubtedly the boy had become very amorous and had broken down some of her resistance to necking, arousing strong guilt and conflict in her. Apparently, she had not dated at all in high school and seldom in college.

FAMILY BACKGROUND

Phyllis came from a religious family that had been very active in a rural, fundamentalist Protestant church. They lived on a farm. Her father was active in church affairs, sang in the choir, and had a good reputation in the community. He was apparently very outgoing, and demonstratively fond of her three brothers, one older and two younger than Phyllis. The older brother had been killed in a freak automobile accident. This had been a calamity for the family and community, and the father had never fully recovered from the shock.

Very little information was obtained directly from Phyllis about her family, but John had indicated that her mother was very conservative and overprotective and that her father had a casual attitude toward Phyllis. He showed interest in her mainly by teasing in a manner that she felt was demeaning. When she arrived at college, she realized that she had strong negative feelings toward both parents. She felt that they had definitely *favored the boys over her*. To Phyllis, her parents' attitude toward her seemed to represent psychological rejection, although she never expressed this idea and her parents would probably have denied it. They seemed to appreciate her mainly for her ability to get good grades and for being a quiet, withdrawn girl. They had not encouraged her to participate in extracurricular activities nor to fraternize with her peers. When the boy she met at college began to respond to her interest in him, she became very serious. Although he had been gone from the campus for six months, she could not forget him. As she talked with John about the problem, she seemed to be developing the same feeling toward him (John). He undoubtedly represented a security that the first boy did not.

COUNSELING EVENTS

First interview

As John had predicted, the counselor found it very difficult to establish a working relationship with Phyllis. When he suggested that she do most of the talking, she simply turned her head and said nothing. She had begun the interview by saying that she thought nothing could result from counseling and that *she did not think anyone ever changed*. She answered questions with single words and simple phrases, or silence, and then stated that she just could not talk about herself. The counselor tried to show acceptance and understanding of her defensiveness by such statements as, "You find it difficult to talk to someone for the first time." He suggested that she had nothing to lose by talking out some of her feelings and that she could feel free to talk about any aspect of her life.

The only topic she would talk about was John, and she described in detail her great respect for him. In fact, she stated that she came to the counseling session only because John had insisted, and she felt guilty about taking so much of the counselor's time. She hinted that she experienced some slight *rejection and stigma* because John had referred her for counseling. After a slow start, Phyllis's reluctance eventually gave way and she talked at some length.

She said that her work as a graduate student was a wall that she had built around her personality. By studying hard and getting a second degree, she had been able to keep busy and thus prevent people from seeing how sensitive she really was. She expressed disillusionment in not being able to work out her problems by herself. She had great faith in logic, and it bothered her that *a rational approach was not very helpful in dealing with her emotional difficulties.* She hinted that she was a selfish, vain person and that this was a horrible trait.

Second interview

The second interview was even more difficult. Apparently she said more than she had intended to in the first interview; fearing she might do the same thing again, she was almost mute in the second session. She did say, after many minutes of silence, that she had had a long talk with John the day before. Then she began to cry vigorously and loudly. The crying was to continue through many of the early interviews. The counselor found her more difficult to handle than almost any client he had had in ten years of counseling.* He had conflicts about the wisdom of continuing the relationship for the following reasons: (1) Phyllis seemed unwilling to accept a counseling relationship; (2) the loud wailing and apparent loss of emotional control made the usual kind of office counseling almost impossible; (3) Phyllis's perception that the counselor saw this as a very difficult situation; and (4) John's realization that he could do little more for Phyllis unless she got professional assistance. The counselor considered suggesting to John that Phyllis's family seek private psychiatric consultation. However, he knew this would represent further rejection to Phyllis — that she was a seriously emotionally disturbed person. It might also put her parents into a situation they could not easily handle. After weighing these factors, the counselor decided to continue to see Phyllis professionally.

She said during the second interview, amid sobs, that she was very *frightened* being in the counselor's office and wished John was there. She was encouraged to come back for further interviews, even if she did nothing but sit in silence. Finally, after several unproductive interviews, she agreed to come back only if John were allowed to come with her. This suggestion resulted in a mutual agreement

---

* The difficulty involved the necessity of understanding all of Phyllis's nonverbal means of communication — her facial expressions and deliberate postural responses; her weeping and sighing.

between the counselor and John for him to accompany her for a while.*

Subsequent counseling

Phyllis was planning to go home for a spring vacation. The counselor asked John to find out from her parents whether they had noticed any difference in her behavior since her visit. Apparently they had not.

Phyllis seemed a little less tense when John accompanied her in the sessions. During one interview she jumped from her chair, pulled her chair over next to John, grabbed him by the arm, only to sit next to him and say nothing. This established a pattern of behavior that she later used on several occasions. She continued to bring John with her, but the conferences were still verbally unproductive. Although she sat next to John, she remained tense and sighed heavily as the counselor tried to express the feelings he thought she had.

In one of these conferences the counselor happened to ask her what she would be doing the following year. This proved to be a provocative question. She had saved her pin money throughout her life and put it in a savings account. Now she had decided to join a student group, and use her savings to make a trip to Latin America with this group. This was news even to John.

About this time in the course of counseling, John contrived to arrive late, and the counselor was able to talk a little with Phyllis before he came. When John arrived, she repeated her action of previous sessions: she moved next to him, sometimes putting her head on his shoulder, sometimes crying hysterically. The counselor did not know the full meaning of Phyllis's crying nor its role in her past history. In addition to being a response to despair and a release of tensions, it may have been a bid for sympathy and a means of controlling others. It did not achieve this end in the counseling situation.

John had a few interviews with the counselor in which he offered information about some of Phyllis's reactions to the counselor's behavior. The first interview with John alone came after Phyllis had remarked to the counselor that one of the interviews was so painful to her that she felt as though she had taken a physical beating.

---

* This is highly unconventional in counseling and was agreed upon because it seemed the only way to get Phyllis to deal with her problems. John had been seeing her periodically before, as a friend. It was agreed John would accompany her but remain silent.

She indicated that she was always very disturbed when she discussed personal problems, even when she talked with John, but never as upset as she had been during the last few interviews. John stated that by and large she seemed to be tolerating the interviews better now than she had previously; perhaps because of this greater involvement, she reacted more fully to them. John finally persuaded her to come in alone, but he pointed out to the counselor several aspects of the interviews that were particularly disturbing to her. One was that the counselor reminded her of her father when he tended to take a light teasing attitude toward her. She also objected to the good-bye pat on the shoulder which the counselor was in in the habit of half-consciously giving her. She told John that the counselor's remarks made her feel that he was laughing at her. The counselor had noticed that the last few interviews were freer. She tended to talk about impersonal matters — her trip to Latin America, her thesis, and her graduate adviser, whom the counselor also knew. Her attitude toward her adviser was strongly negative. He had many of Phyllis's own traits — he was highly perfectionistic, moralistic, critical, and insisted on much painstaking work. As Phyllis began talking more openly about her problems, the counselor expressed acceptance of her feelings and punctuated the interviews with "Yes," "Of course," "Um-hum," etc. Occasionally he repeated her statements by way of reflecting the feelings Phyllis expressed. This is an example of the use of client-centered counseling, which places greatest emphasis on the client's capacity to grow by ventilating his feelings, having them accepted, clarified, and thus reflected back more clearly. The aim is to produce greater perspective on the part of the client (Rogers and Dymond, 94). The counselor had found that if he took too active a role, Phyllis tended to reduce her flow of speech and remain quiet. It was difficult to predict the effect of any casual remark the counselor might make.

During these interviews Phyllis mentioned that nobody cared or ever would care about her, and it wasn't right to waste the counselor's time. She was still writing to the boy she had dated the year before. Although he barely replied to her letters, she decided, with some ambivalence, to visit him when she went through Texas on her way to Latin America. The large city in which he now lived was on her way.

Phyllis was beginning to talk a little about the superficial aspects of her correspondence with this boy. She continued to weep during part of each interview and to cling to John, who accompanied her until after the eleventh interview. At that time the counselor began to see her less often, about twice a week. She was beginning to talk about many of the things John had mentioned before he introduced her to the counselor — her attitude toward her parents, her felt rejection by them, their criticism, and the pressure they put on her. Although she came into the interviews alone, she rarely looked the counselor in the face. Much of the time, even at this point in the counseling sequence, she began the interview by turning her chair away from the counselor, sometimes even turning her back to him. We might raise the question as to what Phyllis was saying, consciously or unconsciously, by this nonverbal gesture.

In the next few interviews she raised questions about such matters as the ambivalence she felt toward her family, the fact that her mother assumed she would marry, and her feeling that she never wanted any financial support from her father. She pointed out that she was very fond of him and had groomed especially to meet his many suggestions. She also ventilated her hostility toward her adviser. She began to talk about the interview itself and her slightly changed attitude toward it. She analyzed some of her own attitudes, such as her tendency to "try too hard" on examinations. Now and then tearfulness during the interviews returned, especially when she made remarks such as "I am in a trap," "I can't quit," "I don't even expect to find peace," and "I don't deserve anything better than this suffering." She appreciated what John had done for her, but felt he should not do these things because he did not love her. [A graduate student reading the case commented that John was a good example of Sullivan's "significant other" (47).] She expressed her feeling of guilt about not loving her parents and dealt with similar feelings that she had been unable to accept in earlier sessions.

Dynamic trends shown

At this point, what are some of the dynamic trends that can be seen in Phyllis's recent past that may account, at least to some extent, for the emotional difficulties discussed above? Certainly Phyllis's conflict over her parents and her feelings of rejection by them are important. Of equal importance are the conflict between the puritanical and rigid sense of right and wrong; the physical attraction aroused by the boy (who did not love her as she did him); her actual attitude toward her work, and the attitude she regarded as appropriate. In the interviews she was expressing in her own way aggression, the need for dominance by manipulating the counselor, and the need for affection, shown by her behavior toward John.

There were probably other frustrations and conflicts which had so far eluded verbal expression. Phyllis was receiving very few satisfying social responses from other students, even from those she might find admirable, because of her defensiveness and prim, aloof attitude. She belonged to a choral group, but fraternized little with the other members. They were aware of her only when she criticized the less inhibited students or the poor diction of the music leader. She engaged in few activities that were widely need-satisfying to an energetic girl who seemed basically to be sensitive and responsive. She enjoyed listening to music, reading, and studying; but these pleasures did not satisfy her deeply felt human needs.

Results of projective tests

John had given Phyllis several projective personality tests, before the counselor saw her, as part of a practice series for a course in projective techniques that he was taking. These included the *Rorschach Inkblot Test** and the *Thematic Apperception Test (TAT).***

* The *Rorschach Inkblot Test* is a projective test which uses ambiguous inkblots presented on a series of cards. The subject is asked to tell what he sees in the inkblots. His responses are usually more revealing than his replies to a personality inventory. A trained examiner who is familiar with the commonness or uniqueness of responses, with the overall pattern of responses, and with behavioral correlates of various responses, can piece together valuable data about the inner life of the individual, which might otherwise be unavailable. This is illustrated by the following excerpts from John's report, giving his interpretations of Phyllis's Rorschach responses:

"The general picture is one of compulsion, in which needs are successfully met in reality adjustment; there is, however, a liability in her adjustive responses to life (instability in emotional life). She shows a tendency toward *impulsiveness* in meeting emotional situations. This is enhanced by contact shyness and the *fear of being involved in these emotional situations.* . . . There is, therefore, an unsuccessful meeting of the situations, and she tends to be *explosive rather than controlled.* Her *lack of self-acceptance* is not buffered by self-inspection or analysis but seems to lead to inner tension. This tension is also related to the difficulty in successfully controlling effective contacts.

"Her adjustment to reality is somewhat unsuccessful. She conforms to social situations acceptably but compulsively. She has a *high level of aspiration* and drive to achieve high goals which are not necessarily beyond her capacity. However, there is *compulsion toward perfection and hypercriticality.* She *does not seem to be emotionally mature,* as shown by impulsiveness in an emotional situation — not wanting to become involved until she can successfully meet the situation. There is a lack of inner acceptance of impulsiveness. There is every indication of superior intellectual capacity."

** The *Thematic Apperception Test* is a set of ambiguous pictures given to the subject. He makes up a story about each picture, telling what the central character is feeling and thinking, what led up to the situation pictured, and what the outcome will be.

The first card presented to Phyllis was a picture of a very old, wrinkled woman and a younger woman. The older woman has her chin in her hand. The follow-

She wrote sixteen TAT fantasies. The nature of the themes not only reflected some of her own feelings, as for example, the marked willfulness shown in one of the stories, but also demonstrated a capacity for attitudes of optimism and reality. Much tragedy was represented — a woman with a talented child who had been killed; success accompanied by personal unhappiness; illegitimacy; suicide; a parish priest who, in his old age, felt he had been a failure; accidental death; theft; heartbroken parents; and a wealthy man who lost everything and became homeless.

The following year

A summer elapsed, and the trip to Latin America was largely successful. Phyllis returned to school, dropped all her courses (she had by this time received her Master's degree), and found a routine stenographic job. She was no longer thinking in terms of the boy who had ignored her.

The character of the interviews had greatly changed. There was no weeping, and she *talked more freely*. She did not turn her back to the counselor, but still looked away as she talked. She divided the time in the interviews between talking about John and Latin America and talking about matters more relevant to her personal adjustment. She showed much more *concern about her parents*. She felt that they were worried about her. They did not understand why she wanted to be away from home, supporting herself with a low-level position after she had received a Master's degree in a specialized field. She began for the first time to give some evidence that she felt her family needed her. There were still long periods of silence in the interviews, but the general improvement was quite evident.

It was still very difficult for Phyllis to take the initiative in an interview, but she responded positively or negatively to various subjects as they were brought up. She seemed to *accept the counselor's ver-*

---

ing was Phyllis's response to this card: "The younger woman has decided upon a course of action completely contrary to the ideas and wishes of the old woman, her grandmother. She intends to do exactly as she pleases and will let nothing stand in her way, even though what she intends is wrong. Her selfish, willful disposition is partially the result of her grandmother. The old woman, although terribly disappointed, has enough strength of character to endure her disappointment."

Phyllis's response to another card was as follows: "This girl is posing for a painting by her husband, a famous artist. She was a model before marriage, and it is easy for her to assume a natural and lifelike pose. Her expression reflects the peace and happiness she has found in her marriage. Her whole life will probably be characterized by this serenity."

balization of her feelings as he perceived them. About this time she began to question whether she should continue the counseling because progress was so slow. The secretary of the mental hygiene clinic said she had noticed great changes in this young woman. She was less tense and was beginning to make friends more easily and less cautiously with other students.

Phyllis raised some question about continuing to receive counseling free of charge, since she was no longer a student. Consequently the counselor arranged for her to compensate by coaching a twelve-year-old girl, in whom he had an interest. Phyllis was somewhat doubtful about how well she could do this, but she undertook the project. The counselor did this partly because he had noted some slowdown in progress. Phyllis often came into the room, put her head on the table, and said she was tired. She again became sensitive about the counselor's mannerism that she interpreted as "teasing." John continued to talk with her, as she frequently called him on the phone. Her feelings toward John remained very strong. For the first time she was able to talk about her relationship with the boy whom she had loved but who failed to write to her after he left town. She said when he was in town she waited several days for him to call; when he did not call, she called him. This behavior on her part was shocking and difficult for her to accept. She was also able to talk about her conflicts concerning her former graduate adviser. She was learning to accept her hostility toward him, despite "all he had done for her." She talked also about her ambivalence toward the young girl she was coaching.

Discussion of feelings

One of the big differences between this period of counseling and the previous one was that she was able to come to grips with her feelings and to *express the impulses which she previously had not been able to accept.* There were times when she talked quite freely, in her precise, stilted manner. She handled the interview better when the counselor did not intrude; however, she often seemed to change from a free, relaxed attitude to a very tense, still, and defensive one. She talked about John and how he was advising her, making her take more initiative, and reassuring her concerning her sensitivity about being on the campus while not matriculating. John suggested that she discuss with the counselor some of the things she brought up with him.

On one occasion during this period she came in with John. She reverted to the old practice of sitting very close to him, holding his hand, and putting her head on his chest. She started crying again, but later in the interview talked about her feelings of great guilt — including a feeling that she was eternally damned. She thought that if she were punished every day for the rest of her life, the scales would be righted. The counselor mentioned her perfectionism and her unduly high standards. She admitted this was true but thought that nothing could be done about it. The counselor did not make any clinical interpretations about her sense of guilt or her masochistic tendencies (her need for punishment). After she had finished a combination of crying and talking, she seemed to be relaxed and talked with John quite pleasantly. Although this interview had some of the characteristics of the earlier ones, there was one very striking difference, namely her *free discussion of strong inner feelings*. In subsequent interviews she stated that she had felt very good for a week and that she no longer had the tired feeling she used to have.

She again referred to the counseling experience as a punishing one, and again expressed a need for punishment. However, the fact that the counselor was kind and accepting disturbed her, because punishment, she felt, should not be given by that kind of person. The counselor accepted these statements and reflected her feelings about them in a traditional Rogerian* manner with statements such as, "You feel that these counseling experiences are punishing"; "You feel you need to be punished"; "It is puzzling to you that these sessions should be punishing when I don't seem to be the kind of person whom you associate with punishment." The counselor did not push the implications to the interpretation by statements such as, "Maybe the punishment comes from yourself — your feeling of guilt and wrongdoing." She later brought up her feelings of guilt.

She began to talk more freely about her ambivalence toward John — she needed him, yet felt guilty for leaning on him. She intimated that she was falling in love with him, but that he did not reciprocate her feelings. She saw him as trying to make her more sociable, so that she might be more accepting of contacts from other people.

The emotional fixation upon John, which she was beginning to verbalize and accept as unrealistic, was a conflict she was to resolve, though not without guilt and concern. John, a well-integrated and mature young man about her age, was a help here, in that he used the relationship to further Phyllis's growth.

Phyllis talked more and more frequently about the young girl she

* This term refers to client-centered counseling, discussed briefly on pages 2, 3.

was coaching. Her attitude toward this girl was mixed. She appreciated the spontaneity and lack of inhibitions that the girl showed and once said, "My mother would think she was a very naughty child." Her inability to completely direct the activities of her charge bothered her.

The interviews continued to be more open. She was even beginning to discuss her relationship with the counselor. She said she had never been able to figure out her relationship to him or his role. She expressed the hostilities she sometimes felt. These interviews in which she discussed the counseling relationship were, like many others, free and open for a while; then she became tense and defensive and withdrew into stiffness, wearing a fixed expression.

In a discussion about a friend of hers she commented that this girl was able to talk freely about her inner experiences, while she, Phyllis, was not. She discussed her inability to use her religion as she thought she should. She had the feeling that she had no right to change herself and that she was destined always to be the kind of person she was. Her father was mentioned in the interviews, and she talked of her inability to please him, thereby implying resentment of the favoritism she believed he showed to her brothers.

It disturbed Phyllis to feel that she could not show the affection that she thought she should toward her parents. She noted that her attitude toward her brother's fiancée was different from that of her parents and neighbors. This girl smoked and was a little freer in attitude than they thought she should be. This led to a discussion with the counselor of right and wrong and rigid attitudes toward them. She discussed the contrast between her own attitudes toward contemporary manners, morals, and interests of youth, and those of other people her age.

Phyllis was beginning to loosen her rigidity a little and accept the fact that she could not meet her perfectionistic standards. She stated, however, that she could not give them up. What concerned her was that she seemed unable to earn the love of anyone. This statement was followed by sobs. Here we see an increasing tendency on her part to face her feelings about events close to her. This blanket statement probably referred to her felt rejection by her father, her relationship with the boy who did not reciprocate her deep affection for him, and John. She talked about a friend who seemed to be accepting her, but she felt that the girl would not accept her if she knew her deeply. She mentioned that her job was forcing her to meet reality and to see life as it really is. She referred to little things that bothered her on the job, such as people looking over her shoulder when she was writing. Privacy seemed to be very important for her. The matters discussed in the interviews of this period were deeper than those of earlier ones. On the whole, matters were discussed after a year of counseling that could never have been brought up previously, such as her behavior as a child.

She said that she had been a naughty child and deserved to be punished; when she was not punished, she tended to punish herself. She felt no resentment when her parents punished her. She described herself as being bossy to her brothers and having very strong ideas about what was acceptable behavior and what was not. She defended her parents, saying they were not stuffy and they had a lot of fun, but intimated it was clean, wholesome fun.

The secretary in the office, who had known Phyllis casually for several years, reported that she saw Phyllis at a concert with another girl, and she seemed to be laughing and talking happily. During this period of counseling Phyllis cried less often, although every now and then she seemed to try to induce it without success. The counselor made it clear that he would accept any feelings that she wished to express, about any events in her life, or even her feelings about him.

More overt reaction to daily events

Phyllis seemed to be disturbed whenever the counselor greeted and talked with her at times when she was in the building for purposes other than counseling. There were other little matters that upset her. The counselor often stopped the interview when the time period was up, rather than continuing with a subject. When he indicated that the interview was coming to a close, Phyllis often became quite tense, withdrawn, and somewhat pouty. When the girl whom she was coaching failed to show up or came rather late, this bothered her also. Her rigidity seemed to be waning, or at least she was beginning to see that most people were less absolutistic in their standards than she was. The interviews varied from productive ones dealing with feelings, attitudes, and conflicts, to others in which she sat with her head down and said very little.

She was becoming more involved in relationships with people around her, even though she was unable to handle them well. She described an incident at her boarding house. Girls were talking rather loudly downstairs, and she went to the head of the stairs and said, "What has happened?" At first they ignored her, and then they "insulted her." This was shocking and puzzling, but she was able to think it through and realized that she had little in common with the girls and that she had not been at all friendly to them.

She found it easier to go places around the campus, such as the library and the museum, even though she was no longer a student. Some time earlier she had been quite self-conscious about being on the campus as a non-student.

She began to discuss the personality differences between herself and John. She probably was beginning to see that her basic temperament was more spontaneous and open than she could accept, and that her standards acted as a defense against somewhat natural spontaneity. She said, "There is something in me that forces me to adopt these standards. I can't relinquish them. My goal is perfection; I must try and continue to try. I must live with these standards though I don't necessarily like them." Then she tried to cry, but, unlike the interviews of the previous year, she was not successful.

About this time John was becoming seriously interested in a girl who had certain characteristics of openness and spontaneity that Phyllis did not have. Phyllis was frankly critical of the girl and hostile toward John. John described the situation as one of clear-cut jealousy. Phyllis knew that in a few weeks John would be leaving the city to take a job. She was, however, planning to visit the place and was going to see him at least once or twice during the summer. One time when she was talking to John, he indicated that he had to leave for a date. She began to pound him with her fists, something she could not have done a year or so earlier. At that time she would have brooded and hated herself for the feeling. She was becoming more realistic, but was unable to control the tendency to act out her emotions.

At this stage in the counseling the counselor not only listened but pointed out some of the trends in Phyllis's personality, such as rigidity, perfectionism, absolute values about what is permitted and not permitted, and her irritation at behavior that differed from hers. At times the relationship between her and the counselor was discussed. Her attitude toward being counseled was one of shame; she lost a certain amount of independence when she depended upon counseling. The counselor pointed out that she was now dealing with feelings and aspects of her life she could not have touched earlier.

With encouragement from John and the counselor, she was going more places and doing more things. Although her contacts with others were not free and accepting, at least she did not consider them absolutely wrong and herself absolutely right. When she had first made arrangements for counseling, it was at the instigation of John, but now, at the end of the year, the counselor pointed out that she would have to make the choice as to whether she would continue counseling the following year. She reluctantly decided in favor of continuing the interviews. During the summer she even wrote a letter requesting an interview.

The third year of counseling

Phyllis was even freer in the interviews this year than she had ever been before. There was a stronger tendency to accept the counselor as a person, and at times she looked him in the eye — something she had never done before. She occasionally reverted to mannerisms used earlier, such as turning her chair slightly so that she did not see the counselor, and unsuccessful attempts at sobbing. The interviews varied in productiveness. Usually the counselor had to start the interview with a discussion of her interests and activities during the previous week. Such matters as her dependency upon John and its effect on her personality were discussed openly. If, after several attempts by the counselor, she still refused to communicate, he picked up a paper or magazine and read. This infuriated her. She expressed her anger, and then the whole relationship was discussed.

For the first time she began talking about her dreams, which she referred to as "nightmares." They usually consisted of someone pursuing her. In one dream she was in a prison, and John and the counselor were helping her to get out. She saw obvious implications of this dream, and she may have seen reflected her changed attitude toward the counselor. She more readily admitted her own "stubborn traits," and looked upon them as a handicap rather than as righteousness.

The counselor discussed with her her intolerance of ambiguity and what conditions of life brought it about or prevented it. She was typically in a much better humor when she arrived for her interviews, was much more cooperative, and voluntarily referred to decisions she had to make, such as the kind of job she should choose. She wanted to avoid any kind of job that involved responsibility or choice, such as being a departmental secretary in the University, or continuing graduate work, which would entail getting a thesis problem and carrying it through. On the other hand, the humdrum kind of job she had at present was not entirely satisfying to her.

John was living in another city and was engaged. Her contacts with him were relatively few. She seemed to have been weaned somewhat from her dependence on him.

Romance and discontinuation of counseling

During this year Phyllis met another graduate student who was kind and affectionate toward her, although she seemed unwilling to accept his overtures at first. She spoke of her attitude toward him, which was one of increasing interest. There was a tendency to compare him with John and with the boy she was in love with when she first came into counseling. There was also a tendency to make him fit into her rigid life pattern, but with time she was gaining perspective on this tendency. Apparently their differences were discussed openly. Once during the relationship he became ill, and she seemed to enjoy bringing him food and taking care of him. As a couple they were participating in more social activities with other graduate students. In the spring he proposed to her; this presented a conflict and a choice which she openly discussed with the counselor. She seemed to realize that marriage would entail certain compromises that her rigid viewpoints would make difficult, but she accepted the challenge.

Phyllis's fiance objected to the counseling, although the objection grew less when he realized that discussing matters in the counseling session helped her to have a more positive attitude toward him. However, she became less spontaneous and more rigid during the sessions; because of loyalties to her fiance, she felt unable to discuss with the counselor her changed behavior and her fiance's objection to counseling. The counselor learned more about this conflict later during a follow-up conversation with John.

FOLLOW-UP

Two years after the beginning of counseling, Phyllis decided to get married, and she left the city with her husband. The counselor did not hear of the marriage nor did he ever meet Phyllis's fiance.

John later explained to the counselor her disagreement with her fiance over counseling. This was the reason she had left abruptly at the end of the semester, without any discussion of terminating the counseling. John gave this explanation on one of two special calls that he made to tell the counselor how Phyllis was coming along. Both times John reported favorable progress in general.

The first report came about three months after Phyllis had left.

John called the counselor to thank him for helping Phyllis. He said as far as he could see Phyllis was getting along very well as a bride, and that just before the counseling relationship broke down she had been getting a great deal out of the sessions and had looked forward to them. John thought that many of the things she discussed with him and not with the counselor earlier in the sessions were later discussed openly with the counselor. John said he doubted that she could have "pulled through" without the continued counseling. When she first came in, he had thought she might have to be hospitalized because of her emotional state, but now he thought she had gained enough security and capacity to adjust to life's problems.

About six months later John made another call, again expressing appreciation and pointing out the continued progress that Phyllis was making. She had a child and her husband had a new job. John had visited them in their new home, and Phyllis seemed to be in better emotional health than he had ever seen her.

PHYLLIS: Personal Trends and Relationships

What in particular do you see in Phyllis's life history? Recall patterns that impressed you before turning to the questions below.

Personality characteristics

a. Suppose you lived in the same house with Phyllis. Which of her traits would attract your attention most readily?

b. In what ways might you systematically alter your behavior and attitudes toward her so as to exert a maximal therapeutic impact on her life? How much of this could you do without specialized training in psychology?

c. What traits would you fail to see that are shown more clearly in the total case?

d. How do you explain her scrupulous, unrealistically high moral standards, and her guilt when she fell short of these self-imposed standards?

e. To what extent did she use her symptoms to manipulate people around her?

Important relationships and events

a. Since the information about her early family life is sparse, try to reconstruct the relationships that may have made Phyllis the sort of person she was.

b. What in the counseling situation was instrumental in bringing out favorable changes in Phyllis?

1. her emotional behavior, contrasted with her prim, reserved conduct outside of counseling

2. the supportive rather than interpretive role of counseling, which did not destroy her essential defenses

3. a relationship which allowed her to display and deal with her own self-defeating behavior, rather than one which gave her rationally valid answers

c. Were friends, family, and associates therapeutic agents to any great extent?

Concepts helpful in understanding Phyllis

a. Defensiveness (11, 121)

b. Cognitive dissonance (36, 99)

c. Passive aggressiveness (59)

d. A rigid superego (74, 121)

e. Authoritarian personality: dichotomous thinking (24, 116)

f. Transference (99, 121)

Other concepts which may have some relevance to this case: reaction formation; intolerance of ambiguity; "significant other"; resistance; dreams; working through; release therapy.

RALPH

The Confused Hobbyist

Ralph's story began with some interviews when he was a
graduate student. He was followed at irregular intervals
over a period of approximately fifteen years, which included an attempt at graduate work, an inauspicious stint
in military service, and eventually settling into family life
and a satisfactory existence as a store-keeper. With Ralph's
case we can open the question of what constitutes a satisfactory, effective, mature adjustment to life.

IDENTIFICATION

Ralph was a good-looking fellow of twenty-six, somewhat above
average in height and weight, and in good health. He was friendly
and appeared to have a good sense of humor; he smiled frequently
in social contacts and seemed to enjoy life. He was taking graduate
work in forestry, mainly because it was compatible with his interest
in the outdoors. However, he had some doubts as to whether this
was the right field for him.

OCCASION FOR INTERVIEW

Ralph filled out a *Pre-Interview Blank* when he was taking a course
with the counselor. He attempted to express his general attitudes and
feelings as follows: "By ordinary standards I think I am happy, but
I cannot say that I am extremely happy and bubbling over with it.
At times I feel depressed, but never what I would call sad. Lately
I have been feeling tired. I think it relates to my major source of
worry — myself. Mainly, I seem to fail in understanding myself and
lack self-mastery.* I have a feeling that I could do much better work

---
* Italics mine.

164

and much more work than I am doing now. I am in graduate school and much is expected of me. I have a strong desire for self-improvement, but I don't understand why I never get started; or if I do, why this desire weakens and dies, only to pop up later on. In short, I am dissatisfied with myself and the ways I regulate my life. I do want to have better *control* over my own affairs and ways of thinking. I sometimes wonder if I have enough ability to be in graduate school. I told the fellows in the forestry program my I.Q.; they say I am crazy for telling it and that it couldn't possibly be that low. Frankly, I wonder." *

PERSONAL HISTORY

Parents and early life

Ralph described his father as a nervous, irritable man; his mother was also nervous and tended to worry too much. His father graduated from high school; his mother had a college education. Ralph's conflicts showed that he was responsive to his parents' pressures on him to achieve, but apparently he had resisted them. Both were hard-working people. They had a small home-appliance store which sold some second-hand goods. Their economic status appeared to be low for their educational background. They lived in a neighborhood which was slightly below the average for the community. Several of the children, including Ralph, had worked in the store while going to school. Ralph was not specific in describing his relationship with the other members of his family. He had two older sisters, one of whom took an interest in him and attempted to encourage him. He described her as having artistic interests and skills, and influencing him somewhat in the same interests. This influence may partially explain his unusually wide range of interests and hobbies. He had a younger brother whom he considered dependable and skillful as a mechanic. (He apparently felt that his siblings had made a better adjustment than he had; that they knew what they wanted and were getting it.)

We have no clear picture of the nature of the *parental discipline* in Ralph's developing years. From some of his comments the counselor hypothesized that it was *not consistent*. He did state that at present his parents thought it was "high time that I was earning my own living," and he agreed.

* He either had an erroneous idea of his I.Q. or, more probably, quoted an exaggeratedly low I.Q.

He stated that as a small child he did not have any playmates and that he made friends slowly. By the time he was ten or twelve, he was able to play with gangs and groups; in fact, he was usually the leader. In high school he tended to be quiet and retiring and to retain his interest in earlier hobbies rather than in adolescent social life; however, he was not unlike a good percentage of his class in this respect.

He did not date until his sophomore year in college. He found, however, that when he showed interest in a girl, she was very responsive. He had traveled more widely than the typical boy of his age. His travels included much of western United States and some parts of Canada.

Religion

In giving religious aspects of his history, Ralph said, "I am a member of the Baptist Church — I used to go quite regularly but haven't gone at all in the past year. I have lost most of my ideals, so they are probably of little value. Nevertheless my early training greatly influences my own personal religion and moral code." As an adult he represents a superior moral and ethical code. He is a responsible citizen and active in the Boy Scouts. There was a rowdy bar across the street from his parents' store and often people wandered from there into his store. He is known to have ordered some of the louder drunks to get out.

Sex experience

In filling out the *Pre-Interview Blank* Ralph was more frank than even the average male college student. He stated that he began to masturbate at the age of ten or twelve. He did not have his first date until he was nineteen years old. At twenty-two he had his first experience with sexual intercourse. He makes no comment about further experiences but adds, "I have never been to a dance." When the counselor first saw him, at twenty-six years of age, he gave the impression of having some heterosexual interests but less than the average man his age; in fact he seemed adolescent in heterosexual and social attitudes. His friends were students who paid little attention to clothing styles and who dated less than the more socially-oriented students.

COUNSELING EVENTS

An interview followed, and Ralph expanded a little on the statements he had made on the Blank. The counselor attempted to be reassuring by pointing out his assets. In terms of the total population Ralph was not low in ability. He had graduated in the middle of his high-school class and had gone on to receive a college degree. True, his record was in no way remarkable, and he probably would not have been admitted into most graduate programs, but he happened to get into a new program in which there was a need for students.

Counselor's impressions

The inconsistencies in Ralph's physique and grooming were similar to those found in his ability and school achievement. He seemed to be superior in health, vigor, and general good looks, but he was untidy and carried excess weight. He seemed to *lack confidence*, and tried to cover this up with blustering and teasing. He admitted that he felt uneasy in the presence of other people and that he had expressed this uneasiness in high school by stirring up trouble and actually getting a bad reputation — mildly bad, that is — talking in class, playing pranks on the other students, and similar mischief. He had never engaged in any activity that could be classified as delinquent, but he had a way of annoying the teachers, perhaps to get attention from them and the class.

In the Blank he filled out, he constantly referred to his underachievement and his inability to use his assets in an effective way. He said, "For example, I spend four hours a night in study, but I don't accomplish what the average student accomplishes in less than half that time. [This is one of several examples of Ralph's tendencies, at least in his adult life, to *disparage himself* and his capacities when talking to others. He always did this openly and with a smile.] In high school I rarely participated in extracurricular activities." But he did spend a great deal of time with hobbies.

Interests

Ralph followed a wider range of interests and hobbies than the average collegian. He had a stamp collection and many good classical records; he was a good photographer and had constantly improved his equipment by second-hand purchases; he had books on natural history; he was interested in Indian relics, bird-watching, and botanical and zoological specimens. He said that he had a great many acquaintances and an average number of friends.

Self-ratings

When asked to rate his present degree of happiness, he checked the middle of a ten-point scale. His ratings for adjustment and outlook for the future were at the same place. He gave a very low rating for his mental integration or oneness of purpose, and for consistency and stability of attitudes and desires. In describing himself, he underlined these adjectives in a checklist: self-confident, restless, easygoing, friendly, absent-minded, shy, lazy, shows initiative, individualist, cooperative, sensitive, indifferent, easily distracted, cheerful, stubborn, critical, weak-willed, imaginative, egocentric, and self-conscious. At the end of the list he added much more comment than the average student. He said, "I have a tendency to spend beyond my income. I lack poise, and I neglect my personal appearance. I am always waiting for the right time to begin putting ideas and plans into action — waiting has become a permanent habit now. I am quite timid in meeting strangers; I lack ability to express opinions and ideas definitely; I am slow in reaching decisions; and I am lacking in tactfulness, in manners, and in speech. I show a lack of concentration on my studies and I am sarcastic and offensive in my conversation. I have self-confidence but apparently I am losing it. I seem unable to concentrate my efforts."

About the same time that he filled out the Blank, he took a brief psychoneurotic inventory.* Some of the traits he checked corroborate his own descriptions. He indicated he was conscious of the following characteristics in himself: fright, sensitivity, ideas running through his head so he could not sleep, shyness, tendency to daydream, frequent change of interests, easily moved to tears, feelings easily hurt, self-consciousness, and inability to make up his mind. Yet, despite all of these symptoms, he said he was in general self-confident about his abilities and admitted that there were some inconsistencies in his answers.

How would one describe Ralph's self-image? Could it be described as clear and realistic? Did he know who he was and what he was? Did he have a well-integrated identity? To what extent could he

* This was a list of the 42 most discriminating items of the "Personality Schedule." See L. L. Thurstone and T. G. Thurstone, "A Neurotic Inventory," *Journal of Social Psychology*, 1930, *1*, 1–30.

accept himself as he saw himself? Was there a disparity between his concept of himself and what others seemed to see in him?

Ralph had developed a number of skills in solitary outdoor pursuits. He could swim, and he was a good hunter and marksman. Unlike many young men his age who were oriented to the outdoors, he also had an interest in aesthetic pursuits, including good music. Ralph did not consider himself athletic. He made this statement on the *Pre-Interview Blank* in connection with "Recreation and Athletic History": "None — very quiet and retiring in high school. As a boy I greatly enjoyed playing by myself." It will be noted that many of Ralph's recreational pursuits were solitary and non-competitive.

Ratings by acquaintances

When Ralph took the above inventory, he asked if he might have some rating scales* to give to his friends to fill out anonymously. These scales were filled out by two close friends and one housemate. He was rated as "average" by all of them on efficiency; "good" by two of them on emotional stability, "average" by one. One rated him "good" in social adjustment, another "average," and a third gave him no rating on this trait. His appearance was rated by two as "poor," by one as "average." Two rated him "average" in leadership, one "did not know." On integrity or the tendency to live up to his representations, he was rated as "average" by two and "poor" by one. He was rated "below average" in motivation by all three raters.

The housemate remarked, "This is the type of fellow one would expect to find in high school. He brags about his female conquests to all who will listen, yet he would admit that they were untrue. He does not have a great deal of sex appeal; he is untactful; and he remarks to other people about their physical defects. I have seen him almost daily for years. His tendency to talk too much seems to be his most undesirable trait and I have told him this."

His two close friends were more generous. They both felt that the rating scales gave an inadequate opportunity to appraise Ralph. They both pointed out that he had a number of likable traits. Some of the adjectives on which they showed agreement were: good-natured, friendly, often procrastinates, enjoys people, cheerful, reliable, imaginative, and individualist. Two of the raters underlined the following words or phrases: avoids responsibilities, retiring, capable, appears unemotional, and submissive. If we compare these observations with Ralph's, *he apparently saw many more negative traits than his asso-*

* See page 32 for a sample of the rating scales.

ciates did, particularly those dealing with his motivation and inhibitions.

FOLLOW-UP

Ralph never did get his Master's degree. He married, entered the service, and was commissioned as an ensign in the Navy. He remained at that status throughout the war. When he returned, he opened a small, dimly-lit and poorly-painted toy store on one of the side streets in the small city in which he grew up. A relative had owned and operated the building for the last fifteen years. A few second-hand novelties in a dusty, portable show window, which he moved out on the sidewalk each morning, reflected his hobbies and interests as a youth. His merchandise attracted a number of parents and children into the store. Except for the one day a week that he closed the store to allow himself a day off, he was generally found, dressed in old clothes, standing smiling, arranging the stock. There were always two or three customers in the store. He seemed to enjoy them, and they talked pleasantly with him. His diction and poor grammar were more compatible with theirs than with that of the students he had met in college. He brought his lunch from home in a paper bag.

For a time his wife, who was quite competent as an office worker, held a position of importance in the State House. They had two children. On his day off and during his summer vacation he closed the store and went camping with his sons.

Ralph seemed to enjoy life thoroughly, although he functioned at an occupational level below that for which his education had prepared him. He apparently eked out a living. He clearly was not a status-seeker, was not at all interested in the country-club crowd or in owning a new car every few years. He had many acquaintances and loyal friends, as he had always had; a large group of congenial relatives; a simple, family-oriented social life. Although Ralph has visited the university community ten miles away and has had casual contacts with the counselor over the past fifteen years, Ralph has never mentioned the cause of his earlier concern nor commented upon his inner life. Evidently he has been living the kind of life he enjoys most. Ralph seems to possess many of the traits that he had regarded as undesirable when he was in college. But now he behaves as though he accepts them and seems quite content with life to those who know him.

The writer has no information about the welfare of his children or the attitude of his wife, except that her job must have yielded more than Ralph earned in the store. They both came from a similar middle-class background. Also, their grooming and general appearance were quite similar.

Most people who know Ralph would not regard him as a success in the usual American sense of that concept. In fact, he seems to see relatively few of the friends he made in college. They are in other cities working in the fields for which they had prepared. The sort of life he now lives is not incompatible with his campus activities or interests, since he had not joined a fraternity and did not strive for social achievement there. He continues to have many hobbies and enjoys them on his days off and on Sundays. He enjoys a number of cultural experiences, such as classical music, educational television, and the slick magazines. He is highly critical of the run-of-the-mill movies and television programs and seems to be conversant with some contemporary fiction. He also is in touch with current events. He does not feel that he has to conform and is perfectly frank in expressing opinions which conflict with the popular ideas.

RALPH: Personality Patterns and Relationships

What did you see in Ralph as you read his case? Give your own impressions before turning to the questions below.

Important personality characteristics

   a. In describing Ralph's traits, how important are (1) his preoccupation with masculinity; (2) his abundance of acquaintances and apparent lack of confidants; (3) his buffoonery as an adult?

   b. To what extent do you perceive Ralph's personality as unified and integrated?

   c. To what extent does Ralph show three important characteristics of mental health: (1) adjustiveness; (2) integrity; (3) realism?

Significant persons and relationships

   a. What roles do you think Ralph's mother and sister played in his development?

   b. Can you see the influences that caused his identity and interests to take the form they took?

   c. Do his interests and vocational life pattern serve as avenues of growth or as defenses against early anxiety?

Concepts helpful in understanding Ralph

   a. Self-actualization (73, 76)

   b. Life-style (2, 7)

   c. Consistency of personal dispositions or traits (3, 102)

   d. Repression–suppression (79, 103)

Other concepts which may have some relevance to this case: mental health; integrity; adjustiveness; realism.

DAVID

The Self-Fighter

David was a bright youth with a physical handicap and homosexual leanings. He was a youth with intense sensitivity, who attempted suicide, was hospitalized, and received treatment. His many pre-hospital contacts with a psychologist, with whom he had a good relationship, are described, as is the long-term, post-hospital follow-up, showing later attitudes toward life and attempted adjustment. Excerpts from David's letters and a brief psychiatric report are included.

IDENTIFICATION

David was a college freshman. He was above average in height and weight, neither handsome nor physically unattractive. However, his overall appearance gave a slightly negative impression. One failed to appreciate the effect of his expensive, stylish clothes because his glumness, awkwardness, and uninspired grooming overshadowed his desirable qualities. He came into the office with his head down and shoulders hunched. His initial approach was submissive, tense, and nervous, but outgoing. One felt almost immediately that he thought little of himself as a total person, despite occasional awareness of his bright mind and verbal superiority. Once he began talking, one readily saw that his vocabulary, and probably his intelligence, were superior. Although the counselor did not notice it when he first walked into the office, David was crippled and wore a specially-made shoe on one foot, which he felt made him awkward and self-conscious. This boy had come a thousand miles from home for a college education, for two reasons: an uncle of his had a clothing store in the community in which the University was located; and David was interested in literature and creative writing, a field in which the university was widely known.

OCCASION FOR INTERVIEW

David made an appointment with a psychologist in the mental hygiene clinic after he had taken a personality test along with a large number of other freshmen. They met in small groups to learn and discuss the results of the test. At this time they had been encouraged to make an appointment if they wanted more information about the meaning of their scores. David was taking advantage of this invitation because the scores he had received indicated he was having difficulty in some adjustments, and he wanted to talk about them.

PERSONAL HISTORY

Relationship with parents

During the course of counseling, David brought out the fact that his relationship with his father was very poor. His father was a big man with a strong, masculine orientation toward sports and a definite idea as to the kind of son he wanted. This idea was somewhat shattered, first by David's congenitally crippled condition and later by the interest and competency he showed in more aesthetic pursuits. "The Colonel" (he was a member of the National Guard and at that time had the status of Lieutenant Colonel — a title he cherished) had apparently tried out for football in high school, but had never been an outstanding athlete. Now he wanted a son who would be. He was highly critical of most of David's personality characteristics.

David's mother was a bright, well-groomed, upper middle-class woman who fit the stereotype of the suburban, bridge-playing wife. The family belonged to the country club and entertained often. They wore the most stylish clothes, doubtless lived up to the last penny of their current income, and strongly wanted to please a wealthy bachelor uncle who was very fond of David. In fact, the granduncle was one of the few sources of real affection and acceptance that David had. However, this relationship was tenuous — although he showered gifts upon David, the hours they spent together were relatively infrequent. He was a man to whom David might take his grade card and his early writings and from whom he might receive appreciation for his wit, creativity, and aesthetic interests.

David's mother was probably ambivalent toward her son. It is conjectured that she shared some of her husband's disappointment in David, and furthermore, felt the brunt of her son's displaced hostility growing out of his lifelong rejections. Yet, her basic tenderness allowed her to give solace to David when he needed to withdraw or throw a temper tantrum, which may have unwittingly reinforced this kind of behavior. David and his parents were part of a large Italian-American family — intelligent and successful people, conscious of their social status. Despite the fact that they were members of a minority group themselves, they apparently had strong attitudes toward Italians of lower economic and social status. It seemed to the counselor that David had never gained the basic trust or the clear personal identity that are so necessary in coping with the problems that he faced as an only child who was bright, creative, and crippled. His father's and mother's possible jealousy of the uncle's acceptance of the boy tended to confuse rather than promote David's integration.

From David's behavior in the fraternity and toward the counselor, it might be hypothesized that he was a boy who had had his own way and could threaten his parents with temper tantrums or reports to his granduncle, whom they wanted so much to please. David remarked at one time that he did not ever remember his father's complimenting him on anything. He knew that his father had sometimes been pleased with the intelligence he showed, but, at the same time, had been revolted by the thought that David might turn out to be a "fairy." Apparently, one member of the family was blatantly homosexual, exhibiting and encouraging in himself effeminate mannerisms and bizarre clothing. The Colonel would have liked to eliminate this relative from the family, and he constantly held him up to David as a horrible example. The difficulty was that this man was also creative, witty, bright, colorful, and skillful in aesthetic endeavors. There was some indication that David found his status as a cripple of some value. His father would not whip him; but David must have realized that any tenderness his father showed him was partially motivated by pity, and perhaps guilt, for his son's physical condition.

Apparently there were many scenes in which his father raved and shouted, berating David because of his irresponsibility. This did not curb David's tendency to spend all the money his uncle gave him or to misuse his parents' charge accounts as well. This situation was aggravated when David went to college. Both his mother and father became highly anxious with every telephone call from their son confronting them with bills and obligations. They looked upon him as a bottomless pit into which they and his uncle were pouring an indeterminate amount of their resources. David felt guilty about his behavior, but it seemed to be compulsive in nature.

COUNSELING EVENTS

A good rapport was established early with the counselor so that during the first interview David volunteered much miscellaneous information about himself and his early adjustment to the campus. The counselor noted that David appeared more immature than his physique suggested and speculated that he had been greatly overprotected as a child, possibly because of his physical defect. He had pledged a posh social fraternity whose members were sons of rich and socially prominent families. David indicated that he liked the campus very much. He had made more friends in the fraternity than he had had in his earlier life. Although the fraternity practiced hazing of pledges, David was exempted from the fraternity paddle (punishment for minor infraction of rules) because of his physical handicap. He mentioned this voluntarily.

Very early in the interview David talked freely about his interest in writing and mentioned the fact that he had boxes of poetry and stories at home that he had written during high school. He stated that he had been fairly active in extracurricular activities in high school, particularly in journalism. He enjoyed writing humorous doggerel and reading it to the other fellows for a laugh. The counselor got the impression at this time, and in later interviews, that the laughter and attention of his contemporaries was very important to David. Yet he had perspective enough to know that even though they enjoyed his caustic humor (a form of aggression), they did not accept him as completely as he hoped.

Behavior in the fraternity house

David often engaged in daring, unpredictable behavior, such as humorously ridiculing the fraternity chaperone behind her back, and even at times imitating derisively the parents of an unpopular fraternity brother. On the other hand, when his fellow students irritated him or engaged in the normal pranks directed at him, he flew into a temper tantrum of such intensity that the boys withdrew. His sudden furies strained normal, easy relationships with other members. He was highly sensitive and tried to hide it; when he was rejected by them, or found them withdrawing from him, he retired to his room and brooded.

Another of David's peculiarities was indulging in elaborate prevarications, which got attention but also taxed the credulity of his listeners. It is doubtful whether any of his fraternity brothers considered him a "regular guy." It became obvious then, as it had been in the past, that he was included in some groups simply because of the status of his family and their efforts to have him included in the group.

David had *difficulty being frank* and straightforward. For example, one of his pledge brothers, Bill, who had no place to go during the spring vacation, openly asked David if he could go home with him. David did not like Bill and said bluntly, "He certainly wouldn't add to my prestige." Yet, he could not bring himself to tell Bill that he would not invite him to his home. Instead, he circulated the rumor that he did not want Bill to visit him, hoping that it would get back to Bill.

David was openly snobbish. He intensely disliked the sons of *nouveau riche* fathers with foreign accents, who had been highly successful in business, moved into good neighborhoods, and were able to furnish their sons with the best clothes and expensive automobiles. He called them "wops" and humorously burlesqued them in front of their socially established brothers.

Attempted avenues of satisfaction

David spent his money for valuable possessions, such as classical records, books or artistic reproductions, novels, better magazines, and expensive liquors. Every now and then, when he had just received his allowance, he took four or five of his better "friends" out for a Sunday evening meal at the most expensive restaurant in the college community. Clothes represented another craving, and David had acquired handsome and expensive ties, shirts, and suits.

David's relationship with the counselor continued to be one of mutual respect and warmth. The counselor accepted him, was interested in his poetry, and encouraged David to use his talents as a means of becoming a more secure member of the fraternity and the university community. David had participated in journalism activities in high school and had received some recognition in the school paper for his writing. Within a small group he had gained attention because of his caustic remarks about well-known persons. His poetry was devoted to death and sadness; and his outpourings during the sporadically arranged interviews contained depressive expressions as well as ventilation of feelings about some of the more boorish members of his fraternity.

Suicide attempt

One night a physician in the Student Health Service phoned the counselor and said that David had taken a large quantity of a mild poison. This had necessitated having his stomach pumped, but he was expected to recover. David had asked for the counselor as soon as he began to feel better, but had stated to those around him that it was useless to try to save his life because he would try suicide again.

The counselor saw him the next day and David said something like: "I am a complete failure in life. I have *failed in everything* I have ever tried to do. I thought if I backed out of this existence, I would be doing a favor to everybody. I have just failed two courses. My mind is my major resource and I have failed in that." Most of his comments were of a depressive sort, although there were times when the nurses reported that he seemed to be in a better mood.

His parents had arrived but David had not yet seen them when he made the above remarks. He said he did not want to see them. "I couldn't face them now after doing this." The counselor told David he had no alternative. His parents had come to see him, he was their only son, and they were greatly concerned about him. They were just outside the room and would be right in. David readily accepted the situation and found them very forgiving and kind. After he had talked with his parents, he felt much better.

David's parents

The counselor noticed that "the Colonel" and his wife actually gave a very different impression from what David had led him to expect. They had all of the social charm found in people who spend a good part of their time in social activity, and the enthusiasm for those whom they considered to be the "right people." They were handsomely dressed and groomed, very appreciative of what the counselor had done for their son, and ostensibly were willing to do anything to make amends, even to the point of mortgaging their home to give David the best medical and psychiatric care.

The chief physician of the University talked with them and insisted that David withdraw from school and enter an institution, the customary treatment under such circumstances. When David was informed of this, he vacillated between displays of temper and depression. He had hoped to go to another school and begin again. He said that if this did not work out, he always had an alternative; that next time he would succeed in his suicide attempt. Later in the day the counselor found David much more hostile toward his parents, particularly toward his father. He began to verbalize freely the fact that his father had never accepted him for what he was, but wanted to make him over. He wanted him to be a big strong man. The chief physician of the University had assumed the same attitudes as David's father, and doubtless aroused the same reaction in David as his father did. He told David, "You have committed a crime by attempting suicide, and you have to face this responsibility." David behaved as he had when his father laid down the law — he listened with resentment and later said to the counselor, "I did this not only because I was a flop but because I could do one great service for the world, namely to eliminate myself from it." There seemed to be a certain amount of revenge motivation in his attempted suicide. He knew that both of his parents and even the chief physician of the University would be inconvenienced, embarrassed, and upset by his death, and possibly would feel sorry for him. At times he even showed some of his bizarre humor to the counselor. He mentioned the various methods of self-destruction he had thought of using and then described certain of them as being rather crude and messy to clean up. The counselor just listened.

Institutionalization

David's parents were completely intimidated by his continued threats of further suicide attempts and followed explicitly the advice of the insensitive, authoritative chief physician who equated, in this case, therapy with punishment. David was transferred to a good, expensive psychiatric hospital after spending a few days in a general hospital in a city near the University. After a few weeks he wrote to the counselor. A few lines from the letter indicate his attitude and behavior in this hospital.

> *The die is cast. The Rubicon is crossed, and I am institutionalized. As you might have noticed from this stationery, I am in the C_____ sanatorium. It is rather, and only rather, nice, now that I have moved from the booby hatch I was in last night, my first night here. At H_____ (the general hos-*

pital), I made another suicide attempt which was even more unsuccessful than the last one. I was hanging myself this time, but I was just making the preparations when I was caught in the act. I was then taken to a real loonie bin, where I have been for about a week and a half. It is quite bad, but they tell me it is good for me. I don't agree, but then I am not expected to. My last attempt was caused by my emotional state after confessing all to my psychiatrist. I shall now go into the gory details.

I was busy psychoanalyzing myself one night when I decided it was time for me to tell what was really at the seat of my trouble, namely, that I had homosexual cravings. I knew this had not turned up on my Rorschach and that no one but me knew about it. Well, I called the psychiatrist on duty in the middle of the night and confessed all. Then I was so depressed and felt so horrible that I tried it again. It now develops that this is not at all the cause of my difficulty but only a minor symptom, which will disappear as I mature. So now I have given up all ideas of self-destruction in favor of an attitude of not giving a damn. I have been saying that I was dead and was brought here to be buried. I really don't believe this, but I do think it is quite analogous to my present state. I am enclosing some of my more morose poems, that I wrote while I was locked up at H_____. So here I am in a real booby hatch. I feel that the whole thing is rather stupid, that I should have gone back to school.

Psychiatric interview for reinstatement in the university

When David returned to school after his hospitalization, approximately a year and a half after the counselor first saw him, he was examined by the University psychiatrist. Below are some excerpts from the report:

This is a twenty-year-old sophomore who was referred on return to school after being out about a year because of emotional illness. He became ill with numerous hysterical, and at times psychopathic, manifestations, about two years ago. He was sent to a sanatorium where he received insulin and electric-shock therapy, along with the other total-push program.*

* Such a program attempts not only to alleviate conditions producing the patient's symptoms, but to provide for him varied forms of therapy and many avenues of need satisfaction — social, recreations, and occupational.

Following this, he made considerable improvement and related himself well to his position there.

When he left the hospital, he got a job in a furniture store in the large city in which the hospital was located and got along well with the support of his physician. He continued this relationship until August before the opening of school, at which time he went home and then entered the University. He was apprehensive about how well he would be received in the fraternity when he returned.

He seemed to have good insight into the fact that he needed treatment, and the treatment which was given him in the sanatorium was quite proper. He said he felt that the eight electric-shock treatments were the determining factor in his improvement, and following that he was able to get along quite well. He also seemed to have a partial and comforting insight into certain difficulties with his father and possibly, his mother. His relationship with the psychologist here (at the University) is good and he recommended that David have periodic interviews with him. He was reassuring toward David; he reported David was getting along quite well and saw no reason why he wouldn't do all right here. Although he was originally hostile to the health authorities because he was required to leave school, he no longer holds any resentment.

The diagnosis of the student could be as follows: immaturity reaction; emotional instability ties, which are chronic, moderate, and manifested by suicide threats; antagonism toward people in authority; recovered.

Post-hospital period

When David returned to school, he looked thinner and acted more relaxed and more mature. He seemed to have a somewhat more realistic perspective and to have gained some insights. He said he realized that he was using his illness as a means of controlling his family; that he could scare them into doing what he wanted, and that he knew this was not the right thing to do. He also realized that he had been using his doctor as a crutch. He was surprised and pleased that he was accepted so well by the fraternity, apparently without any stigma.

During an interview with one of the psychiatrists, he had experienced what he thought was an important insight. He realized he would have to find a major goal and lose himself in striving for it, and that up to the present he had been too much of a dilettante. He said contact with other patients in the hospital was very valuable to him; he now looks back on his experience in the hospital as not unpleasant. After he left the hospital, he obtained a job in a store and continued to see the psychiatrist a few times a week. This proved to be a very valuable transition, and it was one of the first experiences he had in which he was able to take some responsibility for supporting himself.

He was a little more interested in extracurricular activities; he had already joined several organizations, and had become active in them. He was somewhat sensitive to people who indicated that they knew he was a psychiatric patient. One of the boys at the house mentioned "electric shock" in a conversation, and this upset him. He had seen the movie, The Snake Pit, and had to stay in his room the next day. He said, "People judge me to be twenty years older than they did before I went to the hospital." For example, he had been mistaken for an instructor. A girl he met asked him if he was thirty. (At that time he was only twenty.) This did not displease him.

Interview with fraternity brother

One of David's fraternity brothers came in voluntarily to see the counselor and wanted to know if there was anything he could do to help David. The counselor said, "The only thing he needs right now is a couple of good, understanding friends." This boy said that at first the members of the fraternity were reluctant to accept David back. Their attitude, however, was no different from that toward one of the other boys in the house whom they disliked, and who did not have the stigma of being a mental patient. However, they had decided to pledge him again when he returned from the hospital. It was this boy's duty to call David's father and tell him the fraternity decision. He said David's father had cried over the phone when he was told that David would be accepted again into the fraternity.

Life as a fraternity member

As time went on, David was able to bring a certain amount of prestige to the fraternity house through his publications in one of the college papers. The members also asked him to write the lyrics for their annual skit and to furnish ideas for decorations at their parties. He was very frank in various interviews about reporting the ups and downs that occurred. He said one time he had gotten angry at a boy, then returned to his room, locked the door, and drank himself to sleep. He felt guilty about it the next day.

He objected to taking gym and wanted a medical excuse. The psychiatrist who interviewed him about this reported in his notes that David's primary difficulty was that he felt inferior when he went into the gym. He often got sick when he went into the dressing room and saw others undressing. He was upset about having to participate in activities such as volleyball. His effeminate physique and interests explained much of his difficulty. The psychiatrist pointed out to him that he had nothing to conceal and that his request for an excuse because of his physical condition might not be the best thing to do. He may have been concealing a bigger problem that should have been dealt with. However, he was given the excuse.

Most of the interviews after his return from the hospital were *supportive* in nature rather than *analytic* or *interpretive*. David did most of the talking; the psychologist was not completely passive but was essentially client-centered. David reported being under tension as a result of living in the fraternity house and adjusting to the majority of the boys' interests, which were opposed to his own. His relationship to his parents was not different from what it had been before. They still attempted to use his uncle to control him, which infuriated him and caused him to become more hostile toward them.

At the end of that one semester David again *failed* enough work to be eliminated from school, but he returned the next fall. He reported that he had spent a great deal of his time writing at night and sleeping during the day. He thought psychoanalysis would help him; he was trying to get his uncle to pay for it, but had met with some resistance on his uncle's part.

After a conflict in the fraternity house David came to the counselor, and a valuable conference resulted. Someone had borrowed some of his clothes; David had gone into the room of the boy he thought was guilty and had broken a piece of furniture in a temper tantrum. He was fined for this. The counselor talked with him about this tendency to become aggressive, to frighten and hurt other people. He did not see his aggression as the outcome of constant inner conflict but said, rather, "These people are stupid. They don't amount to anything." David said it was true that he did frighten people, including his parents, but this was one of the few ways he could get results. He said he sometimes actually lied to get results, and he admitted he was pretty good at concocting an effective story. At the end of the interview he admitted that much of this behavior was immature, that he was beginning to see what maturity meant, and that he had a much greater desire to be mature than he had before. He realized that he did shocking and socially disapproved things to hurt the people he disliked. He mentioned how frightened he was of being hurt physically. He indicated that, whereas he had much more *insight* into his behavior than ever before, he had not yet gained the necessary *control.* Life seemed to him a masquerade — a game which he had learned to play, often without involving his feelings.

EVENTS TOWARD PROGRESS

A crucial conflict

At no time did David mention his physical handicap, nor did the counselor bring up the matter, even though this was probably central to his social frustrations and identity conflicts. Many of his defenses and withdrawals were probably due to felt rejections of one sort or another by his fellow students. The psychiatrist who examined him in reference to an excuse from physical education mentioned his "effeminate build and interests." This psychiatrist came as close as anyone ever did, in the counselor's knowledge, to confronting David with this major conflict when he said, "You don't have anything to conceal. By avoiding gym you may be concealing a bigger problem that you ought to deal with." *The problem was David's self-image as a man* — *physically, mentally, and behaviorally* — something that David could have worked out and seemed to do in a certain manner by himself later.

Difficulties and accomplishments

Throughout the year David had conferences with the counselor about once a week. During these sessions he mentioned his problems, frustrations, and achievements. Seeing Tennessee Williams' play, *The Glass Menagerie,* bothered him to some degree. He did not mention the factor that aroused the anxiety; possibly the counselor should have encouraged him to do so. After one interview the counselor conjectured that he had identified himself with the crippled, withdrawn girl in the play, and perhaps saw the mother, who had unrealistic hopes for her daughter, as having some traits in common with his own mother.

He was beginning to think *realistically* about a career for the first time and thought he might enjoy getting a Master's degree as preparation for teaching English. He discussed the pros and cons of this and showed some guarded enthusiasm for the project. About this time he began to develop a strong affection for a younger fraternity brother who often used to come into his room and talk. He thought that he identified with this boy, who possessed many traits that David would like to have had but did not have. His emotional involvement with this young fellow aroused anxieties in him about teaching high school. Could he be objective? Would he develop crushes on his students? On the positive side he said that for the first time he was able to listen to the typical kind of erotic, male talk that goes on in a fraternity without being upset by it. Also, he felt that he had, by this time, and through his own efforts, established the idea in the house that he was an acceptable individual who was fairly well adjusted to life. Many of the new boys thought he had been in the hospital for a serious operation rather than because of *mental illness*.

One of the great differences between David now and before his suicide attempts was that he now acted out his feelings and behaved as though he *belonged* to the fraternity. He was not one of the most popular boys there, but he seemed to be respected as an individual. Previously, he had been accepted only for his wit; otherwise he was regarded as essentially a nonentity. He had not been able to act on his own initiative and at times had become quite dictatorial in ordering fellow students out of his room, even showing cruelty toward pledges. Later, these same actions aroused guilt and shame.

During this year in college David had participated in many extracurricular activities, had assumed an ascendant role, had fought openly with fellow students in the various activities, and had often gotten his own way. Some of the student committees of which he was a member had produced interesting projects, in which he had played a *creative* role.

He was concerned about some of his lascivious ideas and felt considerable guilt about them, with perhaps some fear that events could lead him toward some unacceptable sexual behavior. He said, "I feel that I am going to flunk out of school or something scandalous like that." He was becoming much more realistic about the hazard of going into teaching with his present suppressed erotic feelings for his own sex, that he thought the high-school situation might arouse.

David had from time to time missed an interview, and he said he was sure this was a mistake, because he always got a lift from them. Although there were times when he hated to face some of the things he knew he had to discuss with the counselor, he regarded his present existence as almost vegetative and was disgusted with it. Going to the interviews thus seemed the lesser of evils. His physician at this time had prescribed the drug, seconal.

An unsuccessful romance

After David left the sanatorium and was working in the furniture store, he met an older girl who was an heiress. She had fallen in love with him and wanted him to marry her. He was toying with the idea but knew it would be unfair to her because he did not love her. He stated frankly that he doubted he would ever meet the obligations of a husband. He talked openly and freely about the possible unfortunate consequences of this affair. He had taken the girl out, and although he went through the motions of necking, he found it unpleasant. He was beginning to realize that probably no one would ever love him as much as this girl did. She was willing to sacrifice for him and even change her religion. On the other hand, he said, "Although I am a heartless person to some extent and a heel, I am certainly not going to take advantage of her." So, with reluctance, but with support from the counselor in his decision, he ended this romance.

Elimination from school and a job

By the end of this year David had failed to make the grades necessary to stay in school and so had to make a decision about what to do next. He returned home and spent several unhappy weeks with his parents. He wrote and said that he saw it was impossible for him to live at home. The friction with his parents was so great that it was having a very negative effect upon both him and his mother. He was afraid he would develop a psychosis and that his mother would become ill too. His mother appealed to the uncle for help; he had a long serious talk with David. He tried to show him how childish he had been, and how, for his own pleasure and selfishness, he was deeply disturbing his parents. This impressed David, because his uncle was one of the few persons for whom he had any deep feeling. However, little real improvement resulted; when he finally decided to move away and live by himself, all parties seemed relieved. He wrote:

> Perhaps I am growing in insight daily. Just yesterday I saw
> there was no use looking for a job that fitted me. There is no

such job in the world. I must adjust to whatever I decide to do or what is decided that I must do. This doesn't sound like me. How do I know this will be the truth, even though I shall forget it as soon as my job becomes trying? I still have the idea in the back of my mind of writing a book. Perhaps something will come of it. I will talk it over with my uncle. I plan to see him tomorrow.

He ended the letter saying:

Your discussion has been of great value to me. I shall be happy to let you know when I can settle some place, if you still want to know the outcome of the tragedy.

The above lines were written about five years after his suicide attempt. They were part of a warm and generally objective letter written from his parents' home.

The next letter came from New Orleans. He went there on his own, took an apartment in the French Quarter, but realized that he could not live comfortably on the income his uncle had arranged for him to receive all of his life. He had previously attempted to arrange for psychoanalytic interviews at an outstanding institute in the country, but they would not accept him after an initial examination because he lacked sufficiently deep motivation for growth toward maturity and because at that time it seemed he would not profit greatly by the sessions. An excerpt from the New Orleans letter reads:

My life here is one of which you would heartily disapprove. I live quite alone and listen to the radio and read. The many people I see each day in my search for a job are quite enough for me. I somehow doubt that I shall make many friends. As soon as I get out of the habit of being surrounded by people, I cease to desire their company; with the exception, of course, of those people whose company I have desired for quite some time, but have never had and do not intend to have, at least, not now.

Do you know the name of a good clinical psychologist or psychiatrist, just in case I decide to end it all in a dramatic dive off a Mississippi River bridge?

FOLLOW-UP AND INTERPRETATION

There were periodic letters over the next ten years. His uncle died and left him a legacy. But it was not enough to live on, at least in the way he was accustomed to living, so he got a clerical job with an accountant who specialized in income tax returns. It involved contacts with people. He began to fraternize with many of the less conventional people in the French Quarter and seemed to live two lives — one, the well-behaved business clerk, and the other, the familiar face in dubious bars, catering to the denizens of the Quarter. At those times he wore less formal clothes and adopted some of the blatant mannerisms of the uninhibited who frequented these bars. When he spent an evening at home, he listened to good music, enjoyed his collection of art reproductions, and read fairly good literature. Some of his contacts in the French Quarter were with serious, talented, creative people. He enjoyed decorating his apartment and entertained his parents when they visited every year or so.

Most of his letters were much more objective than they had been before. An excerpt will illustrate some of his general attitudes:

> I work as little as possible, leading a rather useless life on the whole, but at the same time enjoying it. I find, in having joined the unconventional society [homosexual group], I have become somewhat frenzied, where I used to be so inhibited, but I am much happier. I have not had a severe depression in years. Of course, my family is not too happy about the state of affairs. They wanted me to be a big success in business, marry, and make a lot of money. I still try to write occasionally but have not been able to produce much in recent years except in unprintable and unmarketable poetry. I have joined a dramatic club, and believe it or not, they have made me secretary of the organization. I am still quite socially acceptable when I want to be and quite the reverse a good deal of the time. As I said, on the whole I am about as happy as I feel I have a right to expect.

David in perspective

It looked as though David had definitely not taken advantage of the opportunities afforded him by the background and financial status of his family, nor had he exploited his unusual intelligence in a creative way. He did not finish college. He was not a success by any of the world's standards. He shocked society by attempted suicide, lived for a year in a mental hospital, had counseling for a period of about five years, and at all times fought the unconventional, homosexual impulses that he had developed during the first twenty years of his life, only to accept, finally, the kind of life they dictated. He found that as long as he attempted to live the way his parents and the prominent people in his social group expected him to live, he was tense, irritable, and hostile, and behaved very much like a spoiled child. When he finally went to another city, lived alone, and moved into an unconventional world during his non-working hours, many of his symptoms disappeared. He was not dissatisfied with this state of affairs, at least so it seemed from the letters he wrote the counselor. He was building up interests in the arts and in literature that might serve him in good stead as an older individual. Whereas there were some elements of the social parasite in his life, he did hold a job — however, far below his intelligence level — and spent a certain amount of his time living, superficially, like many of his young associates. He built a few friendships, but it was not clear whether any of these would sustain him as the loneliness of middle age and old age descended upon him. What can one say about the present adjustment of David at approximately thirty-five years of age, in view of his history and potentialities?

What aspects of David's life were important in causing him to have the crisis that developed in college? We may speculate that a person of a different physique, constitution, and temperament might have reacted differently. What information do we have from case material that may shed light upon David's constitutional make-up? How would one obtain information from which to hypothesize that part of David's crisis could be attributed either to his inherited anatomy and physiology or, on the other hand, to very early experiences which developed or failed to develop a personality make-up which could withstand great frustration? Would an interview with both of his parents and living grandparents about other members of the family have been helpful? Assuming that little could have been done to change David's basic constitution and temperament, what factors in his early life might have brought about a different adjustment during his early college years?

What factors either within David or within his environment contributed to his emotional breakdown? In what ways did these conditions change later? What role did counseling play in different phases of his college adjustment? It might be noted that what happened during the counseling sessions varied at different periods in his college years. Some of the later interviews dealt with problems that were deep and basic to his personality. This was four and a half years after his initial contact with the counselor. Their relationship was always good, but at the period of most profound soul-searching it seemed to be excellent. It was probably as good a relationship as David had ever had with another human being in his life. Moreover, he was attempting then to deal with problems that were significant, but which were very disturbing as they were brought to the surface. More and more he was searching for answers to questions such as "Who and what am I?" and "What can I become despite the self-defeating traits I have built up through the years?"

At one time in this soul-searching, he reported a dream. There was a person sitting next to him who seemed to possess all of his traits. He was able to look at this person in great detail. He saw this fellow as fat, greasy, slovenly, and noisy. "This is the way I inwardly look at myself," he commented, "and although I would like a prolonged psychoanalysis, I cannot be too hopeful." The counselor was reassuring. He thought that most of his strongest needs were blocked from satisfaction by his being the kind of person he was. For example, he could neither give affection to others nor receive it from those who wanted to show it to him.

The homosexual pattern

David recognized at the time of his first attempted suicide a pattern in his personality that disturbed him greatly — a tendency to have affectional attachments to members of his own sex. The psychiatrist who saw him after his second suicide attempt was quite reassuring and told him that this was not the real basis of his problem but a reaction to it, and that it would disappear as he grew toward maturity. As David failed to make a satisfactory adjustment to the average member of his own sex or of the opposite sex, this pattern became even more dominant in his life. Finally, after he decided to take an apartment in a strange city, he gravitated toward a homosexual sub-group, and this became a part of his life. He said he lived the life of a conventional young businessman at work and lived among his unconventional companions the rest of the time. It was his opinion that he was happier living the kind of life he had always dreaded — certainly a kind of life that in our society is fraught with disgrace and potentially scandalous consequences.

There are a number of questions that this raises: (1) What factors made this pattern initially so important in his life and later so dominant? (2) Since many individuals have homosexual trends, yet are able to make a heterosexual adjustment, why was it so difficult for David to do so, despite the fact that he had strong conscious motives to become the socially acceptable young man that he admired in his fraternity? (3) What conditions might have allowed him to make some sort of heterosexual compromise? (4) Why did he value this (resigning himself to living as a homosexual) as being the best kind of adjustment he could make? (5) Will it serve him in middle age and old age, even if he continues to live in a community in which there is a homosexual contingent?

We might review some of the factors in his life which may enable us to answer the above questions. Certainly his atypical physique and his inability to discuss it openly is of primary importance. We alluded to this above as the crucial conflict. He seemed unable to accept his physique or himself as a man. It is possible that all his life he had regarded himself as an imperfect male. There was, in addition, his father's unspoken attitude toward him (which to him was a rejection), together with his father's explicit dread of the possibility of his becoming overtly homosexual. His atypical aesthetic interests and accomplishments, superior and satisfying to him, were constantly in conflict with what he had come to believe was the ideal male role. It is possible that a more adequate adjustment might have been made, had he been able to view maleness as a broader category, inclusive of many forms, such as an imperfect body and aesthetic interests. Would he have been aided by closer association with companions who were less rigid in their definition of what is acceptable in a youth than were the members of his college fraternity?

We do not know enough details of his relationship with his mother, but we can speculate that there was a strong rivalry in the early years between him and his father for the mother's emotional support. She may well have over-protected David and kept him from associating with average boys when he was younger. It is possible that, had he been able to establish earlier relationships more like those that he later had with his fraternity brothers, his development might have been different. For a long time he seemed to keep these strong anxieties about his inadequacy as a male to himself. He probably developed a number of feminine attitudes, since he identified himself with his mother rather than his father during the early period. We need also to know more about his relationship with his uncle and about when their close contact first developed. Had conditions been different, so that his uncle, who accepted him more completely than others, became a substitute father, we might have seen a different development. Why was he unable to establish a satisfying relationship with girls, even though he did date them under pressure from his fraternity? Why did he find satisfaction in his fantasy experience with the boys he admired? He had an insight at one point in his development — that, in effect, one reason why he became sentimental toward certain younger boys in the fraternity was that he could see in them all of the things he was not; and by identifying with them he was experiencing the deep satisfaction of being the kind of boy he secretly idealized and desired to be.

In trying to understand why such a socially disapproved way of life was finally chosen, we may point to certain factors. In rejecting his father, he may have been rejecting the highly conventional, upper middle-class life that his father espoused; and by his later, apparently blatant homosexual behavior, shocking to the average person, he may have been punishing the society that his father represented by being the very thing they despised. Then, in physical homosexuality, he may have had an intimacy and a certain kind of acceptance by males, despite his crippled condition, that he had never enjoyed before.

It might be clear from the above discussion that, despite the fact that the average person in our society assumes one homosexual is much like another, the pattern varies greatly from individual to individual. Although there are certain recurring dynamic elements, many factors tend to influence the development of homosexuality, and the tendency can be quantitatively different in different persons. Moreover, like all other defensive and escape patterns, it can continue either as a self-defeating pattern of personality or it can lead to positive growth and acceptable social adjustment. David's adjustment after working hours finally developed into one that is beyond the pale of acceptable behavior in our society. Do we see both aspects operating in the later part of David's life as described here? Would the trends in his life have resulted in a different adult status if he had been able to define masculinity so as to include sensitivity (not found in the more conventional, masculine male), aesthetic qualities, some kind of effective male peer relationships, and a heterosexual adjustment which, though less than ideal, might have been mutually satisfying to the individual and his partner?

David in the light of Adler's theory of personality

It might be interesting to examine David's personality in terms of the psychology of Alfred Adler, an outstanding analytic psychologist who put a great emphasis upon an individual's unique style of life — a predominantly social adjustment, which has meaning to that individual. Adler emphasized the person's striving toward expectations in the future, toward an ideal self, and toward superiority. He looked upon the individual as growth-oriented and creative in nature and placed a great emphasis on organ inferiority as a block toward this striving. He noted that persons with defective organs tried to compensate for this weakness either directly or indirectly.

When we examine David's life in terms of the above emphases, we see that there were many factors that kept him from being socially oriented and creative, and from living the style of life which his talents and abilities might have allowed. Not only did he probably regard himself as defective and inferior; this defectiveness seemed to hamper his socialization early in life. In addition, his father's attitude toward David's unique kind of creativity made it less worthy in his own eyes. It is likely that his caustic humor, his snobbery and cruelty — all forms of aggression — were compensations for his inability to achieve in other ways.

What did his two attempts at suicide mean in terms of the above theory? After his first attempt he stated that he was helping society by eliminating himself. When he attempted suicide he was, no doubt, thinking of his parents and their reaction to it. Could he have been thinking also of the effect this would have, not only on them, but on the community and all the people that knew him? It has been observed that a person who attempts suicide acts as though he will be an observer and will see the effect of the act upon those around him after it is consummated. Was the first suicide attempt a meaningful act on David's part to achieve, at least in this respect? From what he indicated in his letter, how is the second attempt compatible with this hypothesis? Finally, one might speculate about how David's life could have been more creative, more socially meaningful, and more acceptable to him as a unique contribution to others. What would have been necessary for this to occur?

DAVID: Patterns and Relationships

What do you see in the case of David? Give your spontaneous reactions to David before turning to the questions below.

Concerning patterns of personality, did you see:

    a. self-punishing tendencies?

    b. ambivalence and aggression toward certain classes of people?

c. needs for recognition shown through dramatization of himself?

d. potentialities and possible future difficulties?

What was the nature of the important interpersonal relations he had throughout life with:

a. permissive persons?

b. authority figures?

c. his peers?

What was the effect of their behavior upon him and his upon them? If certain of the above interpersonal relationships had been different, would he have developed differently? How do you think he would have developed?

Concepts helpful in understanding David

a. Motivation for superiority because of organic inferiority (2, 7)

b. Guilt and self-punishment, leading to suicidal tendencies (12, 74)

c. Masculine-feminine imbalance (47, 62)

Other concepts which may have some relevance to this case: mental illness; shock therapy; suicide; homosexuality.

DAVID: Comments by a Graduate Student

Parents of children with congenital defects often are burdened by feelings of guilt, because they assume that they have sinned by either omission or commission. The guilty parent often blames the child and is spiteful toward him because the child is a constant reminder of the parental guilt. Quite aside from the father's frequent berating of David, he seemed to be deficient in filling the role of a firm, consistent, effective parent to his son.

The college physician described in the case was informing David (as his parents or counselor had rarely done) of the nature of reality —that he, David, was solely responsible for his own acts.

MORRIS

The Quiet One

Morris, a handsome, neat youth from a family of several
mentally ill persons, was sent away to college at the advice
of the family psychiatrist. He referred himself to the
mental hygiene clinic and was followed by a counselor
periodically while he attended school and for several
months following his voluntary withdrawal from college
to take a job away from home. The case gives some understanding of a young man with schizoid tendencies.

IDENTIFICATION

The writer first met Morris at the beginning of the school year at
a group testing session. He was among a number of freshmen who
had responded to a mail circular announcing that a personality test
would be given to any student who wanted to take it. The students
had previously been given a short psychoneurotic inventory, and at
this session the scored tests were returned and some brief interpretations given to the group. Morris had obtained one of the highest
scores (indicating emotional disturbance) that had ever been obtained on this test, and he approached the writer, obviously disturbed,
with a frown on his face, inquiring what the score meant.

Morris was a very tall, handsome, well-built youth of eighteen.
His clothes were well-pressed and in excellent taste; he seemed
gentlemanly in manner. He had entered college a few months previously and was living in a private dormitory near the campus.

OCCASION FOR INTERVIEW

At the group session, Morris was given an early appointment for
an interview. He was reassured and told that students vary in the

scores they receive, that some have more emotional difficulties than others, and that the purpose of the test was to introduce students to a mental hygiene service which was available to anyone who wanted to take advantage of the services. Morris seemed fairly satisfied with this explanation and enthusiastic about an interview.

Before he arrived for the interview, the counselor had received an inter-office communication from the Director of the Student Health Service saying that a psychiatrist from the city in which Morris lived had sent him a letter referring Morris to the clinic. The Director had had a brief session with Morris, found him to be physically well, but noted this on his chart: "The patient complained of numerous troublesome sensations about his body, seemed considerably introspective and had a tendency to withdraw from the disagreeable things of life." He also forwarded to the psychologist a brief report from the referring psychiatrist, which follows:

Psychiatric report

This is a white male, age 18; single, has an older brother and sister. The brother, Tom, is a schizophrenic. The mother has been mentally ill for a number of years. The father is quite well.

He was a healthy baby. He was struck by an automobile at age two; he was unconscious for a time and spent one night in the hospital, then returned home under the care of the family physician. Sometime later the mother struck him in the head with the metal nozzle of a garden hose.

He wore glasses for a while. He did well in school and appeared to be in good health until his senior year in high school, when he began to complain of headaches. During these attacks he feels like he is "hanging in thin air and can't get through;" he has a blurring sensation in the eyes, things "jump around," and he cannot think.

He finished high school and has worked in his father's store since then. Some eight months ago, he became impatient, restless, and at times more quiet.

The neurological examination is within normal limits. He is very well nourished and well developed. Weight, 185 pounds (five months previously, 220 pounds).

He dresses fairly neatly. It was extremely difficult to establish rapport with him. He answers courteously and readily, but with as few words as possible. Occasionally he talks enough about something to assure one that he knows about things, but frequently "does not finish" what he started to say.

During bouts with headaches, he often complains of feeling "funny — queer and numb;" sometimes falls asleep, often sees red lines, and hears ringing sounds in his ears.

He is not interested in sports; is not athletic. He doesn't care much about being with people or going with girls.

He has weird dreams — exaggerated things, impossible things, stories, sometimes trips. His father states that he uses obscene language in his sleep.

I feel that this boy is a potential schizophrenic and should have constant psychiatric supervision.

The father was advised to let him enter the University, to encourage his association with other young men, while remaining under psychiatric supervision.

COUNSELING EVENTS

When Morris appeared for the first interview, he returned the greeting of the counselor who had talked with him previously; he seemed shy but pleasant. It was not easy to get him to talk freely. When the counselor asked him to tell something about his early life, he showed considerable reluctance, but talked much more readily about his attempts to study on the campus. He stated that he enjoyed being away at school, that he found the boys in the dormitory very congenial, and that they had made numerous friendly overtures to him.

The counselor suggested that perhaps he would prefer to write rather than talk about the events in his life. He gave Morris a *Pre-Interview Blank,* and arranged another appointment for three or four days later. Morris indicated that he thought this was a good idea and, after exchanging a few pleasantries, left.

Second interview and Pre-Interview Blank

At the second interview Morris at first seemed a little more relaxed and somewhat more confident. However, when the psychologist began looking over his *Pre-Interview Blank*, he became more tense and seemed much more resistant. On the Blank he had indicated that he usually spent four hours a day studying, but that he found himself daydreaming much of the time while he was studying. He indicated a strong desire to do well in school, made general reference to his poor health, said he had frequent colds and other ailments and was tired most of the time. He stated that he worried about his health and feared the future. He indicated that he spent a little time with others, but a great deal of time alone, by preference. He pointed out that college had been recommended to him by the psychiatrist and that his father was enthusiastic about the venture.

He wrote that he was rooming with another boy who was studious, good natured, and popular. He indicated that he was looking forward to the interview. When requested to write about his problem on the Blank, he wrote only "fear" and "school grades."

In describing his *personality*, he underlined these words and phrases: restless, nervous, easily annoyed, absent-minded, often procrastinates, avoids responsibilities, lacks initiative, a follower, too serious, sensitive, moody, easily distracted, stubborn, and enjoys being alone.

He wrote that his *parents* did not get along well together. His mother was a very sick person; neither parent had had much formal education, but his father had been very successful in business. His brother was a disagreeable person and usually put him in a bad mood. He added that he was happy to be away from home and thankful that his father was able to provide for him so well. He had a car at school (at that time cars were rarer than they are today). He stated that he had had his first date about two years earlier, and that he seldom had a good time on dates. He had belonged to the Boy Scouts and had attended camp for two weeks. He indicated that he had worked in his father's clothing store and seemed to be a satisfactory salesman.

In the item labeled "History of Inner Life" Morris answered more frankly than he had in other parts of the Blank. Considering how resistant he was to discussing his problems and his feelings in an interview, the statements on the blank were surprisingly open. He stated, "I often find myself in a trance. My mind does not concentrate on anything. I don't hear or see anything, although my eyes are open. I have many headaches; I dream at night and sometimes have terrible nightmares. I am very glad to get away from home and go to the University. I have been unable to get along with my mother and my brother. Both of them have a very bad effect upon me."

The psychologist had obtained Morris's aptitude and achievement scores from the Admissions Office. His percentile score on the Ohio Psychological Test, measuring largely verbal intelligence, was 55; this places him roughly in the middle of the high-school group in respect to general ability. His percentile in terms of high-school achievement was only 24; this places him roughly in the lowest quarter of high-school students in respect to grades. This is interpreted to mean that he had greater ability than he was able to use, which also proved to be true in college. Despite the amount of time that he spent studying and his desire to do well, his college grades were barely average.

On a personality inventory he indicated the presence of almost every symptom known to psychiatric practice. Whereas many students will check some of these symptoms, it is rare to find a student who checks as many as Morris did.

Adjustment on the campus

Despite all these subjective difficulties, the students with whom Morris lived and those that he saw in class apparently accepted him at face value. They evidently regarded him as a nice-looking, well-dressed fellow from a good family, who had the prestige of a car, and who seemed cooperative and well behaved. In fact, he was so well liked at the Catholic dormitory in which he lived that he was elected to represent them in an all-University freshman commission, even though he was not a Catholic. He tried to decline the nomination, but they insisted that he take it. Morris seemed impressed with this acceptance and was also encouraged somewhat by the fact that he was passing his courses. He did not object to the amount of time he had to work in order to earn the grades he made. He was much happier than he had been at home, although his father's frequent letters reminded him of the home situation.

Apparently, Morris saw in himself some of the symptoms that his mother and brother had. He realized that both of them were mentally ill; he once said that there were times when the things his mother said made no sense at all and he intimated that he could see himself developing a similar illness. His brother, on the other hand, was moody, irritable, and aggressive, as well as being disorganized in thought and action.

Subsequent interviews

Although it was very difficult to talk with Morris about his concerns, the material from the *Pre-Interview Blank*, the psychoneurotic inventory, and the report of the psychiatrist, indicated that Morris was concerned about the possibility of developing a psychosis. The psychologist, without alluding directly to events in his home life or memories of early childhood, pointed out to Morris some of the success that he was having at present. He reminded him that he had finished high school, he had participated in the activities of his peers, and he had so far not developed the illness that both his mother and brother had. In short, he had met most of the hurdles in life.

He was reminded that he had worked successfully for his father; that he was making a *good social adjustment* in college; that very few people knew about his inner feelings and concerns; that he had a good opportunity in college to broaden his contacts, to improve his social skills, to learn and prepare himself for a vocation. Morris said very little during the interview, but seemed to be quite comforted by these reassurances. In fact, the following letter, written to his father after one of the interviews, indicated his reaction to it. A copy of the letter was sent, unsolicited, to the counselor.

Dear Pa,

I feel swell, I don't remember the day I felt as good. There are two reasons — first I saw Dr. M. today, he cheered me up and after I see him I feel like a new man. I spoke to him, or rather he spoke to me, for I have nothing to say, his arguments are logical. Pa, you ought to know him, he is a great doctor and a good man. He tries to help me, if you can make an S in one of your subjects, do you think there can be anything wrong with you? Now I am again in doubt, if so, why can't I have a good night of sleep like others, why am I in constant fear? Pa, probably there is a way to refill Dr. D. medicine, I didn't give it a fair trial.

The last meeting of the X House, fellows held an election for the honorable freshman position of University Freshman Commission. I was elected by a majority, all votes of the house, pointed to me. I did not want to accept the position, but they put me in by acclamation. This makes me the first Freshman Council member representing the X House. This entitles me to hold a key of the council and I am very glad. Pa, I imagine if it were not for my severe headaches I would make you proud of me. Dr. M. says when you don't feel well don't study, but I know they are not going to keep me here if I don't make good grades and I like much to be here.

Have you received a bill from Dr.? My eyes are no better. Please don't forget and try send an alarm clock if you can.

Your son,

MORRIS

Counseling over a period of three semesters

At first Morris had appointments about once a week. One session was quite similar to another; he would enter with a smile, then sit down and remain silent. Open-ended questions, like "How are things going?" or "Tell me what's happened during the week?" produced very little response. Specific questions about his feelings or dreams elicited frowns and tension. The counselor soon realized that the more he could get Morris to talk about his contacts with the boys in the house, such as the few dates that they got for him and the times he went swimming with them, the better the interviews were.

The counselor tried to put Morris in contact with various people on the campus who would help to get into activities and meet members of the opposite sex. This was not entirely successful. Morris had very little interest in sports other than swimming, and he found it very difficult to talk to the various sponsors of extracurricular activities. The best results were obtained by merely encouraging him in the casual contacts he made with the boys in the house and with others that made overtures to him during class. This was a learning process, providing reinforcement.

He seemed to be ambivalent about the interviews. He seemed very happy to have the contact, but several times when he came in he was experiencing some of his most severe symptoms. At these times he vaguely alluded to his anxieties and pessimism about the future, and the counselor reassured him.

When he began to make a better adjustment on the campus, he tended to forget to go to the interviews. During the year and a half that he was seen by the counselor, the interviews became less and less frequent as Morris gradually became more involved in campus life. He apparently never felt completely like one of the other boys, but they seemed to take much of the initiative in the relationship. He particularly enjoyed swimming and often went with one of his housemates. Apparently the car was a social help to him, and sometimes he went on double dates. His fellow students seemed to accept the fact that he was quiet, that they would have to take the initiative, that it would be up to them to make the overtures. As far as the counselor could tell, no one seemed to regard Morris as anything other than a shy but normal student.

Morris was concerned at times that the other students might find out that he was different. He said once that his roommate had called to him several times, and he must have been in a trance, because although he was sitting in the room, within earshot of his roommate, he didn't hear him call. This frightened him. He was also worried lest his nightmares would alarm his roommate.

His father wrote the counselor frequently and sometimes included one of Morris's letters to him.* His father had built a confidential relation with Morris, and Morris had promised to write his father whenever he had any severe symptoms. The letter below, written after Morris had spent one semester at the University, is one of the more anxious letters that he sent home.

Dear Pa,

I didn't write you because I was very sick. I didn't want to scare you; neither did I want to lie to you, so I kept silent. I suffered with a severe headache: I was dizzy, shaking, nervous; I couldn't see straight or understand others and I heard bells ringing. So I went to the hospital, but they only admitted me after seven o'clock Sunday, after I telephoned the hospital Dr. The nurse helped me up the elevator. I overheard them saying that my temperature was ten degrees below normal. The first sleeping powder didn't seem to put me to sleep.

Your son,

MORRIS

This letter was enclosed with one from Morris's father to the counselor:

---

* It is encumbent upon the counselor to make it clear to the parent of a youth with whom he is working in a counseling relationship that his primary responsibility is to the client and that the parent should have the client's permission to send his letters to the counselor.

Dear Doctor:

I have received a letter and a postal card from the Student Health Service advising me that Morris had been in the hospital and was allowed to go home. Of course, I immediately phoned Morris but he mumbled and I couldn't get anything out of him. I ordered him to write me a letter immediately, explaining in detail, which he did.

Maybe some day I may be in a position to repay you with some favor. Just recently I recommended a young doctor to take over an old established office of a doctor who passed away and I am sure it is a good stand. Therefore, I am forwarding this letter to you and asking you if it is not too much trouble to please give me a report on Morris and if you will, please do not hesitate to tell me frankly your opinion and his chances for the future. Since I have had dealings with Dr. R., Dr. K., Dr. T., and many other psychologists and sanatorium doctors, the shock will not affect me.

I thank you for all past favors and hope you will accommodate me. I assure you I will appreciate and reciprocate if ever the occasion occurs.

Respectfully yours,

T. N.

On the whole, Morris's father reported Morris seemed happier, more spontaneous, and in better mental health since he had been at school than ever before. He continued to improve during the time he was at school. When he went home for weekends, he was in a good humor the early part of the weekend, but grew more depressed the longer he stayed.

Morris's father

Mr. N. seemed to be a very warm, expansive man, but the counselor had never had an opportunity to observe his behavior toward Morris or his wife when no one else was present. He was an immigrant and spoke with an accent; he had never learned to groom and dress in a manner that might reflect his financial and business success. He had a lovely home in a very good neighborhood and drove a moderately expensive car. To meet him on the street, one might think that he was a day-laborer, from his dress, speech, and manner. However, after a brief contact with him, one could see that he was intelligent and very adept in dealing with people.

Mr. N. stated that when he married his wife he did not realize she was not normal. When she first showed symptoms of mental disturbance, he did not know how to handle them. In the early years of their marriage he had traveled a great deal with her, apparently hoping this would lead to improvement in her personality. She never seemed to be able to take responsibilities in the home or to become a satisfactory mother to the children. He finally hired a housekeeper and began to treat Mrs. N. as though she were one of his children. He said, "I have been very strict with her; otherwise I couldn't handle her."

He seemed to be both mother and father to Morris and in many respects treated him like a small boy. Morris accepted this treatment most of the time. At other times he resented his father's domination, as shown by facial expressions and obvious irritation; yet he knew that there was no alternative. Whenever he became overly anxious and experienced the frightening symptoms that he reports, he immediately went to his father for solace. His father, having had the experience of a psychotic wife and son, hearing Morris's symptoms, was over-protective. Instead of encouraging Morris to get a job in another store, he gave him a job in his own store. Morris adjusted fairly well. The father had cut the strings to some extent when Morris came to the University, but then he continued to write Morris and encouraged *dependent* letters from him.

At this time World War II was being waged, and Morris was subject to the draft. For some reason his classification was not clearly fixed as a deferment, and Mr. N. continued to approach the psychiatrist and others to appeal to the draft board in Morris's behalf. He was a persistent man, and through little thoughtful gifts and pitiful appeals as an overburdened father, he attempted to arrange matters. Mr. N. was afraid that if Morris entered the service the stress there would cause a complete breakdown. He tried to get him jobs that would continue his deferment, but Morris's good looks and healthy appearance made it difficult for him to get a clear-cut deferment, despite the psychiatric testimony. A glimpse of at least one aspect of Mr. N.'s personality and character is shown in the letter below.

Dear Doctor:

It is detrimental to me that I am not equipped with a glib tongue, with eloquent language, and with adequate talent. Had I possessed the above facilities I would call the attention of the world to the good you are doing voluntarily and silently for the youngsters, for humanity in general, and for my son in particular. However, since I am handicapped, all I can do is pray to God the Almighty to ask Him to repay you with the same coin, i.e., to invoke His blessing upon you and on all those who are near and dear to you. May it bring to you the reward which is due you.

Dear Doctor, if you will compare the enclosed letter from Morris with the letters Morris wrote when he first met you, you will find the reason for my gratitude and the good feelings I have toward you. I would never believe it is possible to put Morris in such a good humor; the credit for it is all yours. You did it and I will never forget you.

Respectfully yours,

T. N.

FOLLOW-UP AND INTERPRETATION

Morris gets a job and leaves home

Morris did not do as well in college as he had hoped. He began to lose interest; his grades dropped below the satisfactory level. More and more male students were leaving for military service. He and his father decided it would be better for him to get a job which would give him a clear-cut draft deferment. With this in mind, Mr. N. wrote to a relative in Miami who owned a rather large store, asking his assistance in finding employment for Morris. Morris made the trip south, obtained a job, and seemed to be greatly encouraged by the change of scenery and the responsibility. Below is a letter expressing this encouragement:

Dear Pa:

I like my job very much — it is very interesting, and the day passes terrifically fast. I am kept quite busy okaying and checking saleschecks, bank checks, register receipts, and seeing that complaints are taken care of, that all people are waited on, etc.

I am in the basement — dry goods and domestics — 3 telephones, and boy do they do a terrific business! I think that this part of the store must keep many of the other departments going. Today we had a sale. When they opened the doors of the store, people came down the steps like a herd of cattle. People

were lined up in 4 long lines waiting to be waited on. The report that I made out at the end of the evening showed nearly
$11,000 worth of business, just in small sales. The mark-up on
dry goods must be very very high — for I have permission to
cut the price of any remnant or damaged goods to half the
original price.

Your son,

MORRIS

Morris worked for several months, but he was not an entirely satisfactory employee. After a while he began having the symptoms previously described; he did not have his father to console him, nor
had he made contact with a psychiatrist in Miami. He was quite
disturbed by his boss's reprimands when he became inefficient or
failed to come to work because of illness.

It is not clear whether Morris lost his job or quit prior to discharge,
but he returned home and again went to work for his father.

Interpretive remarks

In the above instances we see some of the inner life of a young
man who had lived with a schizophrenic mother and brother and
an anxious, over-protective, but resourceful father during his whole
life. We see that he had met many of the hurdles, had had a year
and a half of college education, and had been able to work for his
father and obtain employment periodically through friends. His
superficial adjustment to his fellow students was good. He was liked
and sought out by many of them. He had developed good personal
habits of a somewhat passive kind. His adjustment to the opposite
sex was never completely satisfactory, although on the other hand
he was not completely withdrawn from them. The responsibilities of
dating seemed beyond his limited capacity to deal with his environment. We get some idea of his anxieties and symptoms, his lapses
of memory, and his tendency to withdraw. We see that his anxieties
about himself and his future had severely limited his growth toward
maturity and his capacity to use his resources. He felt overwhelmed
by life, with little forcefulness as a person. Morris had not been
hospitalized because of his emotional symptoms; he seemed to respond fairly well to psychological and psychiatric support. Although
his father had been his one source of emotional support and in
many respects had satisfactorily guided Morris to his present state;

on the other hand, because of illness in the family his father was unable to give the secure, objective support that Morris needed. Morris doubtless will make some kind of vocational adjustment, but he will need continual psychiatric assistance and support.

MORRIS: Personal Patterns and Influences

What do you see in the life of Morris that is outstanding? Below are questions to which you may want to turn after you have formed your own impressions.

Distinctive personality patterns

    a. How did Morris's view of himself differ from that of his fellows?

    b. How do you think his father viewed him, and what was the effect of this?

    c. What traits will be sources of strength or weakness in his future development?

    d. What additional information would you seek from him if you had an impersonal contact with him?

Significant relationships (real and potential)

    a. How might some other father have handled Morris?

    b. What role might a well-trained high-school counselor have played?

    c. What role can his friends realistically play in his adjustment?

    d. How would a school for emotionally disturbed children have helped him?

Concepts helpful in understanding Morris

    a. Schizophrenia (115, 121)

    b. Dependency and passivity (54, 62)

    c. Sex-role identification (9, 62)

    d. Ego strength; personality integration (11, 73)

    e. Participation by non-professional persons in mental health programs.

Other concepts which may have some relevance to this case: overprotection; withdrawal; reinforcement; personality inventory; educational facilities for emotionally disturbed children.

MORRIS: Comments by a Graduate Student

Morris begins sentences but does not finish them. In other words, someone else has to finish up for him — which places a burden on his listener. This is clearly a diagnostic sign of a dependent person.

In a letter Morris says, "Pa, I imagine if it were not for my severe headaches I would make you proud of me." Insofar as the headaches are presumably psychogenic, they are to an extent under Morris's control. Could this be a way of (1) striking back at his father, (2) continuing his dependent status, (3) doing both with the same act?

It is very hard to show anger, or even admit to oneself resentment of a parent, especially when the parent is overwhelmingly good.

I suspect there is latent homosexuality — non-athletic, but likes swimming (bodily exposure); expects others to take initiative; dependent; girl-shy.

It is indicated that the mother was so inept that she could not handle responsibility for the home, so a housekeeper was hired. Here is Morris's model of dependency. The father treats both Morris and his mother like puppy-dogs. I asked myself, "What would I do if my father were like Morris?" I am tempted to answer, "I'd go nuts" — and one could very well do that!

The following statement is made, ". . . accepted him at face value." This is one of the best reasons I can think of for having normal people *help* their fellow man rather than letting them depend entirely upon psychologists or psychiatrists.

PAUL

The Successful Wanderer

Paul's story is that of a serious American youth who has
achieved above the average in sports, school grades, and
social interactions, and who has high motivation for
achievement. We trace his explorations in finding the
vocation in which he can gain the greatest life satisfaction
by describing briefly his first inquiries in this direction until he achieves his present career and his status as a married
man with children of school age. The early interviews and
biographical data describe his relationship with his parents
and contemporaries; subsequent communications trace his
life through military service and post-war adjustments.

IDENTIFICATION

Paul may be described as a clean-cut fellow. Although his clothes
were not necessarily stylish, his pants were carefully pressed, and
his shirt was clean and starched. He had much of the "regular fellow" appearance of a boy respected by other boys. His history
showed that he enjoyed sports greatly; yet one got the impression
that he was not going to tolerate much horseplay if serious work
had to be done. Paul was of average height and weight; although
physically well-developed, he did not especially impress one as being
an athlete. He earned superior grades and was majoring in rural
sociology with a minor in agricultural economics.

OCCASION FOR INTERVIEW

The counselor first met Paul as a student in one of his classes. Paul
was a senior in the College of Agriculture. He asked for an appoint-

ment after class one day to discuss his vocational choice. Paul's neatness and decorum impressed one immediately. In class he was highly attentive, took good notes, and seemed personally responsive to every activity of the lecturer.

His manner in an interview was almost military. He walked in an erect manner, responded with a firm handshake, came directly to the point, and took notes on what the counselor said. One got the impression that this discipline that he had imposed upon himself was not of a submissive kind. One felt that he could take charge of a group of individuals and, with a clear responsibility for his actions, lead them with a firm hand.

PERSONAL HISTORY

Events in early life and in high school

Paul was the eldest of six children. The others seemed to respect him and look to him for leadership. He felt that his parents had never been as compatible as they should have been. His father tended to go into rages when conflicts occurred. (We have no information as to how successful his father was, but he was a professional man with a college degree in a city of about 15,000.) Paul worried about the fact that his parents argued and were in disagreement most of the time. He apparently did not take the part of either of them but felt they were both at fault. He said that he had gone to Sunday school at his mother's request until he left home; then the regularity of attendance dropped, and now he views the church as a social institution.

We have little information about Paul's specific relationship to his father. Whether he experienced some of the brunt of his father's violent temper and criticisms is not known. It is interesting to note that Paul did not seek the solace of his mother or any sort of submissive identification with her, but rather sought his identification with older boys and youth leaders outside his home. We might speculate as to the importance of this factor in making him the kind of person he became.

Paul was one of the outstanding leaders in his high school, respected by both teachers and students. He was on all of the high-school teams and remained very much interested in sports throughout his life. He said, "As a boy I always looked up to the older boys who were athletes and got along well with them. I preferred playing with older boys." However, he was always a member of a gang his own age and tended to be a leader. He was president of the student body in high school and won several honors as an outstanding student. He elected to study science while in high school and enjoyed it.

He entered Scouting activities early, won many merit badges, and especially enjoyed camping and outings with the troop. Paul usually had several warm friends. Although he had become separated from them when he came to college, he kept in touch with them. He began dating during his sophomore year in high school, and since there was a tendency in the town for high-school students to "go steady" (or date only one girl for a period), he did so most of the time. He went to dances, although he did not enjoy the actual dancing very much. He did, however, enjoy parties. He said he had petted in high school, as had many of his friends. In the summers during this period of his life, he hitchhiked and covered more than ten states adjoining his own.

Paul's self attitudes

Paul exhibited a certain amount of insight into his own personality. He considered himself energetic, ambitious, over-cautious, and nervous, but self-confident. He thought he was too serious, but recognized that he was alert, responsible, and reliable. He admitted that although he had been in the limelight in sports and in student government, he enjoyed being alone and had some strong introverted traits. Despite his self-confidence he had some misgivings about his abilities. Although he did not state it in this way, Paul had to constantly prove his own worth to himself.

Paul admitted that acne and bad complexion were sources of great anxiety at puberty and in early high school, but his sensitivity about it was a thing of the past. The counselor saw no great evidence of poor complexion at the time he knew him.

Paul rated his *happiness* as average, at the center on a ten-point scale. He rated his *mental integration,* or oneness of purpose, and his consistency and stability of attitudes and desires as slightly above average — six on a ten-point scale. His *outlook for the future* he similarly rated at six and his *adjustment* or ability to fit in with other people in his environment at seven. Looking over these ratings, one would say that his objective achievement exceeded his subjective evaluation of himself. Most of his high-school friends would probably have rated him higher on these various traits.

Achievements

In high school Paul had participated in student farm organizations and in events such as livestock-judging. His interest in this type of activity and in intramural sports continued while he was in college; but his active participation diminished during his junior year, when he turned more attention to schoolwork. Paul was definitely above average in abstract ability. On the *Ohio Psychological Test* he obtained a percentile score of 79 in terms of scores for high-school seniors. His grades showed that he at least came up to his potential and sometimes exceeded what one might have predicted. In college he took the first and second CAA flying courses and pursued advanced military training, winning for himself the honor of being one of the outstanding cadet officers on the campus. Paul went into active military service in World War II, along with his contemporaries. He received a commission and one promotion, which disappointed him since many of his college contemporaries received higher promotions during the period. He served for over two years, and much of this time was spent in active combat.

COUNSELING EVENTS

Paul was the kind of student, as the above account indicates, who showed initiative and assumed responsibility for his choices. He came to the counselor, not for advice or direction, but for *assistance*, through tests and evaluative instruments, in gaining more objective information about himself.

When Paul returned from military service four years after the first interview, he asked for another appointment with the counselor. By that time he was married. His wife was a few years older than he and had been employed as a nurse. Paul had decided that he would like to change his vocation from the agricultural field to something else. Personnel work interested him. In reviewing his work history he recalled that he had spent several summers with a house-to-house magazine-selling team and had done very well financially. Before that, during summers, he had been successful as a clerk in a clothing store in his home town. He liked selling, sports, and aviation; however, he thought possibly the most practical area, insofar as opportunities for progress and satisfaction were concerned, was personnel work. He took the *Strong Vocational Interest Blank* and received a score of B+ in both life-insurance selling and personnel work. He enrolled in the College of Business Administration to work for a degree there, specializing in the personnel curriculum.

FOLLOW-UP AND INTERPRETATION

Business success

After this change in plans, the counselor lost track of Paul for several years. When he saw him again, he learned that Paul had gone into business for himself, with a partner, in a growing community within commuting distance from the University. He had become quite successful, by dint of hard work and good social contacts. His partner handled the sales aspect of the small manufacturing plant, and Paul handled the production aspect. He worked long hours, had relatively little social life except with his family, and was highly successful financially. He often worked along with his employees; if one visited his plant, it would have been difficult to locate the boss at first glance. However, after four or five years he decided that he was not getting enough satisfaction from this work, even though he had been far more successful financially than most of his contemporaries. He found that once he had solved some of the problems of production and was secure financially in this manufacturing venture, it no longer challenged him. There were some definitely unpleasant aspects. It seems he had full responsibility for the quality of the product and it was such a delicate product that unless he carefully supervised the work, the quality dropped. This meant he was always under tension; the job was taxing without being creative, even though the end result was lucrative. His partner and associates were very unhappy to see him leave. He was the heart of the organization, but he had decided that there were more important matters in life than turning out a gadget for business and being a cog in an industrial machine. Since he had accumulated a financial nest egg, he decided again to return to school. Apparently, performing a service to society and having a clearly recognizable top position were very important to him. This may have surprised some who knew him, because in the interviews he had been serious, soft-spoken, and quiet, and showed no marked expansiveness. One did get the impression, however, that this young man had goals and would work doggedly to reach them.

After discussing the pros and cons of this move with his wife, he decided to take a year of graduate work at another institution and prepare himself in the area of police science. This would enable him to take over in a professional capacity responsibility for the technical aspects of investigatory work in a relatively small city. He was well able to remain in school for a year or more. He did not feel he was taking too much risk in doing that; if need be, he could always return to a hard-to-fill position in the little industry he had left behind. One of the most convincing arguments to him was that in this new career he would be doing something for society, would have a position of public prestige, and would be doing work that was varied and of a problem-solving nature — in short, an activity which offered much more meaningfulness than the manufacture of a piece of equipment. (Much of the above was inferred by the interviewer, not actually stated by this taciturn young man.)

New career

Reports from Paul while he was in graduate school indicated that he was enthusiastic about the work. Toward the end of the year he received several offers from small cities in parts of the country that seemed exciting to him. He was sure that the new responsibility he took would give him more time with his family. He cared very little for the typical country-club social life and knew that his need for working with people would be satisfied largely through the business contacts he would have to make.

Interpretations

As one looks back through Paul's history, one sees a greater compatibility of this new career with his extracurricular responsibilities in high school, college, and military service. The duties he anticipated were meaningful to him, seemed to be important contributions to the group, and fit in with his values for a well-run, orderly society. Furthermore, this position was similar to those in earlier years, in that it gave Paul a publicly recognized, prestigious status attained by quiet background planning.

Were there some other trends that might have been noted in his early life which would help explain the development of Paul's life after marriage and selection of the career in which he was apparently happy? He had always been a serious, critical individual with high standards, highly desirous of making his life meaningful. He was concerned about his future, and planned in terms of it, even as a college student. One had the idea that he would not compromise easily on certain matters; he had integrity. One also saw a tendency to be able to endure suffering or unpleasantness; in fact, possibly even to invite the difficult rather than the easy.

The interviewer's observations

The counselor, who knew Paul over a period of almost twenty years and saw him for brief periods intermittently through this span of time, observed a certain amount of consistency in his attitude and behavior. Paul always remained a rather serious, intense fellow who gained the respect of those around him without directly striving for it. He was much more intent on satisfying inner needs.

On some occasions the counselor had opportunities to see him when he was talking with his employees and also when he was with his wife and children. He never wasted words; he came directly to the point, rarely joked, and was very businesslike even in his relationship with his wife and children. If he showed warmth toward them, he did not do so before other people; yet he was highly considerate of their welfare, and this was one of the items he took into consideration in planning his career.

His wife was a quiet, gentle, competent person, with superior intelligence, who had achieved in a vocation before their marriage. She was a little less intense and businesslike than Paul and preferred to spend more time in light talk, whereas Paul preferred to get some little job done. Despite this apparent preoccupation with serious business, his relationship with his contemporaries was good. They regarded him as a competent and highly conscientious individual. Although he never initiated small talk, he was responsive to the jokes and banter of those around him.

The counselor does not know whether Paul developed any warm friendships during his mature years. He mentioned on a *Pre-Interview Blank* as a college undergraduate that he usually had one or two intimate boyfriends. At the time when he filled out this blank, he saw himself quite accurately; he described himself as energetic, ambitious, over-conscientious, self-confident, nervous, aggressive, too serious, reliable, quick, and enjoyed being alone.

The counselor's overall impression was that Paul was physically impressive, superior in appearance and motivation, and highly conscientious almost to the point of being a perfectionist. He was able to satisfy many needs but was not completely successful in relaxing or gaining a detached perspective on life. He was making an effective adjustment, but possibly at some cost in life satisfaction. At times he seemed to be using a sledge hammer to pound a nail.

From Paul's own statements, this serious, somewhat restricted existence had its beginnings in his early years and was probably related to the severe incompatibility he thought existed between his mother and father. This pressure in his life showed in numerous answers on the Blank he handed in as a college student. He said that the family quarrels had placed a strain on all of the children. He did not discuss his relationship with either his mother or his father, but he did say that he always tended to seek out older boys for companionship. It would seem that he did not identify with either parent but looked outside the home for his sources of identity. Much of his subjective life was colored by quarrels in the home. This probably made close personal relationships seem to Paul unpromising, or even risky. Achievement thus became his major source of life satisfactions. One gets the impression that Paul was never complacently happy, but was constantly striving and achieving, though not particularly unhappy. This is quite consistent with his self ratings mentioned earlier.

Latest follow-up

A brief letter from Paul's wife dated twenty years after the first interview, stated that Paul is very enthusiastic about his present activities. He works very hard, goes beyond the call of duty, has received several large raises and recognition from numerous important sources, has expanded the scope of the position, and has many challenging responsibilities. He looks back on his previous business venture with a sense of relief that it is behind him. The letter said, "Paul may not be the most able man in the field, but there are few who can excel him in interest and enthusiasm." She ended the letter by commenting on the good grades and high extracurricular achievement of several of the children, the eldest of whom is in high school.

PAUL: Personal Trends and Influences

What do you see in the case of Paul? Give your spontaneous reactions to Paul before turning to the questions below.

Outstanding personality patterns

    a. What consistencies and inconsistencies do you see in Paul's behavior over the period reviewed?

b. In addition to achievement motivation what do you find to be Paul's strong and weak needs? Consider among others affiliation, dominance, dependency, competence, autonomy.

c. To what extent did Paul show rigidity and adaptability; integration and unity versus conflict and anxiety?

d. What do you think was Paul's attitude toward himself, in relation to his ideal self?

Important persons and relationships

a. What do you hypothesize was the relationship between Paul and each of his parents; between him and his siblings?

b. What psychological role do you think his contemporaries played at various stages in his life?

c. What other factors were important in the development of the traits and motivations he showed?

Concepts helpful in understanding Paul

a. Cognitive dissonance (36, 51)

b. Disparity between self-awareness and ideal self (3, 33)

c. Early insecurity (52, 67)

d. Action as a reducer of anxiety (27, 74)

PAUL: Comments by a Graduate Student

Paul seems never to have experienced the sort of easy security at home which might have enabled him to enter into unconstrained emotional involvement with people.

He left the nest early and did not identify with either parent. Not having deep emotional relationships early in life, he also seems not to be very open to involvement later. In spite of his remarkable effectiveness as a leader of youth groups, he does not seem to have personal involvement with the people.

Having no security at home, Paul had to go out and create his own world. Granting this, we may wonder why, with his need for security, he did not become an "empire-builder" — perhaps in agriculture or business; he certainly was not lacking in brains or drive. What we see, is a number of seemingly unrelated job changes. His hitchhiking all over the states is a younger counterpart of his many job changes. We note that Paul seems finally to have achieved a measure of stability and happiness in police work. What accounts for this? Could it be that the civil service job gave him a feeling of security which his own experience as an entrepreneur — however successful — could never do?

PEARL

The Suspicious One

Pearl was an unhappy young woman with strong achievement motivation who came from an economically depressed farm environment. Many interviews were held
with Pearl and she was followed through letters for about
ten years after first acquaintance and into her marriage.
Pearl brought to the counselor an autobiography as well as
the results of psychological tests administered in connection with a course she was taking. Some of her TAT fantasies as well as the Minnesota Multiphasic Personality
Inventory test scores are included in the write-up. Pearl's
case presents the reader with conflicts aroused by changes
from one American sub-culture to another, and shows us
the thinking and feeling of an individual with strong suspicion tendencies.

IDENTIFICATION

Pearl rarely made an appointment to see the counselor. Often she
arrived during the noon hour or late in the afternoon when the halls
were clear and no one was around. Then her head would suddenly
appear around the corner of the door as though she had tiptoed up
to the office. She would smile in a genuinely attractive and feminine
way and say timidly, "Are you busy now?" She did not want anyone
to know that she was in counseling. Very often she came because
she was having difficulties with her landlady, or her dean, or her
roommate. There seemed to be many natural enemies in her life on
the campus, and she had the attitude that one had to fight for everything he got.

This 25-year-old graduate student seemed hard-working and highly
motivated to earn a degree and achieve a better economic status. She

had grown up in a very deprived backwoods environment in a depressed part of Arkansas. Pearl obviously had very few new clothes and seemed to give little attention and time to her grooming. Although she was much less neat and attractive in appearance than the average college student, she was naturally very pretty, with striking blue eyes and blonde hair, which was not washed or combed often enough. Her feminine mannerisms and build, her energy and vitality were appealing; but after a short period in the office, she became emotional and bitter, vacillating between friendliness and withdrawal. Sometimes she appeared quite shy and sensitive; at other times she exhibited a natural coyness; but frequently her hostility toward those with whom she lived was so strong it tended to dominate the content of the interview.

OCCASION FOR INTERVIEW

The counselor had heard about Pearl from several people before he finally met her. They had all suggested she see him. She lived with a faculty family; the wife met the counselor once and said, "There is a girl staying at my house that you should see. I think you can help her — she certainly needs help. She is able and sweet but doesn't get along too well with other students. She hasn't learned the ordinary necessities of cleanliness, and is not doing as well in her courses as she might. She is a girl who would be quite attractive if she paid more attention to style, neatness, and skin and hair care." (When we learn a little more about Pearl, we may ask whether she merely lacked early examples and training, or whether these early lacks were coupled with an unconscious motivation to appear less attractive than she naturally was when meeting people, thereby involving them in her plight.)

The second person to refer Pearl was her academic adviser, a member of the Department of Classical Languages. He wrote to the counselor, stating that after many long conferences with Pearl and much persuasion, she had consented to make an appointment with the counselor. Although the counselor had an office in the Mental Hygiene Clinic, Pearl refused ever to go to that office. She insisted instead on visiting the counselor during his academic office hours in the Department of Psychology, and acted as though it were a friendly visit rather than a counseling session. Her adviser stated that he thought she had the ability to obtain a Master's degree, but he was concerned about her personality adjustment. He said, "I feel she is becoming less and less promising as a useful member of society; hence, I raise some question as to the desirability of her continuing with graduate work. I would like some advice from you." (Evidence on which the adviser based this statement will gradually unfold.)

The counselor agreed to see Pearl, but he explained to her and her adviser that the counseling situation would be an opportunity for Pearl to attempt to understand why she was having difficulties in social interactions; that she and her adviser would have to make the decision as to whether she should pursue graduate work further. The interview with the adviser had been a very threatening experience to Pearl; several interviews were necessary after the referral before the counselor could begin to build an effective relationship with her.

One of Pearl's immediate problems was that she was receiving borderline grades in graduate courses; if she accumulated any more she could not obtain a Master's degree in Latin. Latin had special significance to her. Apparently in the small consolidated school in the hills of Arkansas where she grew up, the Latin teacher had special prestige. Although she never clearly expressed her need for achievement in this area, it was obvious that if she could obtain a Master's degree in Latin and teach in high school, in her own mind and in the view of those who were acquainted with her development she would have reached a high achievement. The counselor found her highly rigid in her attitude about the correctness of her behavior and resistant to any kind of advice that her professors might give. She expressed strong hostility toward anyone who hinted that she would *not* get her degree in Latin. From her standpoint, this was something she *had* to accomplish. She *would* accomplish it, and nobody was going to stop her. She had the ability; the people who were evaluating her were "narrow-minded, prejudiced, and unwilling to give help to one who sorely needed it." With some feeling she insisted that the counselor write a letter evaluating her positively as a candidate for the degree. She wanted to get this matter over with so that she could get to work on her major project, the degree.

After the first interview the counselor told her the kind of letter he proposed to write to her adviser. It read as follows:

> I have had a relatively short interview with Pearl. As you know, she is a very opinionated and forceful person. She is highly motivated to obtain a degree; her refractoriness has doubtless stemmed from the necessity to make her own living

and from her lack of parental guidance during childhood and adolescence. She is particularly suspicious of people who try to direct her activities. I think I will be able to build a relationship with her. I hope that over a period of time the counseling experience will allow her to understand herself better and make more effective choices.

Pearl finally accumulated enough borderline grades to be dropped from the Department of Classical Languages. She held rigidly to the idea that she could be reinstated by continuing to take courses and get higher grades. She was debating within herself whether this was what she really wanted. She was thinking seriously of going into the College of Education, since she had always been interested in teaching.

PERSONAL HISTORY

Early life and reactions to it

When the counselor questioned Pearl about her early history, she replied emphatically, "I can give you the essential facts in a few sentences. My mother died when I was very small. I lived with my father, younger brother, and sisters for a while until my father died. Then the family was divided, and the children were distributed among distant relatives. This didn't work too well, and ever since I have been in high school I have been doing some kind of work and paying my own way. I realize that in this world nobody's going to do anything for you; you have to do it all yourself. I have taught in a rural school, I have worked as a waitress, and I have even worked in people's kitchens. It is because of my work and ability that I am here, and I don't intend to have my plans disrupted." This obviously was not said to get sympathy, because she spoke in a hostile, defiant manner.

It was not until after the counselor had known Pearl for over a year that she finally, of her own accord, wrote a twelve-page, typewritten document which covered her many unpleasant experiences at the University and in her early life. She sent it with a somewhat formal letter to the Mental Hygiene Clinic rather than to the office which she had been visiting. The counselor had on numerous occasions suggested that between counseling sessions she might find it profitable to write out freely her feelings and attitudes. This activity was to supplement the counseling sessions and could be done at a time when the counselor was not available to her. She had always resisted this suggestion until this occasion.

The material was reminiscent of free association. The outpouring of feelings and attitudes was prompted by a visit to her childhood home. There, in an old trunk, she had found some papers and belongings of her mother, including a letter from a distant relative. In this letter the relative told Pearl's father why she could not take Pearl into her home at the time she was reaching puberty, although her father felt Pearl needed a woman's care. This letter doubtless aroused many feelings in Pearl, among them, possibly, rejection. It is also possible that Pearl, after a year of counseling, was better able to face some of her memories than she had been when the counselor first questioned her about her early life.

Here, paraphrased, are some excerpts from this personal document.

I was one of ten children. My mother was married as a young teen-ager, probably about fifteen years of age. My father was not much older. Both of them came from families that barely eked out an existence from the land. We lived on a mud road, in a house with no electricity, before the days of school buses, and among people who had practically no education. The houses we lived in didn't deserve to be called such.

One of the shocking experiences in my early life was a statement from a preacher visiting in the area. He pointed to the home of my older sister and said, "Do people live there or is that an old chicken house?" Ours was not much better. It couldn't have cost more than $20. It was made of rough boards from a sawmill. We had no glass windows, not enough beds, and were all crowded into this hovel. I will never forget how surprised I was when I learned that people ate meals that consisted of something besides mush, cornbread, milk, molasses, and occasionally, meat. We had a few chickens, which lived in the house until they were safe from the predatory animals around. There was no running water. We carried our water up from a spring at the bottom of a hill.

It is not surprising that my mother lost several children when they were very young and that she died prematurely of tuberculosis. Some of the other children were also tubercular. I did not know my mother well because I was only four when she died, but my older sister tells me she was a fine woman who

tried to teach us manners and lift us out of the squalor in which
we lived. My father tried hard but could never make enough to
feed us well. He was very religious, quoted the Bible, attended
church often (he often sang loudly and his Amens could be
heard above all others). He was stubborn and impatient, and
beat my brothers often and severely. My father died about six
or eight years after my mother passed away. Then we were
really stranded and left to the mercy of relatives. Two of my
relatives, whom I called "Mom" and "Uncle," took me in and
kept me until after I got through high school. They gave me
a home, and I was out of the environment in which I spent the
first eight or nine years of my life. I was about ten then — ignorant, skinny, and insecure. I was still wetting the bed at night
and tried to keep it a secret. My "Mom" tried to be a real
mother. She bought me some dresses and curled my hair, but
I was always making mistakes which made me feel ashamed and
out of place.

In addition to our lack of material necessities, the older children in my family seemed to fall into various kinds of trouble.
One of my older sisters was seduced by an older man with
money and attempted to abort herself. I had a brother who
got involved in moonshining and went to a federal prison. Another one often carried a gun because of a feud he had with
another family, and finally died a violent death when I was
small and impressionable. I saw his bleeding body carried in
and then rushed to a hospital some distance from our place.
Several of the children did better themselves and went to the
city and got jobs. One took night-school courses and has a
pretty good job now; another married a successful but narrow-
minded, small-business man.

COUNSELING ACTIVITIES

Pearl becomes more confiding

During the course of the first interview, Pearl indicated that she
felt inferior to the other girls on the campus because of her poor
clothes. She was getting some help from a distant relative, but she
resented being in any kind of a dependent relationship. She hoped
to save enough money to come back to the University in the fall.
She said, "I hate working as a servant, but there is no alternative."

One bright spot was her respect for an outspoken and somewhat independent professor in the Extension Service of the College of Agriculture, under whom she had taken a course and who was willing to accept her as an advisee. She felt she could earn a Master's degree under his direction.

The counselor felt that Pearl's early experiences had undermined the basic trust and security which she so sorely needed, with the death of both parents and the break-up of the family. This lack of trust and security may partially explain why she had difficulty enjoying a dependency relationship with others; she had never experienced one that was rewarding or enduring. She showed a considerable amount of defensive pride, sensitivity, and hostility to people who had more worldly possessions than she did. During the past semester she had moved out of the faculty home into an inexpensive rooming house, and she had been in conflict with her landlady.

After this first interview the counselor wrote in his notes:

> Pearl appears to be a lonely, rejected, insecure girl, who is not unattractive physically and at times even has considerable personal appeal. She feels she has nowhere to turn. She has apparently had relatively little deep acceptance and love during her life, and seems to be unwilling to accept sponsorship readily. She would like to explain all of her difficulties on a financial basis and has built up a number of defenses which make it difficult for anyone to build a relationship with her. She feels that she has never been really happy and has rarely had good friends. She finds it very hard to talk about her early life. When this comes into the conversation, she closes her eyes and shudders.

Results of the TAT

The counselor was interested in finding out what the *Thematic Apperception Test* would elicit from Pearl in the way of life-fantasies. This test consists of cards containing ambiguous pictures of a person or persons. The person being tested is asked to make up a story about the feelings and thoughts of the central person, and the outcome of the situation pictured. Pearl was able to complete four stories during the counseling period. Since the technique seemed to be productive, the counselor suggested that she take the cards home with her. Pearl showed some reluctance and resistance to continuing the test, but finally agreed. She was cautious in her responses and somewhat suspicious of what might result from the interpretations of them. Nevertheless, the results below seem significantly compatible with previous knowledge about her.

Here are a few samples of Pearl's responses to the TAT cards: (The first card pictures a young boy leaning on a table, looking down at a violin which is lying across a wide sheet of paper.) Pearl's response was this: "He is not doing well because the violin is an old one. He is a very talented musician who appreciates music. If he is ever to be a good musician, the financial status of his family will have to improve. His environment will have to expand so that he will meet others who are interested in the things he likes."

It will be noted that Pearl saw the person in the picture as an able individual, unable to actualize his talent *because of events outside of himself — his environment*, particularly his poverty and the uninspiring people around him.

Card 9 is a scene with a background that might be a beach. There are two young women in the picture; one, in the background is running; the other, in the foreground, is standing behind an object that could be a tree. Pearl's response was: "These two women are bitter enemies. The one in the foreground has been successful in cheating the other out of some happiness. She revengefully knows that the woman in the background will never find the man for whom she is frantically searching on the edge of the beach. She, the former object of his love, has seen to it that he has drowned. The man's death is considered an accident, and the two women become separated." Here we see *hostility, jealousy,* and *aggression* to the point of violence.

Card 12F is a picture of a young woman and, in the background, a very much older, wrinkled woman wearing a shawl. Pearl said: "This is an artist's conception of the outer and inner life of a young woman. Outwardly, she is young and attractive and has the vehemence and independence of a man; but she is looked on by others, and in turn views herself, as unattractive, inadequate, and aged."

Seeing the picture as symbolic and seeing the two people as one is quite an unusual interpretation. Could it be that Pearl saw herself here? Her interpretation suggests conflicts within herself; she was young and attractive and feminine outwardly, yet had many of the ambitious and driving qualities of a man and possibly felt unattractive, inadequate, and worn. It is a fact that she did not groom or take advantage of her natural beauty, and she seemed overburdened by her responsibilities and frustrations.

Card 17GF is a somewhat stylized etching. There is a bridge-like structure in front of a tall building. The sun is shining, and below the building men are loading a boat. There is a figure on the bridge, looking down at the water. Pearl said, "The *girl* on the bridge tries to see romance and beauty in spite of the drudgery and sordidness around her. She is in a dream state. Eventually she lifts herself from her environment."

Was Pearl here trying to give a theme from her own life in her attempt to find romance and beauty, while perceiving her own surroundings as sordid? Was she encouraged by the hope that she could lift herself from the inadequate environment in which she had always been imprisoned?

Pearl wrote a total of twenty relatively brief fantasies with varying themes. In addition to those produced in their entirety above, there were two in which the central character was instrumental in causing a tragedy in the life of someone close to him. *The theme of poverty and drabness constantly reappeared but so also did a theme of contentment, happiness, and appreciation of nature.* Some of the fantasies had optimistic endings, as in the case of a man who was attracted to another woman but finally returned to his wife and became a good family man; and in the case of a boy in squalid circumstances whose anxious mother encouraged him to become more sociable and more interested in the opposite sex. He matured to normal, respectable manhood. Another story had the theme of death threatening the security of a loved one who later developed inner peace. In short, Pearl's fantasies tended to reflect her view of the world as both beautiful and harsh, of life-strivings as both successful and unsuccessful, and of human reactions as both aggressive and supportive. There was, however, *no predominant theme of withdrawal or surrender — rather one of struggle and some kind of success.*

Do we see here in Pearl, at least as we examine her fantasy life, a real person reflecting the many forces in her life? Despite a largely uninspiring environment, Pearl, as the result of inner resources and some positive elements in her early education, saw hope of bettering her status. It was not easy, and in the struggle she seemed to see her difficulties represented in people outside herself who personified the narrow, provincial, selfish forces which deprive people like her of success. We shall see these attitudes again later with reference to her landladies and some of her teachers.

Social conflicts and reactions to them

During the course of five or six of the earlier interviews Pearl talked freely about the difficulties she had with her landladies. She felt they tried to boss her and "push" her. Although they rented *her* a room, they acted as though it were *theirs.* She said, "I don't ever feel like one of the 'haves.' I will always be one of the 'have nots'!"

Among her complaints was insomnia. For several nights she had been unable to sleep; hence, she finally decided to go to the Student Health Clinic to see if they would give her pills to help her sleep. Her troubles included a mandatory conference with the Dean of Women. Her landlady had complained that she was not a desirable tenant and that she didn't abide by the house rules.

Pearl confessed that weekends were awful. She stayed in her room most of the time. Her excuse was that she didn't have Sunday clothes, and so could not go out of the house. On one weekend she had nothing to eat for forty-eight hours. She said, "I am depressed most of the weekend." The counselor pointed out that there were other girls having problems, and that if she could build a relationship with some of her fellow students, it might lead to a more acceptable prospect. She answered, "I don't want to associate with that kind of person. It would just make me more depressed."

On the occasion of one interview she came in with great *hostility.* She said she enjoyed hinting to her landladies and to those around her that she had engaged in some unacceptable behavior. She said it wasn't true (and it probably wasn't), but if these people wanted to talk about her, she would give them something really shocking to say. She said, "I hate church people, including my deceased father, who appeared overly pious and was too rigid in his attitude toward me."

The developments that occurred in the next three or four interviews included some invitations to parties (she was not sure whether she wanted to go or not), and her *ambivalence* toward her own role as a woman. She had strong feelings that women were not given the rights they should have in our society and she definitely did not want to be a parasite.

Her ambivalence also extended to society. She felt that there was a definite caste system in the United States, and thought that she was sometimes treated like an untouchable. At times she wished she could cut herself off from the social system. She regarded other people as predatory, exploitive, and insensitive in their treatment of the economically underprivileged.

These interviews were taking place during World War II. Only once did she talk about the war situation; she remained aloof from it. She said, "I am not worried about what the war will do. It will hurt some people who deserve to be hurt, and it may destroy the social system that has produced so many injustices."

She ended one interview with the statement, "Well, if worse comes to worst, I can always check out. I have sleeping pills." The counselor felt that this was a bid for attention as well as an expression of her depression. She continually showed extreme attitudes as a means of expressing her own feelings and arousing reaction in others. Later, when her relationship with the counselor improved and she began to do some free writing, examples of this tendency were found frequently in her writing. Several times she appended a statement such as, "Please don't take any of this seriously."

There is some evidence that she could not express directly all the hostility she felt in her actual relationships with people in authority. In many of her interviews she stated how she would like to give the two deans with whom she had contact a piece of her mind. She expressed very strong hostility toward the Dean of Women as well as the Dean of the College of Agriculture, but apparently never let them know directly her attitudes toward them.

Pearl as seen by other people

We may obtain further insight into Pearl, as well as her reaction to people with whom she was constantly interacting, by looking at some of her statements from the previously mentioned "free-association" document written for the counselor. In discussing her reaction to her early work at the University, she said:

"I had only two and a half years of undergraduate training when I came to the University. I had just finished teaching in the rural school near home. I took a full load that semester and received C's (an unsatisfactory grade for a graduate student) in four of the five courses I had elected. I was not accustomed to university work and I could never get any sleep in the undergraduate house where I was living. I went out of town to dances occasionally and that took time. One of the classes I elected was considered one of the hardest courses offered, and I had not allowed myself time to work on the boring stuff. After that semester I left to go back to a teaching job. Later I took a clerical job in a state office of a large city, the largest I had ever lived in. I was a clerk and I had to deal with figures most of the time. I greatly disliked the kind of superiors that I had and after a short time, I left.

"A cousin of mine had a job teaching in a southern state, and I was offered a teaching position at the same town. I went down there and found it a crude little town. I discovered I was ex-

pected to teach some things I didn't know about and was not
to have the better position that had been mentioned in the
correspondence with them. I pulled out after I saw the situation and came back to the university and registered late. I got
a job in a study hall at a dormitory, but I dropped that after
a few weeks when I found I could live without the pay. My
grades improved, and I no longer had to worry about being
kicked out for mediocre grades, at least until I ran into my ad-
visor one day and he told me he had given me a C in his course.
I hated that class and felt he had done a failing job in teaching
it. He was a narrow, vacillating, dyed-in-the-wool idealist who
gave a false slant to much of the material he presented.

"He could have been kind enough to mention his dissatisfaction with my work before that, although looking back on the
situation now, I think I was aware of his dissatisfaction whenever I recited in class. I had not used the library at the university because I didn't know how, and I was backward about
asking for help from professors, whom I had always put on a
pedestal. They've certainly fallen off! I am losing respect for
those who pretend to be working for the public benefit and
accept their money grudgingly because they feel it isn't enough.
They use their positions only to hold their monopoly and their
claim that education is for the few, because only a small percentage have the intelligence to go to college. This is conceit
on their part and along with this attitude they try to get rid of
as many competitors as they can. I know a lot of graduate students that have fallen as a result of the actions of these people
and they leave hating the university. I have seen others and
have myself been insulted by remarks that professors hand out
to students. They've always made my blood boil but I have
never answered them back, except in one case — and I was able
to make a lasting impression on that one.

"After all the insults I have received about being a stupe, I
decided to be known as a drunken and immoral bitch rather
than a constitutional inferior. The dean had the nerve to keep
asking me for reasons for my failure. Do you think I would tell
him at this point? I still had to get a degree out of that department, and I was still loyal to the subject that had meant so
much to me. Well, my plan was to do everything to show that
I was worthless morally and to drink as much as I could stand,
which was little enough.

"I knew my landlady would be a stool pigeon and I sized her up exactly. It never occurred to me, however, that she would go to the Dean of Women, who is gluttonous for information about sex and drink. The dean, by involving herself, became a big fool and the ass of the show. She showed less intelligence than any of the others I have met around here, and I have heard from other people some of the things she said about me.

"At that time I had an old decrepit landlady who kept disturbing me by running in when I was washing myself, eyeing me suspiciously, being possessive of my room even though I paid a pretty price for it, and cleaning when I was there trying to work. I tried to get a key from her old-maid daughter, although I knew she wouldn't give me one. It wasn't long before I moved.

"The new place was on the top floor of a big ugly house, with no bath, and a nut of a girl living in the next room. She finally flunked out of school and left, overnight. I had been warned about this house and the unpleasant qualities of the landlady. She had heard that my last landlady was glad to be rid of me. This one was nasty and overcharged me, and at the end of the semester, after promising to keep the room for me the following semester, she rented it. This old landlady spread all kinds of rumors, accusing me of being out until three in the morning once. I did like to walk at night, and this is the little fact out of which she made the big yarn. This old woman told me once that there was no one that would put up with me as a roommate. She had the gall to say, 'You are dirty. Your clothes are filthy.' To top it all she says, 'It isn't what you do academically or how good a student you are, it's what we think of you that determines how you get along here.' You know, I think she was right, because she had a straight line to the Dean of Women, who gives orders to the other deans. You can see the reason why the whole bunch of them are like chicken dirt to me."

There is no indication in Pearl's writing of what she said to these people that made them so angry and caused them to find her so undesirable as a tenant. The counselor, in reading her discussions of her feelings about her tribulations on the campus, and from his acquaintance with her, tried to envisage how she behaved to these landladies. She probably was aloof, cool, and abrupt, making short remarks that spurned any warmth they may have shown her. She may

have acted a little superior to them, and she apparently made excessive demands. There is no indication that she got into any long
verbal conflicts over some of the things she mentioned. They may
have detected, however, her deep hostilities and feelings of resentment toward other people. It is interesting that to these women she
apparently seemed arrogant, condescending, and erring, rather than
a somewhat bewildered, struggling young woman trying to better herself.

Dynamic trends

Pearl at times hated the present social system; at other times she
accepted society and planned to get ahead in it — to reach a high
goal, a plan she expressed in terms such as, "No one is going to stop
me." By attacking the prevailing culture she was using a common
defense against anxiety or threat to oneself — externalizing her
troubles, seeing them as the result of something outside her control.
Pearl's reaction to her inner and outer conflicts also included withdrawal and depression, bids for the counselor's sympathy, and a hostile, aloof attitude to the people in her environment. What was the
basic underlying condition producing this variable, often self-defeating behavior? Was it her anxiety, her lack of stable, enduring inner
resources? Was she essentially still a small child emotionally, without support in an unpredictable world? To what extent did she refuse to accept the emotional support that may have been available
in her environment? Why was she cautious of helpful relationships
with other people? What is necessary in order for a change to occur
in an individual such as Pearl, that she might arrive at a more effective mode of adjustment to her environment?

LATER COUNSELING ACTIVITIES

After a year of sporadic counseling

It was after Pearl had been seeing the counselor for about a year
that she began to show a tendency to have dates with boys and to
associate with other students. She always showed some reservation
and conflict about these associations. About this time she came in
for an interview quite upset and in tears. She thought that her academic adviser, whom she respected, had told the dean that she should
go to another school or drop out of graduate work and teach for a
while. The dean had made this suggestion to her but did not make

it mandatory. She had gone to another of her teachers, whom she thought was sympathetic, and had ventilated her feelings about the dean. She now felt guilty about this. She confessed that she had been frequenting one of the campus hangouts every now and then and drinking beer with a married friend. It was a platonic arrangement. He was a sympathetic man and it was a great solace to talk with him. He was a contrast to another man whom she had been dating and whom she characterized as too aggressive and masculine. This latter individual wanted to take too much of the initiative and she said this was not the kind of man she wanted to associate with.

It might be interesting to speculate here about Pearl's concept of herself, her identity as she saw it, the role she wanted to play as a woman, and the extent to which she might reach her present goal. Also, we might ask what she wanted in a man and what kind of relationship she desired between herself and the man of her choice. Do we know enough about her early life to comprehend what factors produced her present attitudes toward herself and those close to her? What information must one have to answer such questions?

Pearl's positive attitude toward counseling seemed to have increased. She apparently still felt anxious about it, but she retreated from the counseling situation less readily than before. At this time, when she came in for a conference, she knocked on the door and when she saw someone was being counseled, she ducked out quickly. When the counselor later looked for her, he found her reading a book in another room in the department with the door closed. She refused to remain in the waiting room where other students might see her. Another indication that she had built a better relationship and was profiting by it was her own voluntary statement that coming in to see the counselor had been of some help. She began to take the counselor's suggestion to write out some of her feelings. She brought these to the sessions but wouldn't talk about the biographical materials that appeared in her writings.

Scores on the MMPI

During one semester she was in a psychology course which involved taking certain psychological tests. She had previously taken the Minnesota Multiphasic Personality Inventory.* She had a very

---

* This is a personality test consisting of 495 statements about behavior or experience, to which the testee responds with "True," "False," or "Cannot say." Responses are scored in terms of the typical answers given by criterion groups of patients with different kinds of psychological disturbances. The result is a profile of nine scores.

high Pa (paranoia) score, which is understandable in terms of her overt suspicion and feelings toward people in authority — specifically that they were not being fair to her or to others like her. She also had high scores on Sc (schizophrenia), D (depression), Pd (psychopathic deviate), and Pt (psychasthenia). In non-technical language, these test results suggest tendencies in the direction of suspicion, self-centered thinking, depression, revolt against conventions and authority, and fixed ideas — all of which were evidenced in her behavior and comments during the interviews.

Dependency relationships

We might begin by looking at the men and women in Pearl's life and her relationship to them as compared to her relationships with her father and her uncle. We have already seen that she was quite hostile toward her father; she thought he was overly pious and hypocritical and had been unduly restrictive toward her early years. Her attitude toward her uncle was warmer. She went home to visit him now and then. Apparently she felt that she would receive a very small inheritance from her uncle — old furniture and the residue from the sale of his small property. During one interview she talked proudly about some music her brother had written. After this brief display of pride in him and his accomplishments, she admitted quite freely that she had never been close to anyone. She said, "I am as close to you as I have ever been to any of my relatives." In one of her writings she admitted that she sometimes wished the counselor were her father and could do for her the things that a father would do for a daughter. On the other hand, she indicated that she wanted to be somewhat independent of fatherly attachments.

She rarely, if ever, mentioned any of her female relatives. (Remember that she lost her mother early in life and that the children were separated and placed with various relatives.) What does Pearl tell us indirectly about her attitude toward dependence on someone and independence? How did these attitudes develop?

After two years of counseling Pearl began to talk more and more about the possibility of marriage and about the kind of man she might marry. This was a change in attitude; in earlier interviews she had said she would never get married. She had always had some dates, even though she was not attracted to the men. For instance, she spoke of one young fellow who dated her as lacking ambition. He showed real affection for her, even suggesting marriage, but she discouraged him. Others tried to take her out from time to time, but she spurned them. She felt that she must marry a person who would give her some status. She thought she couldn't marry a boy who was going into business, but preferred someone who would move into an academic position, although the academic status didn't mean as much to her now as it had formerly. She was also beginning to regard more realistically the opinion of many of her advisers that her personality might make it difficult for her to go into teaching. Pearl began to be more frank about her difficult relationships with people, caused by her inability to feel love for anyone. There was a suggestion that she was gaining insight into this aspect of her personality. She worked through this insight enough to see some of its implications in her life, but she realized that she had learned to hate a number of people. She indicated that she would like to see some people destroyed and that sometimes she felt she would like to be the destroyer. She disliked the thought of being tied down with any social group. On the positive side, she began to show concern for another girl who was having problems and sent her in to see the counselor.

She talked about another young man who was very much in love with her and wanted to marry her. However, she showed ambivalence about marriage; she realized her need for affection but feared marriage. She said, "I want to be a person with no ties. I want to be free to move around and travel. It seems that I am not suited for the academic situation either, because of my personality, but I don't care. I will work as a waitress as I have before and not have to depend on these people. This is a cultural desert anyhow. There is no research. People are narrow-minded." She continued to talk in this vein and then stated that she supposed she had a great desire for power because she found herself having difficulty in giving herself emotionally to this man or to anyone else. She indicated that she was tempted to use this man to get the things she wanted — prestige and power. She had used people before, and she realized that, from her viewpoint, people are not something to love. She expressed another concern which was probably deep and disturbing but represented insight: she didn't think she possessed the high intelligence that she felt was so important in life.

This realization of her relative *limitation in intelligence* was an important one if she could use it, because it was realistic. Although she was a hard worker, part of her continual difficulty with her advisers and with the dean was due to the borderline grades she often got. This limitation explains why she had been dropped from one department and was seeking a degree in another. Much of her behavior previously had been a defense against this realization. Now apparently she could face it, and if she could maintain and live with the insight, she would not need so many defenses.

From many standpoints she had made progress during these two years in counseling. She had been able to face negative aspects of herself that apparently had threatened her previously. There remained a strong anxiety that she might not get a Ph.D. degree, but *this was no longer her only hope.* However, she definitely did not relinquish either her intention to get it, or the idea that it was highly important to her existence.

FOLLOW-UP

Graduation and marriage

More and more she was facing the prospect of marriage. In fact, in subsequent interviews she indicated that she had already discussed the matter with her "Uncle" and was making plans for furniture and a home. This was interesting in view of the fact that she had repeatedly stated in the early days of counseling that she would never get married. Apparently her suitor was a fairly bright, hard-working, shy, and somewhat submissive fellow. Despite the romantic turn, she continued to ventilate her hostility toward the University administration and some of the faculty. She said, "The University is a place for people like me, but the whole structure repels people who think for themselves and show initiative and individuality."

She finally received her Doctor's degree in Community Development, was married, became a housewife, and seemed to enjoy giving her husband emotional support. She put her energies into her husband's career and his future. During the ten years which followed the termination of this counseling, the counselor received letters periodically that were somewhat similar to the writing she had done in the later stages of counseling. The letters expressed considerable hostility, and she found fault with certain elements in the community. The letters frequently ended with a warning that the counselor should not take everything she said too seriously.

Little can be known about her life with her husband, except that she continued to identify herself with his career. They had a little boy a year or so after they were married. She sent the counselor a picture of him, and he was indeed a beautiful child. She seemed to love him dearly and to be concerned with trying to make a good life for him. Her attitudes toward her husband's advancement and future were similar to those she had had about her own during her graduate years. She talked about the fact that he wasn't appreciated by his employer, that he hated the mundane existence he had to live, but that there was no alternative. He was an accountant; he felt he could better his status by more education, but couldn't see how he could manage it financially. Although she seemed to have more worldly goods than she ever had before, she still complained that she lived in economic need and had to put up with an urban, slumlike existence.

Review of counseling

Do you see any changes in Pearl as a result of the relationship she had with the counselor over the three-year period she was in school? What factors influenced Pearl during this period? Was the counseling relationship different from some of the other relationships that she had experienced, as reported above? How did it differ? What can you gather from the accounts of what occurred during counseling? You might attempt to answer these questions before reading the following discussion of them by the counselor.

As indicated in the account already given, I heard about Pearl several weeks before I saw her, and the first contacts with her were fleeting, to say the least. I hardly felt that I had established a relationship, but I knew that her approach toward the office was stronger than her avoidance, because she continued to come back often for very brief periods. It was impossible for me to get her to enter into the more typical kind of counseling sessions. Whenever I asked her if she didn't want another appointment, she answered negatively. However, very often within a week, her head appeared around the doorframe, and she came in for at least ten or fifteen minutes. Once she started to talk it was not easy for her to leave. She came between appointments and at busy times so that relatively little could be accomplished. At times she was so overwrought, hostile, and involved in rigid attitudes and feelings of persecution that I felt some concern about her. On the other hand, I felt there was not much I could do other than to exploit for a mature growth the relationship that existed.

Our relationship seemed to be one of the few positive factors in her life. I didn't think she was suspicious of me, and I felt that I was less threatening than some of the other people with whom she talked. In time, the relationship grew in warmth, and at one time (in the above report when she talked about her desire for me to assume a father role), I felt that the relationship was a relatively strong one. About this time she wrote a long document giving vent to her feelings and revealing much of her early life and her tribulations on the campus. At no time did I attempt in any way to direct her life. I figuratively kept my fingers crossed, feeling that if she ever were on the point of doing anything drastic, she might get in touch with me first. At times she seemed quite paranoid and emotionally unstable; at these times I was even more permissive than usual in trying to give her emotional support and alleviate some of the anxiety that I knew was so strong in her life.

It may be hard for the reader to discern any of the counseling activities in the above account, largely because the relationship established was a sort of haven toward which she could navigate in stormy weather. Over the three-year period I saw a definite improvement in her, both in the reduction of disorganization and instability and in the amount of objective achievement on her part. She remained in school despite constant changes of address and courses, and despite crises with her adviser and with her committee when it seemed that her education might be terminated. She obtained a degree and established a steady relationship with a man who was more compatible with her than any other man in her past had been.

I regarded the counseling relationship as a fairly successful one, despite some of its unorthodox features. Considering Pearl's early traumas and the lack of inner stabilizing resources, she continued to make a better adjustment. I suppose that during this period I was aware of some of her strengths, although I must confess I did not verbalize them nor was I in a position to present her case at a therapy seminar. She had removed herself from a debilitating environment; she managed to eke out an existence without any appreciable financial assistance; she found a niche for herself after her failure to become what she planned to be early in life — a high-school Latin teacher.

Speculation about Pearl's future

Let us pause here before proceeding to report what actually did happen to Pearl and ask you, as a reader, to predict what might have occurred. What do you think she will be like in ten years? How will she adjust to marriage? What kind of wife and mother will she be? What turns might you expect her life to take as a young adult, in view of the patterns delineated in the above description?

You have seen now how the counselor viewed Pearl at the end of this three-year period. It should be stated that the preceding discussion was written after the final follow-up, but the counselor maintains that his attitudes at the end of the three-year period did not differ from his impression after the follow-up.

Interview ten years after counseling

After ten years she wrote the counselor that she would be visiting the university community and would like to talk with him. She came on a very busy day. The counselor had written her and told her that he would have only a half-hour free on this particular day. She did not appear at the time of her appointment but came late because of car trouble. She had to wait until the counselor came out of a meeting and was free to see her. He saw her for about twenty minutes. She entered the office out of breath because she had run up from the basement when she heard he had arrived. She came in smiling cheerfully, and seemed more eager for the conference than she had ever been for previous ones. She began apologizing for her letter and particularly for a statement she made in it that at times she wished to die. All during the interview she seemed to be quite excited, and much of the time her hands trembled. She talked glowingly about her son. He was one of the things in their lives about which she and her husband both felt very strongly and very positively. She mentioned strong friction between her and her inlaws. She admitted that she fought openly with them and with her husband. However, her great desire was to help her husband get more education and be in an economically better and more satisfying position. She wanted to get a job teaching to allow him to finish his degree, but she had been unable to obtain a position, probably because of the letters of recommendation she received when she got her degree. The counselor again suggested she write out her feelings and then destroy the paper when she had finished (i.e., using the writing merely as a therapeutic outlet).

He remembered that her previous writing had been satisfying to her, that she had enjoyed writing and had at one time hoped to be able to write professionally.* After listening while she ventilated

---

* During several interviews when Pearl was in college, the counselor had reconstructed the interviews and plotted a ratio of negative emotional words to

her feelings about her life with her husband, the counselor began to reassure her. She seemed to accept, without comment, the reassurance. He talked to her in this vein: "You remember that you had a very difficult childhood with relatively little emotional support, that you have received one of the highest degrees, and that you obtained it by dint of your own efforts. You were able to support yourself financially as few girls are, working at menial jobs and living on pennies. Your life has been meaningful. You have been true to certain ideals and aspirations. There is still a great need for the kind of initiative and adaptiveness that you have shown.

"You mentioned that you wish for more friends and associates with whom you can talk over your attitudes and feelings. You don't realize that there are others having problems similar to yours. Working on some common endeavor of a social nature would have some value for you and for others. Certainly, it is important to find others with whom you can share your attitudes and problems. There are many movements in your own city that need recruits."

To this she answered, "Most liberals do not think as I do. They are interested mainly in promoting the integration of the races and I am against that." However, she did seem to agree that friends would be helpful and that she wished she could do more writing.

It was interesting that she never did talk specifically about the problems she had alluded to in her letter, but mainly wanted to use the session to renew her acquaintance with the counselor and to see the campus once again. She very much enjoyed this visit to the campus. She left the office apparently feeling much better, but then returned in a few minutes after saying good-bye and asked warmly about the dean with whom she had had so much difficulty. She asked the counselor to say hello to him for her. Some of her letters over the ten years had been in response to news items she had seen in the paper about the dean, and in them she expressed hostility toward him.

The counselor noted that she was a little heavier than she had been in college, but although she was approaching forty, she still looked younger than her years and was an attractive woman with outward feminine charm. Her grooming still did not bring out her best physical traits, but it had improved somewhat. She had all the energy he remembered. She appeared to be a very forceful person,

---

words expressing release and more positive outlook. He found that the latter increased during the course of the interview, indicating that the interviews were usually cathartic and therapeutic in nature.

but lacking in the capability to use her intelligence, motivation, and attitudes in a manner that would bring her satisfaction and social approval.

She said frankly that some people had told her she was bitter and mean and even paranoid. She did not deny this but felt that it was necessary in order to get what she wanted for herself and her family. The counselor felt, and reiterated to her, that she was an individual whose life had meaning, that she tended to see more problems and hazards in life than really existed, and that she was not using her efforts effectively. He also saw that sponsoring her husband's cause and rearing her child, even though they were taking place in social isolation, were struggles that brought satisfaction. On the whole, she seemed more *integrated and effective* — if not free of problems — than she had been as a student.

PEARL: Pattern of Life

What do you see in the case of Pearl? Give your spontaneous reactions to Pearl before turning to the questions below.

Patterns, trends, and influences

 a. What was her view of life and her role in it?

 b. What is your impression of the effect of some of the people who attempted to deal with Pearl when she was a student, including the counselor?

 c. What effect did the transitions from one phase of her life to another have? Consider her capacity to manipulate people one way or another.

 d. Suppose you had been placed in some kind of relationship with Pearl, such as a housemate or a friend. What role would you tend to play? How would she affect you and how can you account for your conjectured responses?

Concepts helpful in understanding Pearl

 a. The development of paranoid ideas (26, 115)

 b. The role of counseling in preventing full development of paranoia (74, 114)

 c. Personal disorganization; depersonalization (37, 54)

 d. Schizoid personality (115, 121)

e. Culture conflicts (69, 73)

f. The institution vs. the community-plus-outpatient-psychotherapy.

Other concepts which may have some relevance to this case: rigidity of thought; hostility; guilt; ambivalence; self-defeating behavior; manipulation of people; social class.

PEARL: Comments by a Graduate Student

Going to the Mental Hygiene Clinic would have represented a commitment on Pearl's part: (1) *I* have problems. (2) *I* am going to set out to solve them. The counselor's seeing the girl in his office and giving in to her demands encouraged her to think that the problems were the fault of *other people*. I think, therefore, he should have tried to get her to come to the clinic where he saw other students. He seemed hesitant in structuring events.

Pearl showed a strong capacity for involving other people in her affairs, and at times was pretty bossy and demanding. She rarely saw her difficulties as *her* own problem. She projected them onto other people and events.

Could it be that the landlady was doing a favor when she "had the gall to say 'You are dirty. . .'"? The landlady was representing reality to the girl. I am inclined to be critical at this point, because the counselor, either because of his personal involvement or because he was awed by the gravity of the girl's problem, never dealt with her openhandedly. Granting the counselor's inclination toward an active rather than passive approach, he should have made more interpretive statements. His statements seemed to be lectures rather than pointed questions.

The Great God Education! What a shame. So many people fostered her ambition to get an advanced degree without a realistic view as to where all this fancy education would fit into her total personality.

I am struck with the extremism of her position. If something isn't black, then it's white. This is understandable in terms of Frank Shaw's reconciliation theory — rather than trying to deny the existence of oppositional pulls in his personality, the individual must come to grips with and reconcile the difference.*

I would point out the existence of a personality style based on a

* See Kelley (55).

once-accurate perception of a blasted, withered, starved life, where no quarter is given and none expected. This microcosmic view was neither accurate nor adaptive when Pearl moved into a new and different cosmos, i.e., the middle-class world.

1. Pearl's chances at the outset for living a happy, effective life were not worth a plugged nickel.

2. In the body of the case you *describe* behavior and *infer* motives.

3. Ten years later, Pearl returns and, though we find qualitatively the same personality patterns, something has changed. She is living a more or less effective life.

4. Something had happened. What? How? Because of the counselor? What are the psychodynamic mechanisms of change?

5. Some psychologists maintain that when a person begins to try to help another, he is on the road toward helping himself.

6. The first hint of Pearl's capacity for involving herself with others was her marriage.

ROBERT

The Seeker After Self

In Robert's case we present an individual who was neither
seen over a long period of time nor followed after the
interview, but observed through one interview and as a
student in a class taught by the writer. Robert portrays
some of his inner life through a self-oriented Sentence-
Completion Blank. The responses on this Blank are contrasted with those of a male contemporary who differs
markedly from Robert in behavior and self-attitudes.

IDENTIFICATION

Most of the people who interest a writer selecting case studies for
presentation are in some way outstanding, even though the particular aspects of their lives that gain the writer's attention are not
necessarily socially approved or desirable. Robert, the individual we
will observe here briefly, is outstanding in very few respects, but he
was not completely bland in the eyes of the writer or he would not
have been chosen for presentation.

Perhaps there is a need to give more attention to individuals such
as Robert, who blend into the group, who seem passive, and who do
not distinguish themselves on achievement tests either as outstanding successes or as failures. Certainly a large proportion of the students found in our educational systems today fall into this category
— the unspectacular person who is regarded as average and not remarkable in any way. We raise the question now, and will do so
again later, as to how Robert might have benefited from the help of
a high-school counselor who took a personal interest in him and
helped him to assess his assets and liabilities and to explore answers
to the questions, "Who and what am I?" and "What can I become?"
We will see that although Robert apparently did not verbalize these

questions to himself or to anyone else, the answers to them were very important in his groping toward maturity. First, we give a brief physical description of Robert, then a discussion of why he was chosen for presentation here.

Robert was of average size and build, and neatly but not stylishly dressed. He made no attempt to wear clothes typical of the undergraduate. Few people seeing him walk down the street in ill-matched slacks and jacket would judge him to be a college student. He was twenty-four years old, a senior in the School of Business Administration, and the son of a farmer turned mechanic. The teacher of the course in Applied Psychology, which Robert was taking along with eighty other students, described him as follows: "He was a quiet, sad-looking fellow with a masculine build and walk, who usually came to class early and alone. He spoke only when he was spoken to by his fellow students, and dressed more like the younger boys in a small town than like a college student. The only reason I remember him is that he seemed highly alert in class. He attended to my every word and action, although his face was immobile and he didn't react to humor or class interaction. He might have been lost in the sea of faces except for his unflagging attention, his early arrival, and his immobile face. Despite the fact that he initiated very little contact with other students, he did not seem to be living in a world of his own. Rather, he seemed to be standing on the sidelines, observing everything, but giving no clue as to his reaction to the events around him and showing no inclination to enter into them. In fact, one might speculate that he would show resistance and shyness if he were invited to participate."

OCCASION FOR INTERVIEW

Almost everything that we know about Robert was drawn from casual observations in class, from a fifteen- or twenty-minute interview to be described presently, and from a sentence-completion blank in which he explored certain aspects of his self-concept.

One of the special aspects of this case is the paucity of information and the scant contact with the individual depicted. The reader will be asked later to evaluate the productiveness of the methods as used by an experienced psychologist and to state the shortcomings of these methods. Taking note of certain information as it is obtained will be helpful in answering certain crucial questions about

the structure (habits and traits), dynamics (motives), and development (salient events in one's personal history) of Robert's personality.

The instructor had given the self-oriented Sentence-Completion
Blank* to the whole class. He had asked the students to classify the
responses themselves, and had interpreted the results to the class as
a group. An assistant picked from the class approximately six students
who seemed to reflect self-confidence in their responses on the blank
and six others who seemed confused, lacking in a clear identity, and
low in effective responses to frustration or conflict. Robert was one
of those chosen. All twelve were interviewed by an interviewer who
did not know in which group the student was classified. At the end
of the interview the interviewer was to place the student in one
of these two groups without looking at his responses on the Sentence-
Completion Blank. Robert was told, as were all other interviewees, to
sit down, relax, and talk about the events in his life which made
him the person that he was at that time. He was urged to talk freely
for ten or fifteen minutes while the interviewer took notes on what
he said.

THE INTERVIEW

Of several chairs in the office, Robert chose the one farthest from
the interviewer. He seemed tense, and sat rather stiffly, with his legs
drawn up close to the chair. The chair that he had taken did not
face the interviewer, and as he talked he looked off into space rather
than directly at his interviewer. As the interview progressed, he
tended to look at the interviewer more directly. He spoke softly, and
the interviewer noted that this was the first time he had heard
Robert's voice, even though he had seen Robert in class for several
months.** It was more subdued than one would have expected from
his somewhat rough appearance. Robert was cooperative, though
slightly withdrawn; he warmed up gradually during the course of
the interview. He became tense and looked sad when the interviewer
indicated that the period had terminated. Apparently, Robert found

* Robert's blank and that of another student are included later in this case
description.
** It will be noted that the interview begins as soon as the client walks in the
door of the office. An alert counselor is aware that his client is showing behavior
and inner processes at all times. This is revealed in his manner of dress, gestures,
and style of life. See Chapter 19 in Allport (3).

during the interview that he was building a relationship which would allow him to discuss freely some aspects of his emotional life, and then the interviewer, who seemed friendly and accepting, suddenly became mechanical and aloof. Robert reacted to this as another rejection experience.

PERSONAL HISTORY

Early life

Robert began his discussion by saying that up to nine or ten years of age he had lived on a small farm, and then his family moved into the nearby town. He was the oldest child in the family, but he did not say anything about the other siblings or about his relationship with them or with his father and mother.* His father got a job as a semi-skilled mechanic. Although Robert did not say so, the family apparently lived in a low socio-economic section of the city. High school was an uneventful experience, and although no specific information about his activities was given, the counselor surmised that Robert was shy and did not volunteer for any extracurricular activities. He seemed to be a boy who might well have entered into the typical sports activities, but he did not mention athletics as an important factor. He did say that he had several odd jobs from time to time, but that they did not interest him and he did not hold any of them for very long.

Military service and employment

He had been in military service, but he did not mention his branch of service; he had won no distinctions nor had any experiences worth reporting. One might envisage him in both high school and the service as just one of many, going passively through the routines planned for him, sharing little of the pleasure or concerns he experienced. In all of his early life, one would gather he did not develop a clear identity or a feeling of belongingness with any group. He said that in high school he became somewhat depressed when he considered what role he might play in later life.

* Sometimes what an individual *doesn't report* has significance in showing the absence of needed human acceptance or the presence of frustration. The significance of Robert's omitting reference to members of his family should be noted by the counselor, at a relevant time during an interview. Robert may be encouraged to open up this area of experience by a comment such as, "Would you like to tell me more about the members of your family?"

After finishing his military service he got a job in a large industrial plant on the outskirts of the large city near his community. One day, while listening to a fellow worker as he described a soap opera he had seen on television, Robert said, "The idea just came to me then that I was getting nowhere on this job; I was just a cog in a wheel, and I quit." Apparently he then got a job as an itinerant farm worker and worked with what he called "foreign" people. He liked them better than any he had met on previous jobs, in school, or in the service. Although the counselor did not question Robert on this point, he surmised that these people accepted Robert as an individual and may even have looked up to him as having more prestige than they had. We might ask here to what extent Robert's quitting his job was a positive or negative adjustive act in view of where it led him in respect to people affecting his life.

Desire for further education

Some time later Robert realized that to get more of what he wanted, he would have to obtain more education. He acknowledged having a general curiosity about people, about why they behaved as they did, and about the structure of modern society. He thought college would give him some better perspective on these questions. He found opportunities in college to read and mentioned Maugham and Dostoevski as authors he enjoyed. This reading of fiction, particularly its emphasis on the dynamics in the lives of people, he thought influenced his perspective on life. He began to think about his own potentialities and possible destiny.

Initiative, decision-making, and self-attitudes

During this session Robert said he realized that he had just drifted along, with few goals; he didn't know where he was going, and he found it very hard to make decisions. He tended to worry for a while and then forget the matter; but at least in this period in his life he was beginning to reflect on what attitudes one should take toward life and how different people coped with crises.

The interviewer allowed Robert to guide the interview in his own way until there was a lull, and then asked Robert leading questions:

"What are the major forces in your life?"

Robert's answer was, "I don't know."

"What do you think are your outstanding abilities?"

Again he replied, "I don't know." Later he added, "I haven't done too much. I find it very hard to make decisions."

During this part of the interview Robert mentioned something about paratroopers, but it is not clear in the interviewer's notes whether he admired them and had thought about the possibility of entering this branch of the service or whether this had been a part of his military training. It is clear that Robert did not dwell upon this for some reason. He stated that his home environment had forced him to be independent and responsible. The interviewer had the feeling, even though Robert did not verbalize it, that he had not been given sufficient emotional support at the same time that he was being urged to achieve on his own and to take responsibility for himself. We might speculate about the emotional sustenance Robert received at home and the role this played in his present, somewhat withdrawn personality.

His grades in college were above average, although not superior. He seemed to take his courses seriously and to prepare for them. On the other hand, the interviewer had felt that Robert did not show the creative kind of initiative that might have made him a better student. There were hints that he often felt lost, both when he was on the job in the large factory and also while he was a student in a state university with almost 12,000 students. For example, on one blank that he filled out, he did not know his psychology teacher's name nor the exact title of the school in which he was registered.

At one point in the interview the counselor said, "Do you have any questions to ask me?" This seemed to confuse Robert more than it did the others who were interviewed, and he said, "That is an unexpected question. I don't know how to deal with it." This reaction may be Robert's typical response to novel problem situations. Whenever he was not responding in terms of previous experience or habitual behavior, he became puzzled and had difficulty deciding what to do.

He mentioned the term *depression* a couple of times in the interview. He referred obliquely on several occasions to his socio-economic status and its effect on how others regarded him and on what he might become. He said, "Status is so important in this world." He related an incident in which he was in a store and did not have precise information on what he wanted to buy. He said he was treated by the owner of the store as though he were a person unworthy of civil courtesies; instead of walking out of the store in anger, he discussed with the man in great detail the project he was working on and the materials he needed to build it. He said, "I wasn't dressed well and he regarded me as an ignorant nobody. As I talked with him at length, he began to realize that I was intelligent and had done some reading, and his attitude seemed to change; but it bothered me that he judged me wrong at first."

PERSONAL RECORDS

Answer to "Who am I?"

Robert, as a member of a class in psychology, was asked to write out an answer to the question, "Who or what am I?" This was his response: "I suppose . . . I really don't know what to say or how to say it. I guess in a lot of ways I'm like many other people. But in some ways I feel I'm a lot different from many people, but that really isn't a very good statement because I can't tell what others actually feel or think. I feel that we can tell some of what different people think and feel from the way they act, but this is hard and we can never be sure."

This might be contrasted with another senior in the same class whom we shall call John, who was unlike Robert in most respects. John displayed high initiative, participated in class, and obtained high grades. He had many contacts with his fellow students, had a girl, and felt that he was playing an active role in shaping his own destiny. John wrote, in answer to "Who or what am I?": "I am an individual, unlike any other individual, with my own particular set of standards, values, and emotions."

How would you describe the differences between the answers these two men gave to this simple, yet profound, question? You might want to jot down a few reactions before reading the following.

In many ways Robert's awkward but meaningful answer epitomizes his attitude toward himself and toward the world. His answers to questions raised about life situations are often quite satisfactory, but he does not feel secure in what he says. He knows there are quite valid answers to problems, and he is searching for them. After military service, as we saw above, he left a meaningless job on his own initiative, traveled around, studied people, raised questions, and returned to college to look for some of the answers.

Responses to the Sentence-Completion Blank

The *Sentence-Completion Blank* is one of the most frequently used projective devices.* Generally such a test consists of a series of

---

* A test with ambiguous stimuli, to which the individual responds in his own characteristic manner. It is thought that his responses reflect his unique attitudes and interpretations, projected onto the stimuli.

sentence fragments, which the student or client is asked to complete in any way he wishes. In the example given below, which includes two individuals' responses (one of them Robert's and the other John's), the sentence fragments are oriented toward the person's responses to frustration, conflict, and aspects of self-identity.

Look over the two sets of responses labeled "X" and "Y" included in the blank below and choose the set of responses that you think belongs to Robert. In which of the two groups of students, classified in terms of their answers on the *Sentence-Completion Blank,* do you think Robert belonged? Was he in the group that exhibited a great amount of confidence or in the group that showed confused identity and lack of self-confidence?

SENTENCE-COMPLETION BLANK

Here are some incomplete or partial sentences. *You are to complete them in your own way.* Use them to state freely your attitudes and feelings. There are no right or wrong answers. They represent rather an opportunity for you to tell what you think and feel on certain matters. You need not think long about these things. Just write down ideas which come to you. The blank has research value. You are not asked to sign your name. Take as much time as you need. The experimenter will write the time that expires in half-minutes on the board. When you finish, write the number he has just placed on the board in the blank provided. Wait for the signal to start.

	X's Responses	*Y's Responses*
1. My main interest	*people.*	*is happiness.*
2. When something worries me	*I try to forget them.*	*I analyze the cause and what I can do to stop worrying.*
3. I admire	*people that use their own minds.*	*people who have outstanding study habits.*
4. My attitude toward myself	*rather neutral.*	*is analytic but also biased.*
5. When I feel I have too much to do	*I get rather anxious.*	*I eliminate the least important.*
6. I am very fond of	*a lot of things.*	*my girl.*

	X's Responses	*Y's Responses*
7. When I feel I am not achieving enough	*I feel that it's my own fault.*	*I dig in harder.*
8. People	*interest me.*	*need to be understood.*
9. When things go wrong	*I forget or try to.*	*I don't get shook but just try to take it in stride.*
10. My abilities	*rather general I guess, nothing especially outstanding.*	*are well above average.*
11. I look forward to	*getting out of the University and working at something more specific.*	*holding a permanent job and having a family.*
12. You can't go wrong if	*you're really trying; if you do anyway no point in worrying.*	*you buy a Chevy.*
13. When I am angry	*I usually keep it to myself; sometimes it lasts a long time.*	*I don't hide it.*
14. The most important thing in life to me	*do what I want to do, feeling it has meaning to me and in general.*	*is peace of mind.*
15. If the worst thing that could happen did occur	*I don't know — maybe I'd adjust, but I really don't know.*	*I'd be without a girl.*
16. Most of the things I do	*have some meaning and/or are of some interest to me.*	*involve my girl.*
17. In general, I	*enjoy just about everything some.*	*am very well balanced.*
18. I daydream about	*the future mostly; most everything seems to have some future significance.*	*a job.*
19. My ideals	*idealistic I guess, is the best word.*	*are somewhat above standard.*

	X's Responses	*Y's Responses*
20. When I am undecided	*I usually get confused.*	*I analyze the situation thoroughly.*
21. I am different	*not really different from most people I think, in some of my ideas maybe.*	*from most individuals.*
22. My best trait is	*friendly to most people.*	*self-knowledge.*
23. Strong forces within me	*confuse me.*	*are love and honesty.*
24. My greatest fault	*want too much from the future.*	*is lack of consistent initiative.*
25. I am the kind of person who	*not sure about anything.*	*will eventually succeed no matter what.*
26. When I make a big mistake	*I feel bad. I think, but can't think of any really big ones.*	*I don't always admit it to other people.*
27. When I feel I am left out	*I feel like I've done something wrong.*	*I seek to "get in" somewhere else.*
28. My religion	*no preference.*	*is very important to me.*
29. When I am afraid I won't get something I want very much	*I try harder, it becomes an obsession.*	*I seek alternative things.*
30. My friends	*all kinds, some rather weird!*	*are not really very close to me for I will not let them be.*
31. When I am disappointed	*think about it some, then forget it if it won't do any good.*	*I soon forget it.*
32. When someone expects me to do something important	*I get rather anxious to do it right.*	*I do it as best I can.*
33. About my goals	*they are very general.*	*I plan their attainment thoroughly.*

	X's Responses	Y's Responses
34. My recreation	varied, like to do a lot of things some; nothing too much.	usually involves my girl.
35. When something I like disturbs me	this is really a problem, feel very bad, but usually do it anyway.	I don't lose faith in it.
36. Marriage	it's all right when you get ready for it.	is one of my primary goals.
37. My career	very important not the career, but being successful.	is another of my primary goals.
38. My favorite	pastime? None especially.	food is chicken.
39. I need	nothing that I can't get.	my girl very much.
40. I would like to add this to the above:		I am an individual and consider myself as such.

About this blank or the course

You didn't ask	about my family.
You repeated the idea of	
I feel that Psychology	is a tool and not an end.
This course	is a bit slow and draggy.
This blank	has fine parts.

Trends in responses to the Blank

In the responses to the *Sentence-Completion Blank* above, we see how many of the subject's responses indicate a tendency to engage in trial-and-error or problem-solving activity when he is frustrated or in difficulty. Consonant with these are responses which indicate an openness to experience which will lead to learning and growth. Contrary to these are responses which indicate negative emotions — anxiety, confusion, panic, or various kinds of escape and defensive behavior. The latter types of response, unlike those indicating trial and error, tend to prevent behavior which may possibly result in learning and personal development. They are defensive rather than growth-encouraging in nature.

In the responses to the *Sentence-Completion Blank* above, we see two individuals who differ very widely with respect to these categories of response. Robert's responses are the ones labeled X. He shows many more anxiety or negative-feeling responses, and fewer trial-and-error, problem-solving responses than does the other individual, whom we call John. In Robert's blank, thirteen of the forty items could be clearly classified as trial-and-error or problem-solving, as contrasted with thirty-nine for John. Robert gave fourteen responses that showed negative feelings or defensive and escape behavior, as contrasted with none for John.

If you scan Robert's blank again, you will notice, in addition to the descriptions given above, that he shows in his responses an *interest in people* and a friendliness toward them. He particularly admires "people that use their own minds." He seems to have *wide interests that are diffuse* rather than specific and well established. He is very fond of "a lot of things," and his abilities are "rather general . . . nothing especially outstanding"; his recreations are also non-specific. He does display considerable thought about *the future* and some realism in his aspirations. He regards success as important, but he still seems immature. He implies he is not ready for marriage. There are several examples of lack of confidence concerning his behavior. He admits anxiety, that strong forces within him confuse him, and confesses he tries to suppress errors and worries, and keeps anger to himself — all showing his difficulty in handling his emotions.

In response to the sentence fragment, "Marriage," Robert's response that "It's all right when you get ready for it," may reflect his lack of associations with members of the opposite sex in a social or romantic relationship. One might judge from his general behavior and indirect comments that he did not consider himself eligible to date or to approach some of the girls who might have been attractive to him. Robert was definitely above average in appearance, neatness, and masculinity; but he did nothing to enhance his most positive physical and behavioral traits, in order to appear as an eligible young man. Moreover, since we know of his negative image of himself from the above discussion, we might say that his attitude toward himself was the major factor inhibiting him from approaching girls.

ROBERT: Life Trends and Potentialities

What do you see in the case of Robert? Give your spontaneous reactions to Robert before turning to the questions below.

Distinctive personality characteristics

a. Have you known someone like Robert? What *traits* stand out?

b. How do you think Robert *viewed himself?*

c. Robert called his reaction to life "*generally depressed.*" Why does he become depressed rather than hostile or cynical?

Significant persons, relationships, and events

a. Robert talked very little about his *home life.* How do you account for this?

b. What personal *characteristics and relationships* (approach or avoidance) seemed to you to contribute to Robert's life pattern?

c. What potential influences might have made a *difference* in Robert's life as you see it?

d. What *information not given* would be needed for a full understanding of Robert?

Concepts helpful in understanding Robert

a. Aspects of his self-structure (73, 76)

b. Openness to experience but no existential commitment, no clear goals (76, 77)

c. Insecurity leading to sensitivity and self-centeredness (52, 109)

d. Possible rejection by struggling parents (15, 44)

Other concepts which may have some relevance to this case: high-school counseling; "Who am I?"; group identity; depression; social class.

SAM

The Insightful Observer

Sam is a novelist, now receiving national recognition, who
revealed his search for understanding in an autobiography
written when he was a college freshman. He did not seek
counseling in college nor did he take any tests for personal assessment. The case is presented to open a discussion on the dynamics of normal development toward personal identity and self-actualization. The unique aspect
of the case is the availability of a personal document written in college and a later published interview when Sam
visited the campus as a successful writer approximately
twenty years after his graduation. Here we see a youth's
view of himself and the same individual's adult view after
his accomplishments have been recognized.

IDENTIFICATION

As an eighteen-year-old college freshman Sam was tall, thin, blond-
haired, quiet, observant. One might have seen him standing in the
hall, away from the other students, who were busily recording data
in a research office in the department. He smoked a cigarette and
watched them, while they did as little work as possible and enjoyed
each other's camaraderie. Sam was one of the group, but apparently
was no one's special friend. He had seemed, even in his teens, to
have inner thoughts and reserve which his contemporaries respected.
He was witty with little apparent effort. His remarks amused some,
but did not touch others. Although Sam was bright, he did not earn
outstandingly good grades. He was naturally good-looking, with
strong, masculine features, but carelessly dressed. From his behavior
toward the girls in class, he seemed to appreciate feminine beauty,
but was not preoccupied by its presence. He was well regarded and

257

included in the group, but was not particularly sought after. His independence, apparent confidence, and receptiveness may have been the major factors which influenced the attitudes of his associates toward him.

What might he have thought as he listened to the somewhat immature banter of the other students? Why was he so apparently secure and stable in his adjustment to life — or was he? Let us see in his autobiography how he regarded himself in his first year of college.

PERSONAL HISTORY

Approach to autobiography

The psychology instructor asked Sam to tell his story by following a two-page mimeographed outline.* The outline listed a number of factors that may influence a person's development. The list was divided into two parts — one "cross-sectional" in nature ("What I am today") and the other "longitudinal" ("How I came to be myself"). A person following this outline is asked to consider each item in terms of his development and present status — in short, what he is and how he came to be as he is. He is also to include his attitudes toward these factors, or aspects of life, and to evaluate the factors in terms of what each contributes to a stable, mature personality.

Instead of following this outline, Sam chose to give the essence of his life by a simple, direct narrative. Let us note the manner in which he attempts to understand and identify himself by writing a

---

* Below are the major headings of the outline, with a few examples under each category:

I. Cross section (What I am today)
    A. *Social background* — religion, parents' vocation, size of home town.
    B. *Physique and health* — body build, facial features, illnesses.
    C. *Capacity and achievement* — school grades, special skills.
    D. *Active motivations* — attitudes, interests, and habitual tendencies.

II. Longitudinal (How I came to be myself)
    A. *Physical and health history*
    B. *Family history* — discipline, understanding, freedom.
    C. *Emotional history* — fear, temper tantrums, sex curiosities.
    D. *Social history* — friendships, dates, memberships.
    E. *Educational history* — grades, subjects liked, honors.
    F. *Religious history* — devoutness, practices, beliefs.
    G. *Vocational and avocational history* — odd jobs, hobbies.
    H. *Subjective history* — daydreams, ideals, guilts.

personal document. Do we see here the rudiments of his later career as a novelist?

Autobiography written as a college sophomore

"Whereas sex should play an important role in the adjustment of a boy just turned eighteen, I will not allow much space for its discussion — because usually I do not think about sex very much. Although it has been repressed (the sexual urge, I mean) to some extent, the few outlets offered have been sufficient to make me feel normal in that respect.

"The conflicts I will discuss have dominated my being, have colored my whole life — which now seems to be in a state of constant internal conflict, unrest, and insecurity.

"The first I shall discuss had its origin in my childhood — as far back as I can remember. As a child, I continually sought and was given the place that might be called the center of attraction. Although I was never told directly that I was the most important being on this earth, I suspected that I might be one of the most important. (I wish to state now that my family did not at that time make it a point to make me feel that way — but I imagined that they did.)

"I never failed to inject my wit into discussions; I never failed to have my wit applauded. Thus, I felt that if I was not all of life, I was at least a big part of it.

"Then too, while in the company of other kids, I constantly pushed myself forward to the center of things. I was rarely the leader. I was, however, the proud and brilliant instigator. Who thought of 'pulling that swell trick on the new kid'? I did, of course. Who always did the funniest things, making everybody laugh? I did, of course. Who? I! I! I!

"It was inevitable that I should soon discover that all of life was not to be dominated by these 'I's.' And when I did make that discovery, I suffered. About four years ago, I was away from home (the first time that I had no audience) working at a strange hotel. I had made the acquaintance of a boy my own age, who was a guest at the hotel. Naturally, as he and his family had been patrons of the hotel for many seasons, he was well known. One night, while in the ballroom, we both became attracted to a beautiful girl in the corner. Not feeling very bold in these strange surroundings, I allowed my friend to dance with her first. Then as I stood in the darkness and watched him whirl gracefully about the floor, a strange sadness came over me. It seemed as though everyone in the room was watching him. His parents were smiling proudly. People seemed to stop what they were doing to watch him. They were pointing him out as 'very cute'; some remarked that he was an excellent dancer. He was in the spotlight; the entire room was charmed. I was in the darkness, quite alone and unnoticed. A lump grew in my throat — and I sneaked out of the room.

"On the way home, my sadness gave way to tears. I went through all the stages of self-pity. I imagined myself to be the most unfortunate, most miserable being on this earth. My confused mind sought answers; it began to rationalize. My friend was a louse and the people didn't know a good dancer when they saw one. Luckily, this explanation did not satisfy me. As I lay on my bed, thinking more calmly, looking at things from a synthetic viewpoint, I realized that the cause for my recent unhappiness was that my friend was occupying just the same spotlight that I had once enjoyed. I realized that I had come to need being the center of attraction — to have people praise only me, watch only me. I told myself that I could not expect such constant appreciation; that later in life I would experience much the same unhappiness if I did.

"I am trying to correct myself — with some success, too. These last few months, spent here with you hard Midwesterners, have helped me. It is no longer as great a conflict as it was a year or two ago.

"The next problem is, I believe, the more important because it is responsible for much of my personality — for my unrest, for my feelings of getting nowhere, for my discouragement, for my lack of interest in many things in which I should be interested. Ever since I can remember, I have daydreamed. I have been living in a dream world. It seems that the glamour of things rather than their particular essence has always attracted me.

"I was in high school. First, I want to mention an unsuccessful love affair, which I believe threw me back into the dream world, which in turn gave me parts to play. I loved one girl — but she did not love me. However, as she was near me all the time, I loved her madly for the four years in high school, without success, of course. Since reality would not grant me my wish, I turned to dreams; and here I spent many delightful hours reveling in what was the most beautiful love affair that any poet ever created. I want to digress for a moment to say that I was in terrible awe of this girl, the most divine creature — I was the most humble being in her company. This was, I believe, a big cause for my occasional feelings of inferiority in public places.

"The part I now undertook to play was that of the Greenwich Village playwright. His bitter cynicism and absolute indifference toward convention are most modern. Quite casually, he sleeps with women, and he breaks their hearts with even less concern. His clothes must be rugged (they should tell of his indifference toward appearance); his shirt collar must always be wide open. The most important people will leave him very bored, and he will make no attempt at concealing his boredom. Of course, he drinks daily in some secluded, picturesque spot, surrounded by artists, poets, composers, and philosophers. He completely dominates the conversation with his brilliant theories and attitudes (of which I knew nothing). Dissenters wince under his lashing wit. His speech comes fast; the phrases original; the words crisp — all very 'Noel Cowardish.'

"Whether I knew it or not at the time, this was the part I was going to play. The glamour of the fellow drew me to him like a magnet. And so (this was in high school) I defied convention (not knowing why, of course) — until a crisis arose. To my keen delight, the girls regarded my impulses as 'dangerous, but interesting'; I regarded them (the girls) as conquests whether the victory was mine or not. The fellows and teachers thought me rather witty, but 'queer-queer' perhaps, because I appeared to hold great contempt for normal things such as joining clubs and making good grades — especially since I had made high grades in my first two years. To make matters worse, two of my plays (silly things, pure junk) were produced in the school auditorium. Thus, you see, the unfortunate part of it all is that I was made to feel that my characterization had produced the desired effect.

"Now I wanted to write plays — worthwhile plays, not the amateurish junk that was given in high school. I really came to love the drama, there was no doubt about that. However, my motives were then impossible of fulfillment. My pitiful attempts at creating drama left me frantic. I became lost. I was not intellectual! I was not the playwright! What was I? It was all so confusing, so upsetting! I suffered! It was now torture to remain alone with myself, because my dreams would no longer satisfy me.

"Now, I am grateful to those periods of torture, for it was then that I began, for the first time, to distinguish between illusion and reality. My life up until then appeared to me in its true light — in all its falseness.

"Yes, I realize all this — but even now I am still the victim of this urge to imitate by saturating myself with glamour and discarding essence. This is why I feel I am maladjusted at present. It causes me to become depressed, discouraged, and upset. Reality stubbornly refuses to allow me what my dreams will. One day I am the successful, blasé, extravagant writer. But the truth is, I'm not a writer because I haven't written. I can't possibly be blasé, because I really have great affections. I can't be extravagant because my finances are sharply limited. So, I assume an entirely different role — that of the conscientious, thrifty, ambitious student. Am I thrifty because I'm worried about spending too much money? Am I conscientious, plodding, because I have a particular goal in mind? No! It's the damn glamour of the Horatio Alger story. I cannot do either part! (Please remember that I am not conscious of playing these parts at the time.)

"In my saner moments I realize that all my endeavors are colored by this same insincerity and shallowness. The thought is distressing, for I realize how weak is the foundation under me. There is so much of the indefinite — of insecurity! There is so much self-disgust!

"The paradox is, that although I realize much of the falseness in me, I still want to write and believe that I should write. There is so much inside of me that seeks an outlet — so much beauty that I would spread out into life. However, we will stop here — because I cannot do justice to that feeling now."

Questions about Sam at this point

How much of Sam do you see from the above personal document? What traits seem outstanding? Refer again to the outline given him and see how much of his essential nature and its development he reveals as he wrestles with some of the major problems of his life as he sees them. What questions are left unanswered? Can you get an image of Sam as a student in high school or as a freshman in the university? List the questions you would ask if you were to interview Sam at this point in his life with the purpose of understanding him better.

FOLLOW-UP

Development toward maturity

It might be of interest now to observe how well a personal document of this kind furnishes evidence on which one can evaluate development toward maturity. We might do this by taking the characteristics mentioned by various writers and speculating as to their relative presence or absence in Sam's autobiography. Erikson

(33), for example, speaks of certain characteristics which are usually found in various periods of development. He traces development from infancy, at which time there may be established in the individual a *basic trust* in people, and events to maturity, when one shows *integrity* and *acceptance*. Some other characteristics which appear, hypothetically, in the following order, are a *sense of autonomy*, a *sense of initiative*, *industry* and *competence*, *personal identity* (an important development at adolescence), *intimacy*, and *genitality* (at adulthood).

What could we say tentatively about Sam's development toward maturity as a college freshman? Which of the above aspects of maturity are rather definitely shown in the autobiography? What further information should we have in order to make a judgment of this kind?

Another approach to this question is to examine Allport's (3) six characteristics of maturity* and to note evidence in Sam's autobiography of his development in terms of these characteristics. We will want to do this again when we see Sam at a later stage, through the eyes of an interviewer who encounters him as a middle-aged man.

An interview in early middle age

We leave Sam as a freshman in college and go now to another document which will give some more information about his college years and will tell us how he launched into the career to which he has devoted most of his adult life. We jump then to an interview with Sam as the established novelist, making one of several visits to a campus best known to him when he was an impecunious student.

The editor of a regional magazine in the community of the university Sam attended decided to run a feature article about him while he was visiting the campus as an invited assembly speaker. He was interviewed by a young, bright reporter, perhaps similar in some ways to the young Sam who wrote the autobiography reproduced above. The article presents, in addition to items relating to Sam's college days and later life, the reporter's impression of his personality. This was published twenty-five years after Sam had written the

* Allport's criteria are: (1) *Extension of the sense of self* — participation in significant spheres of human endeavor; (2) *Warm relationship to self and others* — without impeding their freedom; (3) *Emotional security* (self-acceptance) — frustration tolerance; (4) *Realistic perception, skills and assignments* — in close touch with the real world; (5) *Self-objectification* — insight and humor; (6) A *unifying philosophy of life* — containing life-direction and values.

autobiography, at a time when Sam had attained a national reputation in his profession. By this time Sam had been a guest of a President of the United States, and had written a series of articles on his craft, as well as numerous mystery novels. Sam Murray's stories had been read by millions throughout the nation and were appreciated by fellow writers.

Now Murray assumes a new role. He sits back and tells *his* story instead of writing the story of one of his characters. The young reporter who excitedly interviewed him knew him by reputation and by then had learned that he was comfortably settled economically, lived in a fine suburban home, had a loving, bright, sensible wife, and a son and daughter in high school and college. He had traveled all over the globe, was acquainted with several dozen of the best-known, contemporary international personalities and was widely respected as a real craftsman by his fellow writers.

He began his life story with events in high school, and the fragments he related from his biography were largely confined to his achievement history. Sometimes we learn as much about an individual's central personality by the topics he doesn't discuss as by those he freely relates. Is this true of Sam's story? Well, let's see what the reporter found:

Edited excerpts from a printed interview

. . . And that's what Sam Murray is: *awfully human.* He bites his fingernails, likes sailing in Long Island Sound, avoids all possible entangling red tape, treats life in a sardonic-yet-serious style, and enjoys people. He is understanding, perceptive, sensitive, and whimsical. After you've spoken to Sam Murray for three minutes, you're sure you must have met him when you were kids.

Murray began his writing career in high school.

"I had a hard time getting on the high-school paper," he said, remembering his first few tries at news-writing. "Then my big break came: I began dating the editor. She started me on writing and soon I worked up to having my first byline — on a gossip column. But we broke up the year I graduated and I got kicked off the paper."

When he graduated from high school in 1935, Sam Murray didn't know what to do, where to go, or how to start. The depression had tightened family finances and choked off Murray's plans for college. What was a guy to do then? Murray had no answer.

For the next half-year, Murray rode a bicycle through the busy 42nd Street area in nearby New York City — as a delivery boy. "But

I was getting nowhere," he said. By chance, he went back to his old high school to see whether things had changed much. "I saw my old English teacher," he said wryly, "and she suggested, with an historic inaccuracy, 'Sam, you could be another Walter Lippman!' Then, she told me that the University of _____ had the world's best school of journalism — and what was more, she thought I could get a part-time job there while I went to school."

Getting off the bus from New York in January, 1936, Murray was a very scared freshman. He was alone in what people back home had called the wilds of the Middle West, and he had no friends, money, or confidence. But he could fire Mrs. H.'s furnace; somehow, the other attributes came along rather quickly.

"At the local restaurant patronized by journalism students," Murray recalls, "everyone used to sit around and talk about what he was going to do after college. The consensus then was that no one would work for less than $50 a week — that was big money then." (His psychology instructor was earning $31 a week at the time.)

At the University, Murray showed no signs of keeping his salary ambition. "I wasn't noted for doing much work around the J-School," he said. "I was assigned to cover the police beat. Every so often I used to persuade the cops to drive me back to school. We'd go roaring up the driveway near _____ Hall, lights flashing, and sirens blaring.

"I guess I was an above-average student who somehow managed to get below-average or average grades. I was a bit of a nuisance to my superiors, I think. On dull days in the news room I used to try to liven it up. Once I sent a number-four headline to the press room — written in Greek!"

Murray also worked part-time at odd jobs. Later, in his senior year, he got a job as a part-time reporter. "In those days, you used to have to vie for the job, and when I graduated, I found a job easily — as a copy boy for a New York daily!" Salary: $15 a week — the envy of Murray's classmates.

After six months Murray was fired: "The assistant city editor now and then let me write small news stories, although I wasn't supposed to. Then one day, the city editor, who was class-conscious about editors and copy boys and a New Englander besides, found out about my writing and ordered me to stop. Suddenly I lost interest and sloughed off. In those days writers were pampered. When they sent you out for coffee, they gave you a list of the delicacies they wanted and sent you to a complete smorgasbord restaurant on 57th Street.

When they sent me out, I played the pinball machine there for a while. I was fired for being 'lazy, inattentive, and unintelligent.'

"I was about to go to work for my fiancée's mother in her retail store. At the last minute the retail business was saved; I got a call from a contact I had made. Would I work doing some rewriting odds and ends for a magazine at $25 a week? It was a raise and a chance to write." So he and his fiancée went to the big city, where they were married.

To his talent and modesty, Murray has added the restriction of taking pride only in a good job. He keeps exhaustive notes, writes slowly and painfully. "I'm a bleeder," he says. "I suffer more than anybody when I write. I'm horribly slow."

Here we see Sam Murray as he talked to an admiring young man who doubtless hoped some day to be as successful. In both of these biographical sketches we catch glimpses of Murray. What important aspects of Sam Murray's psychological development remain unexplored by his autobiography and this interview?

Dynamic trends

We have looked at Sam through his own autobiography and through the eyes of a young reporter. I knew Sam throughout his school years and have had occasional communications with him during his professional life. He seems to me to have a basic emotional security. How much of this can be attributed to *basic temperament*? How much to seemingly good relations with his immediate family and other relatives?

He suggests in the autobiography that he had received much *encouragement from his family* and that he had been the center of their attention. Later in life he once quoted his father in talking with me, and indicated that although his father did not have much education or worldly success, Sam remembers him as being a man of basic wisdom.

It appears from the information available that in early life Sam was allowed to take considerable initiative; that *his superior intelligence and verbal capacities were recognized and rewarded*; and that he came in contact with members of his own age group and made a satisfactory adjustment, except for the major conflict that he seemed to be struggling with in college. The *need for achievement* that apparently had been developed by this conflict did not, however, express itself in essentially aggressive or socially undesirable behavior. Apparently he was able to satisfy this need and to see signs pointing toward further satisfaction in the future. He was definitely not satisfied with achieving below his capacity and showed this by his persistent efforts to get into college. For some reason, he did not measure achievement in college in terms of grades or success in the limelight, but in terms of inner assurance of competency.

We also get a suggestion from his autobiography and from observations of him in school that his relationship with his peers was essentially satisfactory. He said that he was rarely the leader, but often the proud and brilliant instigator, that he had the capacity to understand people and to hold their interest and respect.

Apparently, he began early in life to search for identity. This search is reflected in his autobiography, written at eighteen years of age. He had by this time attained an amazing degree of objectivity and a broad understanding of life. Although he was able to laugh at the foibles of human beings, he retained a deep sensitivity to the individual's personality and subjective problems. He had developed an excellent sense of humor; not only could he laugh at the predicaments of other people, but he was capable of turning this humor upon himself. He was able to retain his uniqueness and to exploit the problems of life and the anxiety they produced in his own growth toward maturity. His individuality did not produce egotism. These are some of the characteristics that empirical studies have shown to be related to creativity in the individual (MacKinnon, 67; Torrence, 116).

Sam belonged to a minority religious group. It is not known whether he was reared in a neighborhood which might have nurtured a feeling of minority status. His associates at college certainly were not conscious of such feelings. Again, he may have used any anxiety caused by belonging to a minority group as motivation for development, rather than as an excuse for aggression or self-defeating hostility. His friends in college and later days were not confined to his own religious group. He dated girls of his religion and married within his own faith.

His excellent discussion of the conflict he experienced, written as a college freshman, shows his capacity to grapple with conflicts in his own life and to bring about some sort of resolution. He appeared even then to be an individual with clear-cut integrity, which he has exhibited throughout his life. He is much more responsive to his own sense of the appropriate and the meaningful than to the pressures of society. However, he is conscious of these pressures; he understands them, and apparently does not fight them directly, except through pranks and minor revolts, as suggested in the interview. His work satisfies many of his needs for adventure and companionship with individuals of similar makeup, but it also requires hours of painstaking struggle with words.

SAM: Life Trends and Relationships

What do you see in the case of Sam? Recall patterns that impressed you before turning to the questions below.

Personal characteristics

   a. What traits do you see at adolescence and middle age? What continuities and changes?
   b. How is he similar and dissimilar to adolescents you have known?
   c. Are there aspects of his development into maturity that were impressive to you?

Experiences and relationships

   a. What seemed to be the significant personal relationships in his early life, and what effects did they have?
   b. Do you see events and processes basic to his achievement motivation and creativity?
   c. What role did adolescent conflicts play in his development?

Concepts helpful in understanding Sam

   a. Maturity (3, 59)
   b. Achievement motivation (44, 68)
   c. Personal identity (32, 76)
   d. Competency motivation (3, 122)
   e. Basic temperament (30, 86)
   f. Aptitudes (41, 85)

Other concepts which may have some relevance to this case: personal documents; creativity; self-actualization; personality integration.

SAM: Comments by a Graduate Student

Sam's habitual introspective style is a basis for personality integration. How was he able to integrate the "Noel Coward" and the "Horatio Alger" schism in his early personality? Can we still discern the traces of these two styles in his present integration?

TOM

The Achieving "Regular Guy"

The case of Tom is really a vignette of a college undergraduate of normal adjustment, with defensive tendencies
and high motivation for achievement. He revealed aspects
of these characteristics in a few non-counseling interviews
and in a Sentence-Completion Blank. The case is included
here to provoke discussion about the adjustive mechanisms
of the normal individual from an American suburban
subculture, who has good study habits, effective peer relationships, and extracurricular interests.

IDENTIFICATION

Tom was not the kind of person a psychologist or counselor would
ordinarily see. He represents the student that might be sitting on
either side of you in class, that you might see in the Student Union,
in the Library, or with other students at football games. Tom, a
junior, was average in size, masculine in appearance, and well
groomed. He was energetic, highly alert, confident, friendly, and likeable, responsive to other students, attentive in lectures.

Tom's father was described as a salesman. His parents were di-
vorced; he had an older brother he admired and a married sister;
and he lived in an upper middle-class suburb of a large city. This
is all that was known about his family background.

OCCASION FOR INTERVIEW

Tom had impressed the writer, who was Tom's adviser, on first acquaintance. He usually came into the office during the registration
period, having thought clearly about some of the course choices open

to him. He was much more responsible than the average student and he readily accepted suggestions. In class there was a strong temptation to turn to him as a volunteer or an assistant in an experiment because one knew he would get the job done and would be accepted by his fellow students. The writer came to know Tom even better when he asked for recommendations to several law schools to which he was applying. Again, he arrived with the proper blanks partially filled out, a stamped envelope, and had all the needed information at his fingertips.

PERSONAL HISTORY

School and work activities

Tom belonged to a fraternity of high social status which emphasized academic achievement. He was vice-president of the Freshman class one year, represented his group in the Interfraternity Council, and was a member of the Student Government Council. In addition to this, he worked about twenty hours a week throughout his college years. He also engaged moderately in spectator activities and dating on the campus. He worked full-time each summer in a law office.

Tom's record in college was superior, mostly A's and some B's. He aspired to enter law school and knew he had to have a good record to gain admission. He applied to three well-known law schools and was accepted by all three on the basis of his test scores, grades, and letters of recommendation from teachers. He continued to be a superior student in professional school, as could be predicted from his work habits, experience working in law offices during summers, and his dedication to the profession.

In high school Tom was an above-average student; he was also an athlete and achieved all-state standing in tennis. He won a scholarship to college. He had to give up intensive participation in athletics in college in order to spend more time on his studies and peer-group activities, but he retained his strong interest in sports and physical fitness. Tom made a real effort not only to achieve in preparation for future success, which for him was a strong motivation, but also to be a member of his contemporary group. He regretted that he could not spend more time "with the fellows" but did not yield to the temptation. Although he was conscientious and hard working, he also had a good sense of camaraderie. One might often see him standing outside the room before class, talking with other students.

Problem solving and defensiveness as an adjustive pattern

Tom was a real achiever in anything he undertook; he recognized this when he filled out a *Sentence-Completion Blank* with items eliciting this information. He admired social status and prestige, thought of his abilities as limited, but was determined to reach his goal as a lawyer, working with people. He daydreamed about his future success as the most important thing in his life. He listed his best trait as *ambition*, admitting he was heading for the top. His older brother was also a hard worker and successful student, and Tom emulated him.

The writer noticed some defensiveness in Tom in several of the interviews, shown by a few minor, inconspicuous mannerisms. For example, he sometimes turned his head and looked aside when the writer discussed matters that might presumably arouse anxiety. This defensiveness was not generally noticeable when Tom went about his usual activities, but it appeared in these several interviews.

In connection with class activity, Tom had filled out the *Sentence-Completion Blank* mentioned above.* Among the outstanding self-attitudes expressed were his interests in people and in understanding them. He seemed to fear social rejection because, he said, if he felt left out, he became depressed. He also felt bad when he was afraid he wouldn't achieve what he strongly wanted. He said people are "a strange and interesting bunch." He considered himself as having numerous friends who could be trusted.

Tom was, it seemed, a good, practicing Catholic, had attended parochial school before high school, and credited "his religion" on the blank as the basic motivation for his behavior, but without identifying his religion. His major interest in school appeared to be not so much the knowledge gained, but good grades, and acceptance by a law school. In response to the sentence fragment, "I need . . . ," he said, "better grades." He thought of himself as different from the average person. He stated that he disliked politics and that his greatest fault was his "bias in life." He indicated on the blank that it was difficult to talk about his dislikes or faults. Throughout the blank, he emphasized getting good grades. The personality trends of strong drive, problem-solving attitude, and defensiveness were shown when the forty responses to the sentence fragments were classified. He had 26 problem-solving, 8 defensive, and 0 anxiety responses. This showed him to be unusually high as a problem solver and higher than average in defensiveness when compared with his group.

* See pages 251–254.

Students in Tom's class were asked to write in their own way an answer to the question, "Who or what am I?" Answers to this question differ greatly among college students, ranging from a cautious statement of objective, observable facts to a revelation of inner self, feelings, and attitudes. For example, two college students responded to the question in the following ways:

(1) I am a homo sapiens with a multitude of idiosyncrasies, but capable of learning, loving, and understanding. I am a selfish person in some things; also strive to satisfy the needs of others.

(2) I am a human being filled with curiosities, fears, anxieties; just like any other person. I live in a world of people and in a world of my own and sometimes I fail to understand either.

How did Tom answer the question of "Who or what am I?" He wrote: "I am a pre-law student, a junior in college, twenty years of age, above average in grade-points, and a member of _____ social fraternity."

This statement merely gives us the facts we may find on a card in the registrar's office, revealing nothing of his inner life except the importance of achieving prestige. This is Tom's self-identity as he revealed it to a teacher on a confidential blank. We might speculate as to whether he was sometimes more aware of his inner life as part of his identity. Perhaps, in repressing what he experienced, he was led to a preoccupation with what he might become, particularly in terms of *external achievement, social recognition,* and *prestige.*

An autobiographical project

A month or so after Tom agreed to write an autobiography, the counselor met him one day at a campus snack bar. He was with several other students and seemed relaxed, cheerful, and inclined to chat briefly. Tom voluntarily discussed the autobiography and the difficulty he was having in writing it. The counselor agreed that it was a difficult project, but pointed out that this writing would be valuable to him and possibly to a reader. Tom assured the counselor that he would continue with the project. The year ended and Tom left, presumably for law school, and the counselor heard no more from him. Doubtless Tom was experiencing an approach-avoidance conflict in connection with this project. He felt an obligation to write it. He may have seen some advantages, particularly since the counselor had said it would have value. It might be conjectured that Tom had difficulty every time he thought of writing. It was not something he looked upon with pleasure. It was an unstructured venture, even though the counselor had given him an outline. The outline, however, was very general, and the counselor had suggested he write a story of his life rather than follow the outline precisely. He had to do more than mechanically fill out a blank; he had to talk freely about his early life, his feelings, and conflicts. He probably procrastinated, particularly since he had many other responsibilities which were highly structured and of high priority in his life.* Tom may have experienced a certain amount of guilt, but probably was able to handle it fairly well with some rationalization such as "I've got other things that I must do and I'll do this later." This speculation grows from one response on the *Sentence-Completion Blank*. In completing in the sentence fragment, "This blank . . . ," he wrote, "is time-consuming."

The writer debated whether to include this case in this collection. There were so many unknowns, particularly about Tom's development. On the other hand, if Tom could be perceived as a real person, the lack of information might allow the reader to reconstruct his personal dynamics and development hypothetically, thereby having the experience of using his own skills to advance hypotheses and employ the theories about personality structure on a case in which there are many unknowns.

Tom was judged by the writer to be an average college student in his *emotional adjustment*, but possibly below average in *emotional maturity*. His associates would probably rate him above average in social and emotional adjustment and superior in other social and character traits.

It was decided to include what was known about Tom, even though the origin of his defensiveness is not clear. Tom does reflect well a common tendency in our suburban culture, and the case might, the writer thought, stimulate an evaluation of it. He was succeeding in the external world. He had a good reputation with his peers and was no doubt satisfying his parents in his achievement. He

---

* It should be added here that the writer has had similar difficulties with other individuals from whom he tried to get further information or permission to use something they had written. In all cases these individuals showed good adjustment to the world in which they were living, but in many instances they apparently had certain conflicts and anxieties which led them to resist corresponding with the writer about the biographical project.

had a promising future — he made good grades, succeeded in getting into law school, and should become a technically competent lawyer. Much of what Tom did would be approved by a large percentage of his peers. His first felt responsibility apparently was to himself and his activities. Many would agree that if there were some things in his life that were unpleasant, that he preferred not to discuss, it was just as well that he forget them. Moreover, his previous life and success seemed to validate this general practice and to discourage introspection about unsatisfactory events which may, from his viewpoint, have interfered with his currently successful activities.

Religion was an important personal factor in Tom's life. He seemed to accept his religious duties, but we have no information as to whether the theoretical position of the church on social issues had any place in his attitudes. The conflicts over the position of his religion on divorce and the action of his parents in this respect seemed to be an area of sensitivity. We do not know the religious conviction of either parent, but we might assume one parent was responsible for Tom's apparently strong conviction.

Tom's good relationship with his fellows at present and his achievement in sports and school subjects seem to reflect conditions in childhood which allowed a balance between play and school duties. Some feelings of inadequacy may have helped to bring about his strong achievement habits and compensatory striving for good grades and a professional career.

We know little about Tom's attitudes toward the opposite sex or about his view of himself as a potential suitor. His behavior on the campus indicated that he subordinated dating and casual relationships with girls to his duties. If he thought about it at all, he probably expected to become a satisfactory husband "eventually," after he achieved success in his profession. He wrote on the blank, "Marriage is far away." How deeply his parents' marital failure affected him is a matter of conjecture.

The attitudes expressed in the early part of this case were not revealed directly, but were implicit in his responses to incomplete sentences. These few lines are all we know about Tom's attitudes toward himself, his fellows, and the life around him. Although intelligent, he apparently restricted his life to sports, a career, the fraternity, and campus and religious duties, attending events pertaining to these areas and apparently ignoring all else. In this, he doubtless had a great deal of support from his contemporaries.

FOLLOW-UP

Tom's future growth as a person

What kind of person do you predict Tom will be, ten years from this writing? What do you anticipate might happen as Tom goes through his early law practice and sees the many problems that exist, particularly in socio-economic classes below his own and as movements toward greater opportunities for the underprivileged increase in our society? Will he continue to be defensive and turn away from problems to a work-filled life and assume the attitude: "If I can serve the needs of the people who employ me, I'm doing my duty"? Would Tom be a more sensitive and effective lawyer and better contemporary citizen if he were able, over a period of time, to broaden his scope? Could the autobiographical project, together with some self-initiated counseling interviews, have begun this process?

This brief and fragmentary sketch of Tom's personality allows us to raise the question about *unity* or *integration* of personality. Personal unity is gained by striving toward a goal that is important to the person and perceived as attainable. But unity is also related to a consistent, accurate self-image, or a striving for identity. No personality is wholly unified, but one might hope to find in an individual, in addition to degrees of congruence and consistent directions of development, some evidence of expanding awareness of the total self (see Allport, 3).

The unknown

A student of personality who has need to see the whole man will find many unknowns in this case. We have no information about Tom's father, whether he had an influence in Tom's life, or the strife between the two parents that led to divorce in a Catholic family. We don't know the role of other relatives — grandparents, aunts, and uncles. We have no information on the personality, emotional stability, or vocational role of either parent. There is a hint that the family break was a source of sensitivity for Tom, and that he may have tried to suppress it from conscious thought. There is also an indication, unconfirmed, that Tom lived in a "good" neighborhood, possibly surrounded by people of higher financial status.

TOM: Personality Patterns

What do you see in the case of Tom? Give your spontaneous reactions before turning to the questions below.

Outstanding characteristics

    a. Can you visualize Tom as a person; what *traits* would allow you to recognize him?

    b. To what extent do you think he *saw himself* as he was?

    c. Why is Tom the kind of person you would find either *congenial* or uninteresting?

    d. What aspects of Tom would you like to *know more* about?

Important persons, events and trends

    a. What *characteristics, events, and persons* do you see as highly influential in Tom's development?

    b. Did you see *trends* in Tom's life that were not highlighted in this write-up?

    c. What *information is not furnished* that you would like to have to understand him? You may find it interesting to try filling in the gaps through speculation.

    d. Tom resisted interference in his life. What specific influences or resources for *further growth* do you think Tom needs? How might they be presented so that he will utilize them?

    e. What conflicts and anxieties would you conjecture are influential in Tom's life, and what are the *personal resources or strengths* which may allow him to resolve them?

Concepts helpful in understanding Tom

    a. Defense mechanisms (22, 101)

    b. Authoritative influences (29, 97)

    c. Suburban culture; conformity (38, 47)

    d. Masculine and feminine models in his life (62, 79)

    e. Relationship (conjectured) with parents and older models (62, 112)

Other concepts which may have some relevance to this case: suppression; approach-avoidance conflict; affiliative needs; personality integration.

DICK

The Self-Centered Lover

This is the case of a masculine-looking collegian with love problems. He was the only son of a doting mother. He had a supportive relationship with the counselor during college, but with no depth therapy. Every now and then throughout a twenty-year period Dick communicated with the counselor. He returned for a long session of marital counseling fifteen years after graduation. An evaluation of his later financial and social success is given, together with complications in his relationships with his wife and mistress. Excerpts from conferences and letters throughout the years are presented.

IDENTIFICATION

When the counselor first met Dick, he was a nineteen-year-old college sophomore. Although he was not heavy, he had an athletic physique and bearing. He had been active in high-school sports and enjoyed this phase of his life very much. On the whole, one would judge him above average in appearance. His most outstanding physical characteristics were a pug nose and black curly hair. Despite his masculine appearance, he was rather mild-mannered and soft-spoken. He had a very convincing social manner, particularly with adults. In conversation, his manner was direct and he talked with warmth and confidence.

EARLY COUNSELING

Occasion for the first interview

Dick was referred by his public speaking instructor; the instructor was concerned about Dick's depressions. He felt that Dick had an

277

emotional problem that he was not qualified to handle and, there-fore, suggested that Dick see the psychologist connected with the Student Health Service. Dick took the suggestion readily; he seemed to react to the psychologist as he might have to an older brother or an uncle.

Most of the counseling was essentially *directive* in nature.* The counselor apparently played the role Dick expected of him, and Dick was highly cooperative. He filled out a *Pre-Interview Blank* and kept notes on his feeling and activities during the early counseling period. The counselor apparently felt a need to get acquaintance ratings. Although Dick was very open and frank, the counselor needed to know more about how his contemporaries viewed him.

It was not difficult for Dick to start talking. He came to the point of the interview immediately. He stated that he was very much in love with a girl who was attending a neighboring girls' college; she seemed to like him very much at times but at other times he seemed to be only one of several. She had told him that her parents were putting pressure on her to continue dating a boy back home to whom she had been engaged. He really didn't know how she felt about this boy, and this was one of his concerns. He says, "When I am with her, she seems very affectionate and responsive, but I have never been able to find out whether I am the most important one in her life or not, and lately I have been quite depressed because I feel that we are about to have a breakup." Apparently he interrogated her at great length to find out her real attitude toward him. He said that no other girl could possibly take her place; she was the one girl for him.

He talked about his own family background. He was an only child. His father was in his late fifties and his mother was about twenty years younger. He said they were devoted to him. His father had suffered heavy losses in the depression, and his financial status was very poor at present. His mother held a full-time job because of their financial need.

Other interviews

In the second interview, Dick was even more depressed than during the first. He seemed to be immobilized. Now that he was about to

---

* This is in contrast to client-centered, or nondirective counseling. In directive counseling the counselor plays a more active role. See the Introduction for a dis-cussion of the early period of the author's counseling experiences.

lose his girl he didn't feel like doing anything; his education had little meaning for him. He couldn't study. He acted as though he wanted to make his problem someone else's responsibility. During the early part of the interview, the counselor listened to him as he poured out his feelings. Later, the counselor frankly stated that Dick seemed too passive about the matter; this was not the only girl in the world. The counselor used Dick's own statements to illustrate that he was preoccupied with his own negative feelings and spent his time daydreaming about what might have been rather than getting into campus activities and using some of his many assets.

Before leaving this session Dick said, "You know, as long as I have a girl who is affectionate and who loves me, I never think about sex. However, this summer I didn't have a girl and I was fooling around with another girl who had a pretty bad reputation." He told this apparently expecting approval from the counselor, who suggested that it would be wiser to develop a fully satisfying relationship than to get involved in some activity which would produce guilt.

Through four interviews Dick continued in the same vein. The counselor attempted to challenge him to use his resources and turn outward rather than brooding over his inward feeling. Dick began reading books, and he talked about them in the interviews. In the third interview he said, "I met my girlfriend in a nearby city and my cousin took us to an expensive restaurant. I almost married her but then I realized I couldn't support her and I didn't want to be a ward of her father." He said, "All my problems would be solved if I had $50,000." The counselor tried at this time to show him how passive and dependent his attitude was.

The matter of "the girl" came to a climax three months after Dick first saw the counselor. She finally told him that she had been lying to him all along, that she really loved the boy her parents favored; much of what she had told him about her parents' obligation to the boy's family and their insistence on her going with him had not been true. As Dick talked to the counselor about his disillusionment, he wept openly. He stated that it had been a long time since he had cried like this; he was deeply hurt and felt that he couldn't give up the girl. His only feeling was vindictiveness toward his rival. One reason for the girl's frank confession was that the rival was to visit the campus. Dick said he felt like telling the boy "a thing or two" about the girl, implying that what he would tell would be damaging to her character.

Counselor's written impression

The counselor made the following notes after Dick left:

This fellow is highly egocentric. He can't understand how this girl could have signed herself in the letters to him as his wife, indicating how much she loved him, and at the same time be in love with another boy in her home town. Apparently there is very little he has thought of or daydreamed about in the last few weeks except this girl. He says he doesn't get along with most girls and that is why this attachment (which the girl seemed also to want) was so important for him.

Supportive activities

The counselor arranged with a dormitory counselor in a nearby girls' school to get a date for Dick.* He had appointments with Dick on several consecutive days while he was going through this period of great disturbance. Dick continued in his cynical and "disillusioned" mood for several weeks; he began to read widely, apparently as a substitute for study. Shaw's *Man and Superman* and *The Arts* by Van Loon are examples of his choices. He said he was beginning to think "There is no such thing as morality, only conventionality; and there is no such thing as kindness, merely sentimentality." While on this culture bender, he talked about the number of books he planned to read. He also decided to try out for dramatics. He had been in plays and skits in high school and had been encouraged by the dramatics coach.

The counselor supported Dick in his reading and urged him to get involved in projects outside of himself. The counselor had also given him letters to several people on the campus who might help him get part-time employment. In a few weeks Dick returned with even greater financial problems. He had been spending beyond the allowance sent by one of his relatives and had accumulated some debts. Dick admitted to spending approximately 20 per cent more than he was getting, but he could see no way to reduce his expenses. As he detailed his expenses, however, many of them were luxuries. After this interview he decided to get another part-time job, and this arrangement seemed quite satisfactory to him and to his employer. Among the other activities suggested to him was keeping notes on

---

* Some professional psychologists would question whether this is appropriate behavior for the counselor. They would insist that the counselor does not engage in manipulating the environment of the individual.

the amount of time he spent in study and in the other activities that were necessary to meet his obligations. He kept this record for three or four days. One time, because he had to report his time expenditures to the counselor, he spent one whole evening studying; he reported that it produced a very good feeling.

At the end of the year Dick found a job in a nearby city; he apparently was successful at it because he received a raise. The job entailed a certain amount of physical work. Dick felt the work helped him to develop in this respect during the summer and this pleased him. The next year he held several part-time jobs successfully. He wrote the counselor periodically throughout the summer and continued seeing the counselor when he returned to school.

Information from Pre-Interview Blank

Dick was pursuing the electrical engineering curriculum. He had lived most of his life in Detroit. He stated that his father had once been in the upper four hundred in wealth in that city. Dick's score on the *Ohio Psychological Test* (given to all freshmen to obtain some index of their college ability) was in the 87th percentile in terms of college freshmen.* But he had been in the lowest percentile in terms of grade achievement in high school — 445th in a class of 450. This disparity would prompt some to classify him as an *underachiever*. His grades in college varied from superior to failure; he admitted that it was rare for him to apply himself properly and to study well. His study periods were frequently interrupted with daydreams.

He engaged in no formal or regular extracurricular activities. He did spend considerable time in bull sessions with other students and hanging around the campus cafes. He dated more frequently than the typical student and did practically no reading. Now and then he would pick up an article, but he had never read a book completely. Despite the fact that he was pursuing an engineering curriculum, he thought he would be more successful as a politician or as an executive in industry. He was frank to state that he was not coming to college for the prestige but as a means of getting better employment than he could get without a college education. He realized that he was quite effective in dealing with people, that he spoke well, and he admitted feeling confident in his social relationships.

He prided himself on being highly intelligent. Money was very

* This means that 87 per cent of the individuals taking the test were below this score.

important in his life. He said, "I have seen both the plush and the poverty sides of life. I have had the silver spoon yanked out of my mouth when I was just beginning to enjoy it and needed it most." He confessed that he had wasted his time in high school, but he enjoyed being "one of the fellows" and participating in athletics. He began dating early, and he grinned over the fact that he chose girls from financially comfortable families but rarely had enough money to buy them a soda or take them to even an inexpensive movie. He had some rich relatives whom he enjoyed visiting; theirs was the kind of life he wanted to experience.

Self-ratings

In rating his attitudes he gave himself a *three* on a ten-point scale in terms of *happiness* — ten being the highest degree. He rated his *mental integration*, or consistency of purpose, and his *stability of attitudes* as seven; his *present adjustment* to his environment as *five;* and his *outlook for the future* as *three.*

In checking items on a blank indicating areas in which he at some time had felt sensitive, he underlined *complexion* and *family economic and social status.* He also underlined *religion* but added the remark that he "didn't give a diddle-de-damn about it."

He said his major problems fell into two categories; one was love, the other was his low economic status. He said he couldn't feel or be normal when he was involved in a love affair. He was disturbed over the fact that "falling in love" with a girl could upset him so much and gain so much control over his thinking and feelings. Yet, he didn't see how he could change this.

When he was given a list of *personality traits,* he underlined the following among his outstanding ones:* persistent and individualist (double-underscored), self-confident, restless, easy-going, friendly, often procrastinates, sometimes too serious, egocentric, and sometimes easily hurt. This is compatible with the items he checked on another blank containing *psychoneurotic symptoms.* Here he indicated that his feelings were easily hurt, that ideas ran through his head so he could not sleep, that his feelings alternated between happiness and sadness, that he daydreamed frequently, that he got discouraged easily, that he was easily moved to tears, was frequently in low spirits, experienced periods of loneliness, was often in a state of excitement, and felt self-conscious about his personal appearance.

* This is the list of traits which are a part of the *Pre-Interview Blank.* See McKinney (74), pages 385–386.

In addition, he was generally self-confident about his abilities and was not burdened by a sense of remorse.

In discussing his family, he mentioned a wealthy older cousin who had been an outstanding success and who was sending him the regular allowance which enabled him to go to college. The cousin took him to fashionable restaurants whenever Dick visited him.

Dick reported that he had very few dislikes, that he was always daydreaming, and that usually his daydreams were about what might be rather than what was. His mother was a Catholic, and she had tried to bring him up as one; but at the age of seventeen he broke away and now feels he has no compelling reasons to believe or not believe, although he thinks religion is important in maintaining morals.

Ratings by peers

Although Dick was given several rating blanks to give to friends and acquaintances, only two completed rating blanks reached the counselor. One was from an acquaintance of short duration, and the other from Dick's roommate. The acquaintance of short duration rated Dick either poor or well below average in almost all the traits considered — namely, *efficiency, emotional stability, social adjustment, appearance,* and *motivation.* The roommate rated him *below* average in social adjustment, leadership, integrity, and motivation. He added, "Dick is too unconcerned about neatness. His mind is too easily distracted from schoolwork by trivial things, and he is too concerned about this girl." The raters agreed with each other exactly in the adjectives and phrases they chose to describe Dick. They both thought him to be an individualist, friendly but moody, easily distracted, stubborn, egocentric, easily discouraged, and jealous.

THE SECOND YEAR OF COUNSELING

A year after Dick first came to the counselor, he made another special appointment and said, "I have forgotten all about the girl that caused me so much emotional disturbance last year. I have a new girl now. She was married when she was fifteen, but has never lived with her husband. It was a secret marriage which was later annulled. She is from a broken family, and I have been seeing a great deal of her recently. I met her mother, and her mother seems to like me." At the time he was concerned about what her relationship had been with her former husband. Apparently he was quizzing her on details of her married life. Most of his curiosity seemed to the counselor preliminary to establishing physical relations with her. The counselor did not encourage him in this direction but listened to him as he talked.

In a few months Dick came to an interview quite agitated. He had been physically intimate with the girl. It was not clear from the conference what her medical problem was, but she had developed continuous vaginal bleeding. He had some guilt about his own role in this bleeding, and in fact was quite ambivalent toward the girl. He seemed to like her, but there were some feelings of guilt and some defensive doubts as to her character. At times he felt that she was "playing him for a fool and really didn't love him"; at other times, because she was solicitous of his welfare and gave him little gifts, he thought she really loved him.

He continued to ask for appointments, and the interviews concerned his relationship with this girl. Apparently the intimacy continued. From his comments, she seemed to be as much involved in the continuation of it as he, but his relationship with her was rather stormy. They argued over various matters. He had discovered that she was dating other boys, and he was worried about her relationship with them. He again reported the same *swings of mood between elation and depression* that had occurred the previous year. At certain times the girl seemed to love him very much and to send him warm letters and at other times she seemed quite cold. Once he waited outside the boarding house where she lived until after her date came out. He got in the car with the other boy as he was leaving her house, introduced himself, and suggested that they go have a beer. The two boys talked rather congenially. When they compared notes on their physical relationship with the girl, they found they were highly similar, but not conventional. He was still strongly attracted to the girl, but realized the attraction was mostly physical and not a response to her as a loved person. He was beginning to realize now that she probably did not have a very good reputation. His own guilt and his disgust with her grew, yet he felt compelled to see her.

During the next two or three months, Dick wrote the counselor whenever he was away from the University on short holidays. He seemed to be very appreciative of the emotional support that he was getting from the interviews. The counselor attempted to accept him as an individual who had certain assets but who lacked stability.

Counselor's further impression

The counselor wrote in his notes during this period:

> The prognosis of this boy is cloudy. I certainly wouldn't bet any money on his progress. Apparently he was greatly pampered in early life and has always gotten his own way. In many respects he is highly superficial. He often makes a good impression because of his easy social manner. At times, following a counseling session, he will study for a while and apply himself at his job; he has gotten several pay increases. Then he gets involved in some shady relationship concerning the violation of University rules. If he becomes a stable, consistent individual who develops maturity and achieves some measure of worldly success, it will surprise me.

Dick was one of the counselor's most appreciative clients. He was constantly reiterating his thanks for the sessions. When he was in financial difficulties, the counselor gave him a job doing some odd jobs in his own home. At this time he met the counselor's children. They grew fond of him as a person, and he seemed to enjoy them.

Letters from Dick

A letter from Dick about this time included these statements:

> Please consider me always your friend and in return I promise you that I will make every effort to improve and effect the changes that you suggested. Perhaps some day I can make you proud of me. I will try my very best. I am going to close with my sincere wishes for everlasting happiness to you all. Affectionately yours.

During the same summer a letter of despair came from Dick:

> My dad is very ill. He has had a stroke and is bedridden. I learned in your course that environment molds a person's mind and character, or something to that effect. I can fully realize how an unfavorable environment can practically poison a man's mind against everything his culture and government stands for. To me, these last two weeks have been a living hell. Day after day I see wops who can't even speak English making $70 a week [a very good salary in 1941] in defense plants just because they hold union cards. Then I tramp the streets and come home

to a dingy, hot, stuffy, little fifth-floor walk-up apartment and see a table full of unpaid bills and see my father, who at one time could buy and sell most of the people in Detroit, helpless in bed and my mother out working to support us. Doc, a fellow can take just so much of that and then money means everything* to him. When he can't get it one way, he will get it another. I am going to keep trying to live and earn my money the right way, but there are times when I can see why so many boys have taken the wrong path and then I realize that the only philosophy is to think of oneself. Of one thing I am sure — my kids and family will never have to live under these circumstances and I'll get power and money someday if I have to go to the ends of the earth to get it. All the psychology in preaching about a nice income and family and interesting work is fine, if it's lived and experienced, but it is getting so objectionable around here that I don't ever even think about having a date any more because I can't be sure of a clean shirt or twenty cents for two cokes. . . . You really have no idea how much better your letter made me feel. It is really swell to know that someone thinks you are worth something. With kindest personal regards to yourself and the family, I remain your friend and admirer as ever. Dick.

Do we get a view of some of Dick's predominant values from this letter? Does he show the importance of success and money? Can we see in his letter his attitude toward people? Are they respected as persons or manipulated for one's own purpose?

Military service

Within a few months after he wrote this letter, Dick had decided to enter the armed forces. He phoned the counselor for a letter of recommendation; he told the counselor he didn't have enough money to call the dean of his college and asked the counselor if he would do it. The counselor agreed to write a letter of recommendation and also to write to the dean, telling him about the phone call.

Instead of writing a recommendation, the dean wrote in the following manner:

Mr. _____'s grades are poor indeed, so poor as to bring about his dismissal; but it is not his grades that make me refuse to recommend him.

* Emphasis mine.

You speak of his unused potential. I assume you mean potential for worthwhile and purposeful activities. Probably you do not refer to his potential for cheating in examinations or for telling lies or for breaking promises — all of which he has and uses.

Of course, I would not question your right to recommend the devil himself to the Army. The Army already has a few and I realize that Mr. _____ may become a good officer. Such things do happen and I admire that quality in you which fits you to deal with the misfits in our social organization. More power to you — so long as I don't have to support your recommendation.

Dick wrote several times while he was in the service. Apparently he enjoyed his experiences very much and met many women. He said he was somewhat disillusioned at the behavior of some of the wives who stayed home while their husbands were away, and very frankly admitted that he played a role in helping them to misbehave.

LATER COUNSELING

Marriage and business success

Two years passed before the counselor heard from Dick again, after he was out of the service. The communication was in the form of a long telephone call from the West Coast, during which Dick brought the counselor up to date. He had been in the Air Force and made a good record as a pilot. He was going with a very stable girl — the kind he thought he should have as a wife — but he had delayed the marriage several times because he was concerned about his capacity to make a good husband. He said, "I have a hard time keeping my eyes from straying, and this might not be too good for married life. I have a very good job." (The job, incidentally, paid about one thousand dollars a year more than the counselor was making.) The counselor accepted Dick's concern as a real one and encouraged him to talk at length about the problem as he saw it.

Dick's higher education totaled two and a half years at two universities, plus whatever training led to his commission in the Air Force, but his academic record would bar him from entering college again. He eventually married the girl, did well on his job, and finally went into partnership with another man in a commercial real estate venture in a large city on the West Coast. He was reasonably successful but felt that he could make more money on his own, since his record of sales far outstripped his partner's. The separation was amicable, and Dick was more successful in business for himself, as he had expected. Over a period of ten years he netted something like $20,000 a year (a very good income around 1950), became the father of two beautiful girls, and built a lovely home in the suburbs.

Extra-marital involvement

His work kept him away from home a great deal and during one of his many excursions, he met a girl about fifteen years younger than himself with whom he fell madly in love. The affair went on without physical consummation, since the girl had strong religious scruples, and her mother, though friendly to Dick, was aware of the irregularity of the relationship. Dick said he was very much in love with the girl but he admitted that one of the major factors in the whole affair was her youth. He made the following *narcissistic* remark: "To think that a girl so young and beautiful would fall for me, and here I am heading definitely into the middle-age bracket, with thinning hair and a developing paunch. I know I haven't been involved enough with my family and this is part of the problem; but the temptation to be with her as often as I could to take her places, mostly on errands that she had to make, and to have her reciprocate my love just swept me off my feet. I don't think too much of my wife and family. I have continued to think and act as I did before I was married."

Dick arranged for a long counseling session, which occurred twelve years after the last one he had before leaving college. The twelve years did not seem to have changed Dick's appearance very much. He was a little heavier, slightly calmer, and on the whole, more mature. He had experienced a number of successes and had even earned a military decoration. He had held several good jobs and had assumed much more responsibility than the counselor had ever anticipated he could. He had encountered some financial problems but had dealt with them quite well, and at this time he was not only in an established business that was yielding a very good yearly income but he also was respected as an aggressive entrepreneur and was given responsibilities by the other businessmen in the town where he lived. He stated that he still felt a little insecure because he had not finished college. He admitted that his life, during the war and after, before he got married, contained many episodes of which he was not proud. Most of them involved women.

In describing his wife, he said: "From almost every standpoint she is a perfect wife. She is highly efficient — too much so. She runs a house well, she has good taste, and she is a good cook and a good mother to my children. I really haven't been as close to my children as I should, but this crisis has made me realize how important they are to me. In fact, my wife has noticed that since she has taken the children and gone to live with her parents, I have been more attentive to the little ones. My wife went to her parents' home when I told her I was thinking about asking for a divorce. Now I don't know what to do, and there is no one I can turn to except you. I don't want your advice. I really want to talk the whole matter over and see your reaction to this. In a way I know what your reaction will be because I know what is the sensible thing to do — namely, to keep my family together and to be a good husband, which I haven't been. However, my wife doesn't mean to me the same thing that these amorous affairs have. She is so cold compared with this girl, and she takes me for granted. In many respects she doesn't need me, and what I need from her she doesn't seem to be able to give me. I know I am egotistical and need to have a woman make a fuss over me, and I don't get this from my wife. This girl is very passionate and also very moral. She is as disturbed about this as I am. Her mother saw that we were falling in love and sent her to the East Coast; but I managed to have business out there and saw her again. She is, in many respects, more responsible than I am and has made it very clear that it will have to be marriage or nothing. But the closer I come to marriage the more I begin to wonder whether marriage with her wouldn't settle down to be the same kind of life my present marriage is. I can see that we would have disagreements" (a perspective of some value).

"I am also concerned about the age difference. She is so young in all respects and I am beginning to feel less like a young man every day. My business life is very important to me and I never think of romance during the day. From one standpoint it seems ridiculous to leave my wife and family for some young girl; but when I am with her, I can't think of anything else.

"I said that this girl was moral, but once we had too much to drink and we became physically intimate. Both of us were guilt-ridden for a long time. I know that my wife and my children need me for the children's normal development, so you can see how I am torn. The physical side of love is very important to me and not so important to my wife. Yet, on the other hand, if I did the wrong thing now, it would bother me. I should say that I have been faithful to my wife all during the time we were married, except this one episode I mentioned. I know I have hurt her. It would be very easy for me to get a divorce now. We are separated and all I would have to do is phone the lawyer and say, 'Go ahead.' This girl's mother wants the girl to be happy and if we can be happy, she is perfectly willing to give our marriage her blessing.

"In talking this over with my wife, she said she realized that she had been giving more time to the children than to me and she realized that she had certain shortcomings. She saw I would have to make up my mind as to what I wanted."

The counselor listened to Dick's story for several hours. During that time, the counselor broke in here and there to point out the realities of the situation, some of which Dick saw. Toward the end of the conference, Dick said that much of his reaction was vanity and preoccupation with the physical aspects of the relationship. He knew that he would have regrets, particularly as his children grew older and as various conflicts would arise in the new marriage. The counselor, by his comments, emphasized the importance of maintaining the present marriage rather than succumbing to this new infatuation.

Dick was highly appreciative of the session and sent the counselor a handsome gift, since he said he must regard this as a professional consultation. He dismissed his lawyer, reunited with his wife, and told the girl of his decision.

FOLLOW-UP

Ten years later Dick crossed paths with the counselor once again. He was passing through his old college town on a business venture and stopped in for an hour's chat. He said the girl for whom he had almost broken up his marriage had since been married but was not happy with her husband. She had phoned him once in the interval and told him she still loved him. He said this call shook him for a little while. But what bothered him most was that the call made him realize that he had not changed very much, because since her departure the experience with her had been almost duplicated with another young woman — this time a married woman. Again he had great feelings of guilt and some concern over involving not only another woman but also her husband. Neither her husband nor Dick's wife knew about the affair directly. This woman insisted, as the girl had, that if the affair were to continue, marriage had to be the ultimate aim, and Dick was faced with the same choice once again. It made him think seriously. He was becoming more involved in his children and more fond of them; he realized that, although he worked very hard to make his business a success, he did not make the same effort toward making his marriage succeed. Dick said, "If I worked as hard on my marriage as I did on my business, it would be far more successful than it is. Of course, there are some factors that are unsatisfactory; my wife is still not attractive to me physically. I know that I am very vain and self-concerned, and that these extramarital experiences boost my ego. It is almost as though I need them. On the other hand, I know that I can't become involved in a scandal, I don't want to give up my family, and it's kind of dangerous sneaking out the back door as the husband puts his key in the front door.

"My wife and I have taken some trips together and they have been pleasant, but they don't begin to mean as much to me as these escapades. I am beginning to realize that I am definitely no longer a young man, yet physically I feel very young. As I thought about this matter not so long ago, I began to realize that my mother played a role in all of this. My mother gave me the sort of attention that these women give me, and most of the women that I have been attracted to are physically and temperamentally very much like my mother. My mother is very feminine and very warm and so are these girls. I realize I am getting older and less attractive, so when one of these girls finds me attractive and is willing to give up the kind of life she is living for me, it is very tempting. However, I know what is best for me, and that is the kind of life I am going to try to live" (another valuable perspective).

Evaluative trends

We know relatively little about Dick's father, but from the information we have, he apparently was a busy and successful man who failed during the depression, in business and subsequently in health. Undoubtedly, from his many comments, Dick respected his father, but their relationship was not so close as that between Dick and his mother. His youngish mother was the important person in his life and apparently she was very indulgent. Can we reconstruct hypothetically the life Dick may have lived as an only child, a bright, outgoing, good-looking, healthy, and well-dressed child with a doting, wealthy mother? There is some question whether Dick ever had to meet any moral and ethical standards in the home; he seemed to be allowed to do and be almost anything he wanted.

He found great success in his contacts with other people. He impressed people by his easy social manner and his "public" role as an attractive man. He seemed, at least to certain people, to be very warm and acceptably responsible. He certainly had won the emotional support of the counselor and, for a time, of his dean and teachers; but in such matters as grades and academic responsibilities, he usually failed those who had high expectations of him. He had entered the kind of business in which he could become a success. He apparently was an excellent one-shot salesman, and in his warm, convincing way was able to excel most of his competitors.

Dick was, at least rationally, aware of certain guiding standards of conduct; but when there was a choice between his own strong needs and these standards, impulsive actions prevailed. Dick was not without guilt, but this guilt usually occurred after the action. The memory of past guilt did not seem to guide his future behavior.

In terms of Freud's thinking, we might say that Dick's behavior often followed the *pleasure* principle rather than the *reality* principle. However, do we see a growth with time toward greater *maturity*, *responsibility*, and greater *realism* as we survey the events in his life that are known?

DICK: Impressions and Reactions

What do you see in the case of Dick? Give your spontaneous reactions to Dick before turning to the questions below.

How can Dick be described to another person? In doing this, you may want to include the following considerations:

   a. What would be your *general impression* of Dick if you were in the counselor's position?

   b. What were the major themes occurring through his life — personality traits that are predominant or needs that are strong and persistent?

   c. What frustrations or conflicts, and the manner in which he dealt with them, seemed to have an important bearing on Dick's life? Would Dick be the same sort of person he is now had his family not suffered financial reverses, or was blaming his unfortunate financial position merely a rationalization?

What are some of the most striking characteristics of Dick's interpersonal life?

   a. Can you infer the sort of parents Dick might have had?

   b. You may have been struck by the frequency with which feminine characteristics appeared in Dick's life. What significance
does this have?

   c. Considering Dick's relationship to the counselor, does it appear
to be different from or an extension of other interpersonal relationships?

   d. To what extent is Dick, in his developing years, ethnocentric in
not being able to accept people different from himself, in social
position or ethnic origins?

Concepts helpful in understanding Dick

   a. Self-awareness with implications for present or future action
(3, 81)

   b. Classical Oedipal theme of psychoanalysis (47)

   c. The search for interpersonal security (47)

   d. Importance of acknowledging some basic value in all men
(93)

Other concepts which may have some relevance to this case: underachievement; ambivalence, mood swing; pleasure principle; reality
principle; responsibility; narcissism; manic-depressive tendencies;
insight; maturity.

DICK: Comments by a Graduate Student

I agree that Dick was egocentric, passive, dependent, etc. — perhaps for somewhat different reasons than the writer has noted. We
see that the girl continued the relationship even though she loved the
other guy. Is it not possible that the reason the relationship continued so long was that Dick — by all his brow-beating, interrogation
of the girl, protestations, etc. — made himself out to be such a dependent creature that the girl would have felt too guilty to be blunt
with him and call it quits.

Note the books that Dick drifted to. They are depressing and
nihilistic, but very existentially oriented. Man finds himself in a
world that's no damn good and he *alone* must create *for himself*

existential meanings. Dick seems to have had an unconscious wisdom here in the way he went about ego-reintegration.

A part-time job mentioned in one of the interviews might have been superfluous had the counselor pointed out the luxury spending.

Dick's flitting around from one casual activity to another was a way of preventing himself from grasping existential experiences. Also, in making someone else (girl friend or counselor) responsible for his happiness, he is surrendering his own existential responsibility. Man is responsible for his own destiny, the existential writers tell us.

What can be said of a person who is not able to find gratification in stable, married heterosexual relations, but must consort with girls of poor reputation (while he was younger), or married women (later in life)? By having these secretive, degrading experiences, he is destructive to women and jeopardizes his own life. He cannot enjoy sex at home, yet he is a sexual virtuoso outside the home. Could he be subconsciously equating his own marital home and wife with his parental home and mother? The classic analytic Oedipal theme may throw some light on this. The young boy's growth to maturity (achievement of genitality) is largely defined, within psychoanalytic theory, in terms of his resolution to forsake his symbolic desire for sexual contact with his mother. The residue of this desire sometimes continues unconsciously into adult life, as evidenced by the person's marriage to a woman who either resembles his mother or is diametrically opposite to her.

Dick has maintained a unity of theme and integration throughout life (illustrating what Allport has maintained in theory). He is essentially the same person years later as he was during therapy — the major difference being an *added dimension* of control.

MAX

The Self-Killer

Max's story presents a very rare case of amnesia for all self-oriented memories. Both hypnosis and narcosis were used to gain access to repressed experiences, and differential memory for various kinds of experience was recovered. The treatment was intensive but of brief duration because Max was transferred by the military authorities to his home area before he regained complete recall. A letter from Max after the amnesic period gives his view of the experience.

IDENTIFICATION

Max was a red-headed, freckled, slight, energetic, nineteen-year-old. He was an Air Force trainee, stationed in a special training unit at a large state university during the concluding phases of World War II.

OCCASION FOR INTERVIEW

This young man came to the attention of a clinical psychologist* in the Student Health Service of the University when he awakened from a period of unconsciousness and reported that he did not know who he was or where he was, and remembered little of his past. When the psychologist visited him on the ward, he saw a smiling young fellow who did not seem very disturbed over the fact that,

---

* A clinical psychologist is one usually trained in a medical setting and often works as part of a psychiatric team. His competency includes diagnosis and psychotherapy. He differs from the counseling psychologist not only in the setting in which he works, but in the fact that his clients are usually more anxiety-ridden and emotionally disturbed.

when he shaved that morning, the face he saw in the mirror was completely strange to him. He could not remember any of his personal life. He recognized his rank in the service, but he did not know what city he was in or why he was there. He had been on the campus only a few days but had gone through the usual registration and examination. His performance on college aptitude tests was in the upper fifth in terms of college freshmen; he gave evidence of alertness and generally high motivation.

His roommate, who had known him before the amnesia, furnished the attending physician with a number of facts about his early life. While visiting Max, the roommate had to introduce himself because he was a stranger to Max at this point. During the visit he acquainted Max with some of his background, including the fact that he grew up in San Francisco and lived on a certain street. Max did not recognize these facts. However, he could conceive that they were true and quite readily recalled non-personal memories. He knew about certain common events that had been published in recent newspapers and magazines concerning economic and political matters and could do algebra problems. He was told that he had played in a high-school band; when handed an instrument, he played with some competence.

COUNSELING EVENTS

Events immediately preceding the amnesia

Max's roommate was able to supply some of the information pertaining to his present condition. Max had been stationed in a hospital and worked as an orderly just prior to his transfer to the campus several weeks before the amnesia. Apparently a patient of whom he was quite fond had died. The story Max told his roommate a few days previous to the amnesia, when he received a letter from the mother of the deceased boy, ran something as follows: The patient, apparently a young man about Max's age, asked him to raise the window by his bed. As Max raised the window, the patient began choking. When Max rushed back to the bedside, the patient grabbed him by the arm and then died, holding onto Max.

This was a highly traumatic experience for Max. He told his roommate he had to be pried loose from the patient.

A week or so after the patient's death, before Max was transferred to the University, he was on the beach near the hospital. Someone, apparently a friend, came up to him and grabbed him by the arm rather vigorously. Max became quite emotional at this moment, trembled, and felt weak. After the transfer the letter came from the dead boy's mother. It arrived on Friday — just a day before Max came to the hospital as an amnesiac. According to the roommate, the mother in her state of sorrow asked Max to describe her son's death. Max delayed answering the letter on that day, and tried again on Saturday to write it, without success. Instead, he wrote a letter home, after which he lost consciousness and had to be taken to the hospital. When he regained consciousness in the hospital, he was unable to recall anything preceding his collapse. He told one of his friends that he had bumped his head on Friday, but he was not concerned about it. Another of his acquaintances said that he had mentioned having a similar episode once before; however, his mother later denied vehemently that this had happened.

We do not know what death meant to Max, what previous experience he had had with death, or what his attitudes toward it were. We do not know what his relationship was with the patient who died, except that he expressed a positive attitude toward him. It is not known whether he had identified with this patient or, if so, how he felt about this identification. No information is available as to whether he had feelings of guilt, either because of this attachment or because he felt he had neglected the patient while caring for him. We do know, however, that the experience of this boy's death was one of the most disturbing experiences in Max's life.

First interview with psychologist

It was two days after the collapse that the psychologist first saw Max. Arrangements had already been made by the Air Force to move the boy to a military hospital. The psychologist knew, therefore, that he would have limited contact with Max. As it happened, Max remained at the university hospital about ten days and then was peremptorily moved by the military to a hospital within driving distance of his home. The psychologist worked intensively with him during this ten-day period, with the results described below.

Before Max came in for an interview, the psychologist perused the literature and obtained as much information as he could on this kind of amnesia, and he *hypothesized* that it was functional. He also read material on frontal lobe injuries to see how the behavior of brain-damaged individuals differed from that of amnesic individuals. He reviewed the studies on narcosynthesis in which sodium pentothal had been used with effective results. He decided to see if Max could be readily hypnotized and if so, to use this procedure, after an initial preparatory interview.

When Max entered the office for the first scheduled session, he jokingly said, "Well, I don't have a friend in the world. I have just met my parents and I swear I have never seen them before. It was upsetting to them. I saw them coming eagerly toward the bed with outstretched arms. There was a heavy-set, middle-aged, bald-headed man and an equally heavy-set, gushy, middle-aged woman. I felt a little uneasy when they began to embrace me and I said to them, 'I presume you are my parents.' This reduced my mother to sobs and the gent that was with her, my father, began to comfort her. He seems like an awfully nice man and I am sure I'll get along well with him. My mother is a little too emotional, at present anyway. They have told me a lot about myself. My father has written out the names of all my friends and now I am beginning to get letters from some of them, which is really puzzling and disturbing. How am I going to write to these people? Many of them apparently played with me in a high-school band and a few of them sound real wacky! I surely had a lot of interesting friends. My mother seems quite upset that I don't remember anything about home or my grandparents."

This interview was brief; the psychologist merely confirmed the amnesia status and allowed Max to talk freely about his plight. He asked a few questions which revealed that Max had amnesia for all personal memories but excellent retention of general information.

Memory under hypnosis

After this successful office interview, which established a good relationship and some understanding of Max's personality, it was decided to try hypnosis as an exploratory technique. At the second scheduled interview the nature of hypnosis was explained to Max, and his cooperation was elicited. He seemed enthusiastic about the treatment.* It was suggested that he relax and that soon he would go into a deep sleep. The psychologist induced hypnosis by having him fixate on a pencil three or four inches above his eyes. Max followed instructions, and before a minute had elapsed, he closed his eyes. The psychologist suggested at this point that Max's right hand was mov-

---

* Dr. Kenneth Brown, a clinical psychologist, read this case and raised certain critical questions which are reproduced throughout the case as footnotes. The first reads: "A good point for speculation! Why was his 'dissociated self' so cooperative?"

ing upward, and this movement occurred immediately. Although the psychologist was not convinced at this point that Max was under deep hypnosis, he began interrogating him about events which were not remembered in the amnesic state. Max readily recalled his mother's maiden name, described his brother in detail, and upon inquiry described the house where he had lived in California. He named some of the teachers he had had as a freshman in college at home, and he talked at length about his band and some of the boys in it. Before awakening him the psychologist suggested that he would have memory of these events when he came out of the hypnosis. *This suggestion was not effective.*

Max was awakened by being told, "When I count to three you will be wide awake." At the count of three he opened his eyes slowly, as though he had been in a deep sleep, and he had no knowledge of what had transpired under hypnosis. The psychologist showed him the notes taken during the interrogation, and Max was highly interested in the facts and enthusiastic about the hypnotic procedure. He said, "There is a lot of information I have got to get, because there are many letters I am getting all the time from my friends and I am in a quandary as to how to answer them."

Subsequent hypnotic sessions

The next hypnotic session occurred after the psychologist had a conference with Max's parents, who were defensive about the nature of his illness. His mother again forcefully contradicted the statement of one of his associates that this sort of thing had occurred to Max the previous summer and that, as a result, he had had amnesia for several days. She was very skeptical of the findings of the psychologist and asked if she might sit in the room during the next hypnotic session. She even gave the psychologist certain questions to ask Max. Max agreed with the arrangement and was as readily hypnotized as in the first session.

Again an attempt was made to explore aspects of Max's memory not accessible in the amnesic state. Max recalled his very good friend Frank, and Frank's girl friend, Ethel — people of whom he knew nothing a few moments prior to the hypnotic trance. Under hypnosis, he described Frank very vividly, saying he was a very friendly fellow, always smiling, and the life of the party.

He gave the full name of Ethel. She was an only child, Frank's girl friend, and a very good friend of Max's. Since he was with Frank a great deal, he saw a lot of Ethel. He was asked about two other friends, both musicians. He answered in great detail some of which is reproduced below. "Ben plays violin. He has long black hair and he, too, is a real good-timer." The other boy was Irving. "Irving is much bigger than I am. He is at least six feet tall and has blonde hair. He plays both clarinet and sax and he belongs to the Blue Skies band — that's our band. We have played in churches, at dances, and in servicemen's canteens. In college on the West Coast I played sax in the freshman band while I was taking some courses in the music department."

Max gave the complete addresses of all his friends and also some of their telephone numbers. He mentioned the names of the popular songs that he enjoyed playing. He gave the names of the professors he had in school and the leader of the band. The psychologist repeated his own name while Max was under hypnosis. He said, "Do you know Dr. _____?" Max shook his head and said, "It seems kind of familiar but I don't know him." Apparently during hypnosis he could recall none of the events that had occurred since his collapse, during the amnesic state. He could recall only the events prior to that time. He described in detail the Air Force base where he had been stationed before he was transferred to the University. He thought he was to be placed in a radar program, but he had been sent to the university instead.

In further exploring early memories, Max was asked to describe the details of the living room in his home. He mentioned where the overstuffed chairs were, where the divan was located, and described the radio cabinet. Upon interrogation, he moved on to a description of his own bedroom. The walls were filled with photographs he had taken, developed, and enlarged himself. He said, "My window looks out over a garden. In one corner of the garden is a circular clothesline and in another corner among the flowers is a bird bath."

He could recall details about his high school and the members of the band. He named the leader of the band, all his other teachers, their personalities, and the subjects they taught. During this session his mother sat astonished, then wept, and finally seemed very pleased.

Inability to integrate the amnesic and hypnotic phases

The next day when Max came in again with his physician and his parents, he again seemed eager to undergo hypnosis. The trance state again occurred quickly. The psychologist merely had to say, "You are going into a deep, deep sleep, you are closing your eyes, you are now deep in sleep," and he immediately went into a hypnotic state.

Max's mother expressed a desire to talk with him while he was under hypnosis. The psychologist talked with him a little while to ascertain that he was in the trance, after which, without any introduction or suggestion from the hypnotist, his mother attempted to speak to him, with no success whatsoever. There was no response at all to her voice. The psychologist said, "Don't you hear the lady talking to you?"

He said, "No, I don't hear any words except what you say. I hear noises but no words." He did not hear any voice except the psychologist's. It was suggested that he would recognize his mother and father and remember them as such when he came out of the trance. He did not show willingness under hypnosis or in the waking state to acknowledge his mother.

Max's emotional attitude under hypnosis was a little more sober than his happy-go-lucky phase before the trance. However, on only two occasions could the psychologist elicit expression of hostility or negative response while he was under hypnosis. In the first, it was suggested that he open his eyes and yet remain under hypnosis. He frowned a great deal, and the psychologist withdrew the suggestion.* The second occasion of negative reaction occurred when an attempt was made to establish whether or not he was hit in the head prior to his collapse. He could remember being hit by a baseball bat and the recall of this produced a frown. His description of this event was as follows: "I was playing baseball at the other military installation when one of the other players threw the bat and it hit me. I saw red and blue rings. The boy immediately came over to me and said 'I'm sorry.' It really didn't hurt me greatly; it was a little bat." Max immediately went on to say, "We won the game," and gave the score.

His parents continued to talk with him at his bedside much of the day about his interests and hobbies at home. He could recall many things about the city in which he lived but *nothing specifically related to his own personal life*, such as the street on which he lived, an image of his house, or images of his friends. The only vague personal memory he thought he could recollect was that of handling some snakes when he was at camp as a young boy. He reported that he could arouse an image of his hands going into the cage. He was wearing some thick gloves. At this point, he corrected himself. He said, "No, I don't remember them as being my hands. I just see somebody's hands going into the cage and there is an unpleasantness

* Dr. Brown comments: "A common response on the first attempt. It's difficult."

that goes along with this." He seemed to show emotion while recalling this.

Once, when the psychologist was reporting to him the facts recorded during hypnosis, he said, "You mentioned that you used to play in the Blue Skies band," Max at that moment cried with great enthusiasm and apparent insight, "I remember that," but followed this quickly with a disappointed, "No, now I remember that somebody told me I was in the Blue Skies band."

The next day under hypnosis the psychologist asked him, "Where are you at this moment?" He replied, "I don't know just exactly where I am. I am someplace waiting for orders to move — maybe to a university, maybe to a combat zone, or maybe to further training. I don't know yet, but I probably will know soon." He went on to say, "Recently I had a leave and went home. It wasn't as much fun as I thought it would be because I couldn't locate many of my friends. So many of them are in the service and scattered all over the United States. My family was there, however." He answered that he liked the Air Force, had made a number of new friends, and now did not like leaving them. He was happy on the whole; he had not had any unpleasant experiences recently and he was satisfied with his military life.

Max was asked, "How is your memory?" He replied, "I think my memory is good; I have been able to get good grades. I don't have any trouble with names or dates. I think it is real good."

"What work are you doing at this place?"

"I'm not doing anything much; I just sit around and play pool now and then."

The psychologist then asked, "What do you like to talk about nowadays?" Max replied, "Well, I don't know. Just anything that comes up." He was queried about his girl, Sylvia. He said, "She is a very nice girl and I like her a lot. We have had a lot of good times together." He was asked about Frank, his best friend. He answered, "I like Frank very much. I have known him practically all my life and even a change of neighborhood didn't separate us. He's a musician too. He's a smart guy and he does everything easily and well."

"What music have you played recently?"

He said, "I haven't played any recently. There are no instruments around here."

He was asked, "What is today's date?"

"I don't know," was the answer.

"Are you in a hospital now?"

"No, I've never been in a hospital."

"Did you ever see anyone die in a hospital?"

"No, I don't know of anyone who died in a hospital. I am the kind of fellow who doesn't worry. I just take things as they come." All of Max's memories about his previous life were of a pleasant nature. He liked the C.O. and talked freely about routines such as drilling, classes, everyday events in the barracks, and playing pool.* He knew nothing about the geographic state in which he was located at present, and when it was mentioned, he said he had never been there. Although he did not know the exact date, he thought this was the month of August, when it actually was the month of September. He was living, under hypnosis, in a period which just immediately preceded the present university period.

The answers to the above questions indicate that he had repressed the memory of the hospital experience and the death of the young man from the other memories that were clear through hypnosis. The psychologist went on with questions. "Tell me some of the things that happened in the course of the day yesterday." His answer was, "The same as always." However, the remainder of his answers were different. He did not use the personal pronoun I. He said, "You get up, you get the mail, then you go and sit in the park with Don and Bill." (All of Max's comments under hypnosis were related to events that occurred before the amnesia.) His answers implied that he believed he was back at the military installation where he was located just before he came to the University.

On several occasions he was asked to open his eyes and look the psychologist in the face while he remained in the hypnotic state, in an attempt to bring the two phases of experience together. This always failed and usually produced an apparent conflict, often reflected in frowns and facial twitches. At no time, however, did the psychologist pursue this attempt after Max showed discomfort.**

Once the counselor manually opened Max's eyes while he was under hypnosis, but as soon as his eyes were open he immediately awakened from the trance. By this time he could pass into and out of the trance very easily and rapidly, but there was a very definite break between the memories accessible to him during hypnosis and those accessible to him before and after hypnosis. There was no bridge between the two sets of memories and, consequently, no experience common to both periods. There was a slight difference in

---

* Dr. Brown's remark: "Ah, sweet repression."

** Dr. Brown's comment here is: "Getting the 'core' out of a boil hurts!"

his personality under hypnosis and during the waking state. During the waking state, he was freer, more spontaneous, and had a greater sense of humor.

At the next hypnotic session, when he and the psychologist were alone, the psychologist grabbed him by the arm. This was disturbing to Max. *He reacted more violently to this than to anything he had undergone under hypnosis.* His face began to twitch. His mother had also reported that as she talked with him, trying to elicit past unpleasant memories, he failed to recall any content, although he seemed to be bothered when the memories dealt with experiences known to be unpleasant to him at the time they happened. Consequently, they decided to discontinue the exploration of previous vivid experiences.

One of the things that his father reported before he left was a little memory experiment he performed. He wrote down a list of the names of well-known people, such as movie actors, actresses, musicians, and noted baseball players, as well as friends and relatives. He asked Max which of these people he knew or could remember. Max remembered practically all of the well-known personalities, but failed to recognize any of his friends or his relatives.

FOLLOW-UP

Abrupt transfer; follow-up letters

After this last interview, Max was moved abruptly by the military service at a time when the psychologist was out of his office, and, therefore, did not get to say good-bye. Less than three weeks after Max left the hospital, his father wrote the psychologist the following letter:

> I am so very happy to be able to report to you that Max has completely recovered his memory as a result of only one treatment at the hospital. You will, I am sure, be interested to know that this treatment consisted of the administration of the drugs pentothal and caffein, supplemented with hypnosis. The treatment lasted about two hours. His present memory covers the period from the time of his accident also. We have been assured that he is fully recovered now.

The psychologist answered the letter, saying he would like to receive any other information available in the future and that he would also like to hear from Max. Max did not write, however, until six months later, and then only in response to a mimeographed questionnaire which the psychologist sent routinely to all clients he had seen during the year. He did not fill out the questionnaire but wrote a personal letter instead, most of which is paraphrased below:

"I know that there is absolutely no excuse for my failure to write sooner, but honestly, I have been very busy since my discharge from the Air Force. Maybe I should begin this phase of my story at the point where I left the University.

"In the hospital to which I was transferred, I was hypnotized twice without success and then given a weekend of liberty. I met most of my old friends and, of course, the relatives. I am sure you can understand what a puzzling experience it was to me and that's putting it mildly! The following Tuesday I was given an injection of sodium pentothal. I am sorry I can't report to you much of what happened while I was under the influence of this drug, but the aides at the hospital supplied me with much of the information.

"Apparently the physician had me speaking freely of the past, but his main problem was to keep me from falling asleep. This he achieved in several different ways. He made the aides take turns slapping my face and giving me injections of caffein. The aides told me there was some amusement while the physician was tantalizing me. I came out with quite a few obscenities, the kind one usually doesn't use in the presence of a colonel.

"No doubt the above description of the treatment is a bit on the sketchy side but this is about all I can do. When I finally woke up, I found myself sitting on the side of the bed and at that time I remembered everything — just like that! Incidentally, we once spoke about the possibility of forgetting everything that took place during the three weeks of amnesia. Well, now I remember everything rather clearly and it is hard for me to understand how I could have forgotten everything — particularly why I didn't recognize those very familiar faces, including my own.* One of my friends has a good

---

* Dr. Brown says in this connection: "I very much question this. If he really did remember everything he couldn't have difficulty understanding. He simply was forced to recognize his repressions so that he could be his normal self again — probably because the Army therapist somehow helped him get rid of *some* guilt over the patient's death, but not enough for him to remember it, or at least not enough for him to tell you (nor to answer your questionnaire). I know of no instance where there has been both *abreaction and relief of guilt* (when guilt is involved, as is very probably true in this case) that an individual has had difficulty in recalling obviously repressed experiences."

explanation. He says if he had a face like mine, he'd get amnesia too. I can't put much faith in this particular theory!

"When I was myself again in the hospital, I spent a few months working around the hospital on some kind of clean-up squad. The advantage of this was that I had a great deal of liberty. From there I went to another hospital not far away from home to convalesce. That was really a nice vacation. I was then discharged in January. [This was four months after the psychologist first saw Max.]

"I applied for readmission to the University out here that I attended before I went into the service. Even though the semester had already started, I was accepted and decided to take a chance on catching up with the work that had gone ahead. I had a little trouble. In fact, I didn't think I was able to concentrate as well as I had previously. This was particularly true during lectures. However, there are many possible reasons for this. One is that I have gotten quite involved in extracurricular activities.

"Although these bad experiences I had may become less vivid as time goes by, I remember very distinctly the pleasant experience I had there at the University.

"My friends treat the whole thing as a joke and, of course, I am happy about that. I've always thought that nothing can get you down if you can laugh at it. I believe that this philosophy made it a lot easier for me during the amnesia. I think I can say now that I don't believe my personality changed much while my memory was gone. I looked at everything just as I do now. The surprising thing is that when I saw these people I once knew, before I got my memory back, I placed them in certain niches in which I thought they belonged; and do you know, *I had put everybody in the pigeon hole in which he belonged. The way I felt about these people then — and I really didn't know them — is the way I feel about them now since I have my full memory back.* Maybe this doesn't surprise you, but I thought it very interesting. I don't think I told you but I went into the service before I had finished a term of college. I have gotten credit for all these courses by taking special examinations, even though I didn't complete that semester. Naturally, I was away from books for a long time while in the service and got out of practice. But when the finals came around this past semester, I got good grades in all the courses I took.

"You may remember that I have always enjoyed camp life and I am at present a counselor in one of the big camps in the state. This is an old story for me because I have worked in other camps previously and always enjoyed it.

"That form that you sent me to fill out a few days ago amused me in one respect. You had certain descriptive adjectives that we were supposed to check. One was 'absent-minded.' This amused me and I might answer 'not recently.'

"Well, Doctor, figuratively and literally, this is the last paragraph in a strange story. Like many melodramas, this one has its corny spots but all is forgiven because the ending is a happy one."

Later follow-up

Six years after Max wrote this letter, a friend of the psychologist reported that he had been on the West Coast and had met Max's father, who had asked him to deliver a message. The father spoke very pleasantly about the University where Max was stationed when he had the episode of amnesia. He wanted the psychologist to know that Max was doing very well. He had received a doctoral degree in education, and had a promising future.

Evaluation from the standpoint of personality theory

The case of Max is a rare one. The author has counseled nearly 3,000 students over a period of almost twenty years, and Max was the only case of amnesia that he encountered. What do you see in it that has general significance for the motivation and the organization of personality? It may be helpful to raise the following questions to explore this.

What does Max's case show us about the unconscious stratum of personality? Why did Max have amnesia? What function did it serve in his life? What motivated him to undergo dissociation or a "split" in layers of personality, so that all personal memories were incapable of being recalled? Why did Max take this so lightly? He repeatedly said he was puzzled when he had to write to his friends, whom he didn't "know" during the amnesia; but he never seemed to think this was a tragedy. Can this sanguine attitude be explained entirely in terms of Max's temperament?

Could his amnesia be regarded as an example of defensive repression? Why was he motivated to repress all personal memories? Was it because they were associated with the role he played in his relationship with the boy who died in his arms? We stated above that we have no information on what this relationship was; nor do

we know whether the physicians who finally brought about the recall of repressed memories through narcosis delved to find the motivation for the repression.* Much of the evidence based on Max's
behavior indicates that he very strongly resisted the return of this
memory, as well as the fusion of the personality present in the
trance state with the memories present in the amnesic state. Can
we assume then that there were some very strong anxieties which
motivated this amnesia — anxieties that might have become overwhelming had Max relived this death scene by answering the letter
from the boy's mother?

What does this study tell us about the organization of the *self*?
One of the characteristics which Allport attributes to the self is
continuing self-identity. This is something that Max lost in amnesia.
What was the nature of this loss, and why did it take the form that
it did? You will remember that all known impersonal memories,
those not involving personal *self-extension* to friends, relatives, high-
level intentions, personal plans, and the like (Allport's *propriate
strivings*), were retained. The highly personal aspects of his life, as
a unit, were not available as memories. Does this suggest a certain
kind of organization of the self with personal events forming one
sort of unit, and non-personal, adjustive processes which are a part
of the usual problem-solving activities of everyday life (Allport's
rational coping) forming another? (See Allport, 3, Chapter 6.) Is
this not highly compatible with Rogers' more dynamic self-theory?
Rogers indicates that any experience which is inconsistent with the
organization or structure of the self may be perceived as a threat,
and the more of these perceptions there are, the more rigidly the self-
structure is organized to maintain itself. (See Rogers, 93.) It seems
that the self-process involves defense against threatening experiences
by denying them to consciousness. In Max's case, the extreme personal discomfort and emotional disturbance was avoided by the
amnesia.

Why was it that hypnosis, under a permissive, mild-mannered
therapist, even with Max's consent, was not able to bring about a
synthesis within the time available, whereas a more drastic (drug)

* Dr. Brown's comment here is: "The reliving of *guilt-ridden experiences* is, to
my knowledge, the only reason for the kind of treatment Max described; i.e., he
was placed in a truth-serum trance and tantalized by the physician. I would guess
he relived the experience, or a considerable part of it, but not in such a way as
to genuinely resolve his guilt. Or perhaps this isn't possible. Maybe he did something counter to his basic self-attitude — cursed the patient (or worse) or perhaps
he actually was partly responsible for his death."

therapy, done in a more authoritative setting without the suggestion that Max play any role in the process, was effective? Has the form of this question suggested the answer?

Could it be, too, that Max had a kind of *basic constitution* and early environment and experiences which would have predisposed him to *dissociation* — illustrated by the amnesia — as a means of defense when he was experiencing great conflict? Would there be more information available about Max's basic constitution if the therapist had questioned Max or members of his family about similar experiences in other family members and close relatives?*

MAX: Personal Patterns and Relationships

What do you see in the case of Max? Recall patterns that impressed you, before turning to the questions below.

Outstanding characteristics

 a. How does Max compare with your previous ideas about amnesia victims?

 b. Can you readily imagine Max as similar to persons you have known (except for his memory loss)?

 c. How did he differ in being susceptible to amnesia?

Events and personal relationships

 a. What seemed to you to be the sources of stability and instability in Max's life that may have contributed both to amnesia and recovery?

 b. What events and relationships do you think Max may have tended to repress?

---

* Dr. Brown's final comment is: "On the general matter of interpretation, I agree with your point regarding the rarity of Max's dissociative reaction in one sense (which you might want to point up with regard to self theory): In line with Allport's stress on continuity of self, it is fairly rare that a person goes to the extreme of overtly denying (by dissociation or active schizophrenia, or delusions of grandeur) or destroying (by suicide) his core self, i.e., his self-identity or even organic identity. However, dissociation or repression (as such) is, I think, a very common type of inhibitory control. It's so easy! In the vast majority of instances the guilt-arousing motive and behavior can be circumscribed and repressed as self-alien, i.e., not acceptable in one's awareness of on-going 'selfness.' Sometimes, however, the 'crime' is so great, and so undeniably a part of the former self, that it is banished from heaven also."

Concepts helpful in understanding Max
  a. Unconscious (26, 96)
  b. Repression (41, 96)
  c. Hypnosis (26, 37)
  d. Self-structure (77, 82)
  e. Abreaction (37, 115)
Other concepts which may have some relevance to this case: hypnosis; personality organization; motivated forgetting; dissociation; self-identity; individual constitution; amnesia (motivated forgetting).

Reflections on the Cases

Now that the reader has had vicarious encounters with these twenty persons, he may reasonably ask of me, "What do you, as counselor and author of these cases, find to be the major differences in these persons in later years, as compared to the period of your first encounter with them? In retrospect, how do you appraise the extent of their personal development and their adjustment to life? How do you now evaluate the effect of the counseling process in which they were engaged?"

First, let me say that any generalization must be made with caution. Each of these persons is a unique individual, with his own peculiar *individual constitution*, and subject to different *patterns of environmental influences*. Through the interplay of these forces each developed his own style of coping with life. Moreover, as we pointed out earlier, this is a selected group of cases, despite the fact that they represent a rather wide variety of behavior and experiential configurations. A certain amount of selection necessarily occurred, in terms of each client's willingness to continue his relationship with the counselor. In addition, the follow-up contacts were usually more casual and less comprehensive than the early sessions. Despite this, I do have some impressions about the adjustments these individuals made, *but they are only impressions.*

I was struck with the observation that all of these people were continuing to make *some* kind of confrontation with the life situations they met. Most of them had *learned to live with their problems* — in most of the follow-up interviews I felt I was experiencing essentially the same individual I had known during my early encounters with them in counseling. There was a certain *continuity of self.* Often their attitude toward their problems or difficulties had changed; often they had found new avenues of satisfaction, partially through changes of circumstances, but the basic personality remained essentially the same.

These observations raise many questions which beg long-term research to delineate more clearly what aspects of personality structure

311

and dynamics change as an individual develops through an acutely disturbed period toward one of greater stability. Is anxiety lessened? Does it become harnessed through more effective modes of need-satisfaction? Are defenses reduced, and problem solving and rational coping activities increased? How do such dynamic changes affect the structure of personality? Why are these individuals perceived as essentially the same person?

As I read through these cases after putting them aside for a time, it seemed to me that on the whole counseling was a valuable experience — particularly when a good relationship was established and when the client took some responsibility and showed a tendency to deal with himself in a problem-solving manner. The clients varied widely in the growth they achieved. The cost, in terms of the counselor's time and effort, also varied; in some cases it was considerable. This consideration, together with the great need for counseling services, led me to the strong conviction that group approaches should be exploited more than they are at present. I could not help but notice that many of these people were aided by other, non-professional, persons — friends, associates, teachers, coaches, and other individuals who helped to induce healthier relationships. It was these observations that encouraged me to write and publish these cases and to use them with classes, groups of clients, and peer groups.

In addition, I have devoted more and more time to compiling materials, including short stories, which invite involvement and have potential for personal development. These may be read and discussed in groups, with emphasis on their implications for personal understanding. Wide exploration in the responsible use of such materials will give us information on their value as therapeutic or instructional devices.

Your Own Case

After reading several of the cases in this book, you might find it interesting and rewarding to try to write a case yourself. You may have found that none of the cases deals with a personality pattern with which you are particularly familiar. This personality might be your own, or it may be someone in your family, or possibly a very good friend with whom you have spent considerable time. You might find it helpful to use an outline similar to those followed in the cases presented. If you decide to use an outline, such as the one suggested below, try not to let the many factors overwhelm you. Look over the following pages and use whatever items are helpful in your write-up, remembering that it should be written in your own way.

Identification

Begin by identifying the person. Give his age, sex, present occupation or activity, and follow this with a *physical description*. Give the kind of information that will allow your reader *to visualize this individual*, as he walks into an office or classroom, or as he sits across from him at a cafeteria table. You should include some of his more superficial social traits, his manner of meeting people, his style of dress, and some of his most obvious interests and attitudes.

Occasion for discussion

It might be a good idea to tell your reader fairly early in the case why this particular person was chosen. Does he have some unique characteristics or psychological dynamics not found in the previous cases; or do these dynamics express themselves in a particularly interesting and unique manner? Here it might be well to consider a very important factor that always enters into our observation of another person, your *relationship to this person*. How did he come into your life? Is your relationship with him an objective one? If not, how do you plan to bring objectivity into the study? Do you have information on some objective aspects of his personality? Do you

313

know something about his intelligence, his employment record, his school grades, and the evaluation of him by others who know him? It may be that he has taken objective tests and you have knowledge about his scores. On the other hand, you may not have any of this information and may have to depend entirely upon your impression. In that case, you will have to indicate this as an inadequacy in your study and point up the need for this kind of information in presenting a complete and objective picture of the individual.

One purpose of the case-history technique, particularly at the early stages of studying an individual, is that it serves to encompass and integrate what is known about the individual and what needs yet to be understood. You might formulate some tentative hypotheses concerning the individual's aptitudes, personality traits, and basic dynamics (that is, his personal needs and motives, his conflicts and anxieties, and his predominant ways of meeting the problems of life), and from this indicate needs for more detailed information.

Present status and development

It is perhaps best to start with the person's apparent view of himself, to get a *phenomenological* view* of the individual. If you know him very well and have talked with him, at length, you have some idea how he views himself and his personal world. What are his feelings and attitudes about himself and the significant factors in his life? What does he feel are his outstanding capacities, attitudes, and interests; his dominant needs and personality traits? An outline of important factors is presented in the *Pre-Interview Blank*, which we have used extensively in compiling the cases in this book. Some of the items from this Blank are presented below.**

Another possible approach is to ask the individual to write freely about all of the important factors that he thinks have made him the person he is, particularly items about which he has definite feelings. Below is a list of such factors:

A. *Identification:* date; sex; age; college attended (and class); membership in a social fraternity or sorority; home town or city (and population).

B. *Ability and achievement:* grades for the past semester (number of hours of A, B, C, etc.); scholastic rank in high school; size of high-

---

* The view that emphasizes unanalyzed experience, as might be reported by the layman concerning his feelings or his way of looking at things.

** For a more complete description, see McKinney (72, 74).

school class; transfers from other colleges or courses, eliminations, etc.; college aptitude percentile; study habits (average hours per day of study).

C. *Physical health:* general health; height; weight; eyesight (glasses?); physical defects or handicaps; your attitude toward your physical health.

D. *School activities:* extracurricular activities; extent of participation (very active, moderately active, not very active); offices held; friendships; extent to which the following activities occupy your time (bull sessions, dances, dates, movies, conversations, athletics, reading of books and articles, unaccounted-for time).

E. *Interests and plans:* vocational objective (including plans made and qualifications); most outstanding reasons for going to college; outstanding hobbies and interests; skills and accomplishments; your estimation of your greatest assets; activities and events within the coming year to which you are looking forward with greatest pleasure.

F. *Present living conditions:* home; roommate; financial status; working conditions (hours per week).

G. *Attitudes:* interest in a counseling interview; present degree of *happiness*; present mental *integration* (oneness of purposes; consistency and stability of attitudes and desires); present *adjustment* to environment and other people (degree to which you "fit in" with them); *outlook* for future fulfillment of ambitions; explanation of abnormally high or low ratings given for any of the above items. State any factors about which you are particularly sensitive and which you dislike to discuss (i.e., physique, complexion, facial features, health, home town, etc.).

H. *Problems:* For each existing personal problem, give the nature of the difficulty, source of worry, fear, aversion, etc., and your attitude and reactions to it.

I. *Personality traits:* outstanding traits which you readily recognize and others use to identify you. Include traits which others might not readily recognize in you — for example, ambitious, self-confident, hard-working, nervous, quick-tempered, friendly, dependable, retiring, etc.

J. *History prior to college:* List concisely and frankly under the following topics all the factors in your life which made you the type of person you are today. Include factors from infancy to date, as they are known to you, separating grade-school and high-school periods. (1) *Parents* (temperament, compatibility, education, occupation, age, attitude toward their children, financial status); other members of family. (2) *Health* history (accidents, defects, major illness). (3) *Recreation and athletic* history (games preferred, team membership, honors won). (4) *Sex* history (dating, dances, attitudes, experiences, practices). (5) *Social life* history (early playmates, clubs, gangs, camps, offices held, warm friendships, attitude changes). (6) *School* history (honors, best and poorest subjects, embarrassments, attitude changes). (7) History of *inner life* (fears, dislikes, daydreams, strong attractions, night dreams). (8) *Religious* history (church preference, early training, value of beliefs in your life, attitude changes, disillusionment or loss of ideals, failures in reaching ideals). (9) *Summary* (comment on most important factors in development, whether mentioned above or not, which produced happiness or sadness).

Unknowns

Before trying to integrate all of the material presented in the case, write out some of the present unknowns about the individual. Under ideal conditions, what other information would you like to have in writing this case? Are there certain aspects of personality structure, dynamics, or development that are still unclear? What methods might be suggested for obtaining this information?

Would it be helpful if this individual were given an opportunity to take aptitude, interest, or personality tests? * Would an evaluative interview with a psychiatrist or a clinical psychologist reveal certain trends which would add to the total understanding of this person? What observations not previously obtained would be valuable? In what social or performance situations would it be desirable to observe this person? What kinds of behavior would you observe and what information would you record?

Observed behavior in specific situations

In writing the case, attempt to recall observations you have made on this individual in terms of the significant roles he plays in life, including actual reports on conversations and descriptions of events which give reality to the story of his life. What are his outstanding behavioral characteristics in the home situation, in the work situation, in boy-girl relationships, in school, in play, and in a social milieu? What are some of the roles he does not play and some of the situations he tends to avoid?

Are there certain school, work, health, and military or other

---

* See McKinney (74), pp. 402–407, for suggestions of specific tests.

records that are a source of information that might give objectivity to the individual's self-report? *

Interpretive trends: The individual in perspective

If you wish to make your case write-up more complete, after following the outline thus far, you may find the suggestions in this section helpful. Listed below are several considerations which might help you to look at the case in perspective.

First, what is the personality *structure* of the individual? What are his outstanding traits and characteristics and how are these important in his social and emotional adjustment? A factor analysis of many possible traits has yielded a certain few basic characteristics. The basic traits found by various authors are somewhat similar. (See Cattell, 23; Guilford, 46; and Hilgard, 51.)

Second, you may want to ask, what are his basic *dynamics*? What needs are important in his life? To what extent are these aroused and satisfied by the events of everyday life? To what extent are they blocked? What is his reaction to this blocking? Does it tend to make him *aggressive* or does he *withdraw* instead? What *conflicts* do you see between these needs and forces of motivation? Do you see him being trapped by desiring what he cannot accept or loving what he unconsciously hates? Are some of these conflicts tied up with his own self-structure? Does he have levels of aspiration and ideals which he may never reach because of his basic physical or temperamental makeup? Does he experience anxiety frequently? How does he usually handle *anxiety*?

Third, if this has not been covered previously, what do you see in his *development*? To what extent is he a *mature* individual, in terms of the characteristics given on page 263? To what extent has his development proceeded in an orderly way? Have the events in his life enabled him to gain some of the characteristics mentioned by Erikson in his discussion of development? Consider particularly the attitude of basic trust and a clear identity. Has this individual

---

* The suggestions given here are rather complete, so that they may apply to students at all levels of instruction — undergraduates as well as more advanced students in professional programs. The undergraduate's efforts would depend less upon thorough investigation into the records of another individual, and would be undertaken primarily for general rather than exhaustive understanding of that person. The student in professional training, on the other hand, would be acquainted with professional ethics regarding the handling of confidences, and could be expected to give a more thorough analysis.

throughout his development been able to *integrate* the various forces within himself, to gain some sort of unity? Is he conscious of important temperamental or disturbing aspects of his life that don't fit in with his conscious ideals? Are these in the process of being integrated?

HANK

The Satisfied Laborer

The following case was written by a senior honor student
majoring in psychology after he had read some of the cases
in this book. He embarked on this project after a brief
discussion of several cases with the author. He said, "None
of these cases seem to cover some of the people I knew
well when I was growing up." He illustrated by giving a
verbal description of Hank ("the satisfied laborer"). The
author asked him to read the section here entitled "Your
Own Case" and suggested that he try to write the case of
Hank. What follows is the result of the project.

The following is a description of a 26-year-old mechanic living
in a large city. The area in which he lives is economically depressed,
slowly deteriorating, and soon to be demolished to make way for a new
housing development. Hank grew up in this neighborhood and has
lived there all his life. His family was large — Hank was the fifth of
eight children, four boys and four girls. One of his brothers was killed
in World War II and another in an automobile collision. The
parents, though still alive, are now quite old, his father 74 and his
mother 71.

Hank's appearance is impressive. He is a healthy six-footer, weighing about two hundred pounds. His blond curly hair and clear blue
eyes give his round face a handsome appearance, marred only by his
decayed teeth. His wide, thin-lipped mouth is set over a slightly
crooked jaw which was badly broken when he was twelve. Hank is
not fastidious, but when at leisure he is usually neat and well dressed.
He generally wears slacks with a white shirt, and likes to brag, "I
never wear a tie if I can help it" (and usually he can). Hank is genial
and self-confident when meeting people, irrespective of their social
or business position, but tends to form strong lasting attitudes after

only a brief acquaintance. Thus, if he decides a man is likeable and worthy of trust, he will tend to overlook many shortcomings in the person's character. On the other hand, an initial dislike easily leads in Hank's case to a reverse "halo" effect so that thereafter nothing the man does is right. These hastily formed but stubbornly held impressions often lead Hank into difficulties; for example, if a good friend of his is also a good friend of someone Hank dislikes and a meeting of the three ensues, a good deal of embarrassment is generated for all concerned, due to Hank's outspoken hostility. In addition to Hank's geniality and openhandedness to friends, he tends to be domineering in his social relationships, perhaps as a natural outgrowth of his early training in a large family of noisy, boisterous children all competing for attention and dominance in the family group.

This man is of interest because of strongly conflicting personality patterns. His moods swing from openhanded friendliness to sudden, inexplicable rage in a bewilderingly short time, often over seemingly trivial circumstances. Although often thoughtless in his remarks to others, he is sensitive to the most innocent slight to himself. He is opinionated, yet dislikes opinionated people. He seems self-confident, but is unwilling to try different ways of doing things. His attitude toward women swings from tenderness to an indifference marked by crude and callous remarks.

Hank's attitude toward any group outside the working class is one of suspicion and distrust. Though he seldom comes in contact with any "white-collar" people, Hank has classified them as lazy, crooked, and deceitful. At the same time he is willing to take other individuals at face value, thus reflecting a discrepancy in attitude toward classes and individuals. These and other inconsistencies, his unpredictable temper, and his readiness and ability to use his fists tend to make his friends uneasy when with him and guarded in their conversation. Yet Hank has many friends, possibly because of his generosity, boundless energy, and untiring efforts on behalf of anyone who asks his help. Although Hank is sometimes aware of these inconsistencies in his temperament, they do not often consciously worry him. His attitude is usually one of self-acceptance, but here also he shows inconsistency in sometimes feeling depressed, nervous, and anxious without any apparent cause. Hank feels that he was "cut out for better things," but has little ambition to do anything that would change his present status and roles.

Hank had two brothers and two sisters older than he, and two brothers and one sister younger. The children were all close in age, less than two years apart. Hank's father worked long hours as an unskilled laborer in a factory and was generally tired and unwilling to take an active interest in the children when he came home. As a result of this, and the father's relatively advanced age at Hank's birth (almost 50 years old), the father-son relationship was a distant one. Hank's mother, on the other hand, was a large, active woman, who firmly believed that her children were the chosen few of their neighborhood. Because of the large number of children in the family, however, there was constant competition among them for the mother's attention and affection. Hank held his own in this competition, due to his large, robust frame and aggressiveness as a child. Although the parents were religious believers, they seldom attended church, perhaps because of their large family and the father's desire to sleep late on his one day off a week. Discipline was meted out by the mother, since the father had little contact with the children. This is not to say that Hank necessarily had an inadequate male identification figure; numerous uncles and neighbors lived nearby, and the status and roles of males were clearly defined in the neighborhood. Boys were expected to be noisy, unkempt, aggressive, dominant, and gregarious. Hank seems to have fully lived up to all of these expectations.

Leadership was an early trait of this man. This was manifested even before school age when Hank was the leader of his neighborhood play group. Quick, strong, and fearless to the point of foolhardiness, Hank was by far the most aggressive member of his peer group.

His temperament was characterized even then by sudden changes of mood. This probably arose from his home life, where he was favored by his mother and sisters, and teased incessantly by his brothers. His mother had "ambitions" for Hank, but they were never defined. His brothers, on the other hand, were quick to point out every imagined failing. For instance, they liked to call Hank "pretty boy," and teased him about his affection for his sisters. Good looks and obvious affection, even for his sisters, were not highly prized assets among Hank's peers.

Although Hank is of about average intelligence, his speech and mannerisms reflect his upbringing in an economically depressed neighborhood. He attended school up to the eighth grade, but did not attempt to go to high school because, as he put it, "I was tired of school, the old man didn't give a damn whether I went or not, so why should I keep on going?" He got a job in an automotive shop as a stock boy, and spent his free hours, until he was about sixteen, bowling, shooting pool, and loafing with friends who were usually older than himself. Hank's activities have never included organized sports such as baseball, football, or basketball, which he feels make little sense. He does, however, incline to boxing and other individualistic sports, and he prefers to do things either by himself or with one or two others rather than as a member of a group. He was never drafted into the service; and he never enlisted because he feels that is for "men who can't make a living anyplace else." His wife, whom he married when he was twenty-two, believes that Hank would have joined the service, had he not been dissuaded by his friends.

Hank says that he became actively interested in girls when he was fourteen, and from that time on was seldom without a girlfriend somewhere in the neighborhood. Dates usually consisted of going to a show or a dance. Hank's attitude toward women, to the extent that it was shaped by his friends and associates, is callous. "You take them out for what you can get," sums up his attitude even today. This expressed attitude is in sharp contrast to his actual treatment of women, which can sometimes be tender and kind. Asked about the feelings of girls toward his attitude, Hank replied, "What makes you think they're any different?" explaining that the girl's attitude is usually the same as his, but with money or a good time as the objective. It should be noted here that the sexual mores in this neighborhood are more dependent on the individual's family and friends than upon the society as a whole. Hank's attitude toward his marriage is also ambivalent. He finds comfort and warmth in his home life, yet he sees marriage as restricting. He occasionally spends an evening away from home, sometimes in bars, sometimes with "lady friends." It should be noted here that Hank's attitude toward women and marriage, though it may be a warped one by the *ideal* middle-class standard, is not an unusual one for this neighborhood, nor, for that matter, for many classes of society. It should also be noted that this expressed attitude has little application for married women. A double standard is in effect in this neighborhood, as in many other places. Whether this attitude has any effect on the desirability or durability of marriage in this neighborhood is difficult to check, because of the high mobility rate in this locale, with families moving in and out almost constantly. In Hank's case, however, an apparently successful marriage has lasted five years.

Today Hank is a successful mechanic, hard working, well paid, and according to his standards, lives well. His interests are more or less hedonistic; and he lives largely for the present. His life in the slum district of a large city is one well suited to his upbringing. He is "at home" there and would not, he says, live anywhere else. Hank is a leader in his neighborhood, albeit a passive one. He is looked up to, and respected, by the young men of his community. He stands out even in a "tough" neighborhood because of his quick temper, and ability with his fists. His ambitions are rather short-sighted, and he does not look beyond tomorrow. He is suspicious of strangers, distrustful of the police, and resentful of authority. His attitudes and social and behavioral skills are well suited to his environment and, on the whole, he is pleased with himself. However, he does often wonder why he feels so "closed in" and restless at times, and also wonders about his periodic depressions and impulses to do something — anything — but without definite objectives.

The attacks of restlessness Hank attributes to "nerves," and he finds them little cause for concern when he is in a better frame of mind. Indeed, he says he is satisfied with life as it is. His wife, also, appears to be satisfied with their life together, although she is disappointed that so far they have no children. Hank expresses satisfaction with their childless state, but becomes agitated if teased about this lack.

One wonders if Hank is not really living in two worlds. Although he denies that he daydreams, Hank often seems to resent his world, even while expressing his satisfaction. His restless states are suggestive of mild anxiety attacks, and his statement about his father not caring whether or not he left school leads one to wonder if, perhaps, Hank missed his father's attention. His expressed self-confidence, alongside his resistance to any change in his mode of living and his sudden rages, suggests a basic insecurity in his relations with the world. This is also suggested by his ambivalent attitude toward his marriage, and by his tendency toward strong and fixed attitudes toward the people he meets. Finally, his aggressiveness and need for dominance suggest an authoritarian personality, in need of clearly defined social relationships.

The value of writing a case

After reading the above case the author talked with the student who wrote it and asked, "What did you gain from writing this case?" Below are his spontaneous remarks:

"Well, it was a lot of hard work. I know a lot more about him that I didn't know before. I saw things that I hadn't thought too much about previously — for example, he was the child of pretty old parents; they were very poor people.

"There seems to be more to him than I can put on paper. You miss the essence of a human being when you start to write about him. You tend to mold him into a frame."

The student was asked by the writer, "Was it worth the time you put in?"

"Definitely. If I had the time I'd write out cases on some of my other friends. . . . I'm sure I'd understand them better than I do now."

"Did you learn anything about yourself?"

"I found too damn much of me in him. I was brought up in the same neighborhood. He is an extreme example of what I might have been. There is a little of me there. It wasn't as objective as it might be."

"Another question — would you recommend this activity to someone else?"

"Certainly. I think it is a good idea to sit down and figure out what your friend is like. I began to write before I really read the outline. I think it would have been better to jot down the facts and memories that the outline brings to mind, then write out the story of the life. . . . I had fun doing it and gained certain insights into Hank's life."

HANK: Personal Patterns and Influences

Hank's case may be used in the same way as the others for personal reactions and discussion. The reader is encouraged here to write out his own questions, to bring out (1) distinctive personality patterns, (2) significant relationships, and (3) concepts helpful in understanding Hank.

USE OF CASES

Personal Development—Bibliotherapy

The Preface suggests educational situations in which these cases may be used. Here we will deal more specifically with how the cases may be employed as a means for personal development or for furthering understanding of theoretical concepts. Their use will vary with situations and with the background of the reader, the purpose of the educational experience, and the relationship to the person to whom they are presented. In addition to course use, these cases should have value as an *adjunct to counseling and psychotherapy* and as reading for the layman who is interested in gaining greater perspective on human behavior and on his own adjustment to life.

First, *individual* use. A first reading for enjoyment will enable the student to appreciate and understand the individual as a living, striving person. The reader may find it helpful on second review to underline or to make brief notes on aspects of the case that impressed him in some way. At this point he may speculate as to the nature of underlying forces organized within the individual and about early causes and later results. After each case there is a series of questions, largely open-ended, dealing with personality *structure*, *dynamics*, and *development*, and leading to explanatory psychological concepts. The reader may be required to take notes on his reaction, to be read by or discussed with the instructor or counselor. The reaction of a graduate clinical student in the case of Lewis suggests how these cases may be used for written reports or discussions by advanced students.

The cases may be assigned for reading by members of *large classes* which are later divided into small buzz groups* of six or eight persons. This sharing of insights by group members and the comparison of various impressions of the person depicted in the case will

---

* This is a technique in the field of group dynamics which consists of dividing a large group or class into small units of six or eight persons and having them discuss a given topic freely and report back through one of their members to the larger group the results of their discussion.

presumably encourage objectivity and provide a perspective from which to view personality functioning. The group session should enable the individual to clarify his attitudes and ideas about human development and adjustment to the social milieu.

It will be noted that almost every case is related somewhat informally to certain generalizations and well-known concepts about personality and adjustment. The instructor may want to focus on these suggested concepts in each case, or he may want to motivate the student to think in terms of systems of interpretation presented in class or in nomothetic* readings. With more advanced students, the emphasis may be on what is omitted in the case, and on the instruments of assessment and the results obtained from them which might throw greater light on the underlying dynamics, personality structure, or cultural forces of the person delineated in the relatively brief case.

It is hoped that the chapter entitled "Your Own Case," provides an opportunity for the student to use creatively the information he may have gained through reading and lectures and through the use of the preceding cases. Of the several procedures suggested above, this latter conceivably may have the greatest value for the reader because it more effectively exploits his own initiative and understanding, and is in one respect a climax of all the previous presentation. This chapter is particularly appropriate for those users who believe that the writing of an autobiography, or understanding deeply the life of another person, can provide a basis for personal insight.

The openness, relative diversity, and looseness with which these cases are presented allows considerable versatility in the use of the book, and enables the instructor or the counselor to use it with his own purposes and structure in mind — using few or many of the cases.

It is hoped that this volume will contribute to the kind of teaching that involves critical and creative responses on the part of the student. Some instructors may use these cases to encourage thinking and broadened perspective on the part of students, who spend so much of their time listening to lectures and studying textbooks. At present many instructors have limited time to spend reading long papers written by underclassmen; but students can be encouraged to write brief reactions to the cases, to be read by the instructor or

* "Nomothetic" refers to general or universal principles of behavior — those that apply to the behavior of man in general — in contrast to "idiographic" facts, concerning one individual and the conditions producing his patterned uniqueness.

exchanged among students as a means of giving students experience in applying the knowledge they have gained about personality development and adjustment.

EXAMPLE OF USE OF GROUPS

Buzz groups of approximately eight students were formed in large classes after students had read a given case and reacted to it by writing brief notes with the help of the form presented below.*

REACTIONS TO A STORY/CASE

Student # _____ Class (F, S, etc.) _____ Age _____ Sex _____

Marital Status (S,M,D) _____ Undergraduate Major _____

Name of Story/Case _____

Approximate amount of time in hours spent in reading for pleasure per

month _____

Read the story/case as you would any selection read for pleasure. Enjoy it. When you have finished reading the story/case, write freely and frankly your main reactions to a person or persons in the story/case (their feelings and impulses); and/or your thoughts about them or people and life in general.

To what extent did the story/case read in connection with this project give you some understanding of the problems and adjustments of people, life, or *yourself?* State this by giving *any* ideas about human behavior or experience (your own, the characters', or others') that came to you as you read the story/case. Give *your actual thoughts, feelings, and attitudes* rather than generalizations about, evaluation of, or summary of the story.

Instruction to group leader

One member of each buzz group volunteered as a leader and was given these instructions:

> Your major object is to encourage discussion and help the recorder get most of the ideas written down. If the recorder

---

* The author is indebted to Mr. Harold R. Miller for demonstrating successful experimental use of this form, with the instructions to group leader and group recorder, in an undergraduate class in personality.

raises his hand, this indicates that the student speaking is going too fast; you are to say, "May I try to repeat what you have said?" Repeat what the person has said and ask, "Do you have anything to add?"

You may have difficulty getting the discussion started, but we don't anticipate this, since the person has already written out some of his reactions to a person or persons in the story/ case, and their feelings, impulses, and thoughts. If you have difficulty, however, merely say, "The purpose of this discussion is to share our personal reactions to these stories/cases. People differ in their reactions and all reactions are interesting. Won't someone begin?"

Your role is one of encouragement. You are not to enter into the discussion. But encourage them in any dialogue they engage in. Use words like "fine, good, uh huh, yes," but at no time should you criticize. It should be a free discussion. Don't be afraid of silence, let it occur; someone will finally talk.

Instructions to group recorder

Another person from each group was designated as recorder and was given these instructions:

We have tried to select as recorders persons who have had some experience with recording, who can write fast, and get the major ideas of the discussion. You are to record in as much detail as possible all of the discussion that occurs. By all means get down the major ideas. You should review your notes as soon as the session is over to insure that they are intelligible. During the discussion, you are to sit in a position where you can hear everything said, but do not sit so as to become a part of the group. Rather, take an inconspicuous position so that the group members are not too aware that you are recording what they are saying. We want group members to be spontaneous. Sit where the leader can see you, and if you are having difficulty taking everything down due to the speed of response, raise your hand. This will be a signal for him to repeat what the person has said in order for you to record it and in order for the speaker to add anything the leader did not include. Your role in the group is that of observer — to record, not participate.

At the end of a period varying from 20 to 30 minutes, the recorders either handed in their notes or reported information on them to the class as a whole, in order to share reactions to the case and insights and perspectives about the individuals presented in the cases.

Results of a study on involvement in case histories

Saper* has found that in reading a clinical case history, the case of David, students who discussed what they had read with other students became more involved with the material than those who discussed the case only with the experimenter.

He further reported that both groups of students, those who discussed the case history in small groups and those who engaged only in a personal discussion with the experimenter, achieved a higher degree of involvement than a third group of students who engaged in no discussion of any kind.

Involvement was defined operationally in terms of responses on the following scale, filled out by each reader of the case. This scale may be used to assess students' involvement.

REACTIONS TO MAIN CHARACTER

The following statements pertain to the main character of the case you have just read. Please consider each statement carefully and indicate your response to each in the appropriate space to the left of the statement. Mark +3 if you decidedly agree with the statement, +2 if you merely agree, +1 if you slightly agree, 0 if you neither agree nor disagree, −1 if you slightly disagree, −2 if you merely disagree, and −3 if you decidedly disagree. In summary the scoring system is:

> +3 decidedly agree   −3 decidedly disagree
> +2 agree   −2 disagree
> +1 slightly agree   −1 slightly disagree
> 0 neither agree nor disagree

1. ( ) I find him objectionable.
2. (x) The story was too repetitious.
3. ( ) I feel there is hope for him.
4. ( ) He is a useless human being.
5. ( ) He too often seeks excuses for his failings.
6. (x) This story was very readable.
7. ( ) I would like him as an intimate friend.

* Saper, M., "Involvement in reading a case history." Unpublished Master's thesis, University of Missouri, 1963.

8. ( ) I dislike him.
9. ( ) He is a compelling figure.
10. ( ) He has weak moral fiber.
11. ( ) I would not like to be around him.
12. (x) His achievement does not measure up to his ability.
13. (x) Some religious counseling would be helpful.
14. (x) The writing style detracted from the enjoyment of reading the story.
15. (x) He is obviously repressing something significant.
16. ( ) He does not deserve to have a friend.
17. ( ) He is not the kind of person with whom I would associate.
18. ( ) He merits contempt and scorn.
19. ( ) He lacks the ability and intelligence to lead a normal life.
20. ( ) In spite of his problems he is to be respected.
21. (x) His problems can be traced to his parents and home life.
22. ( ) People like this disgust me.
23. ( ) He is basically a rotten human being.
24. ( ) He has more good in him than bad.
25. ( ) I like him.
26. ( ) I felt drawn to him.
27. ( ) He deserves sympathy.
28. ( ) Others should have tried harder to understand him.
29. ( ) I wish I could have helped him.
30. ( ) He has only himself to blame for his problems.
31. ( ) I admire the way he tried to overcome his problems.
32. ( ) I would try extra hard to get along with him.
33. (x) He should try to be more realistic.
34. ( ) He is interesting, the sort of person I would like to meet.
35. ( ) He is a coward.
36. (x) He needs extensive psychotherapy.
37. ( ) I feel sorry for him.

The involvement score was obtained by adding the absolute score of each of the twenty-eight involvement items, disregarding whether the scores were positive or negative. Thus a score of −3 is considered to be as high an involvement score as +3. The twenty-eight items to be scored are those considered to be of either positive or negative implication in regard to the case. There are nine neutral items (the items preceded by an "x" in the list shown above). These items are to be omitted in scoring.

The mean score of the thirty individuals who read the case of David was 54.3; the median was 54.0; the range was from 28 to 79. The mean score of those who felt themselves to be "slightly involved" was 46.6, those "merely involved," 52.5, and those "decidedly involved," 63.8.

Here are some excerpts from the spontaneous reports of readers in each of the three above-mentioned experimental groups, alleging some degree of involvement:

Reader who was slightly involved

"It is hard for me to understand David."
"A lot of people are crippled; that is no excuse for David's lack of success."
"He is not the sort of person I would want to know."
"David lied a lot; people who need psychiatric help always lie."

Reader who was involved

"I would like to have met him to see if he was really like that."
"I would like to have helped him even though he was beyond help."
"I admire him for coming for help."
"I felt sorry for the way his parents treated him."

Reader who was decidedly involved

"While reading of David, I tended to analyze myself."
"I was amazed that he kept bouncing back; I certainly felt sorry for him."
"People didn't understand him, so they didn't accept him."
"He had much insight into his own problem; I learned from him."

SUMMARY

The preceding sections suggest specific ways in which the instructor using this book can make fruitful and instructive use of the cases. He can encourage the reader to record in a specified or informal manner his reaction to the cases, or assign a brief exercise on the value of a concept mentioned at the end of a particular case. On the other hand, he may be satisfied with the indirect effect of the case in stimulating thought and understanding as he observes the students in group discussion. Finally, the user of this book may discover a creative device of his own for using these cases to illustrate personality dynamics and organization.

Selected Bibliography

1. Adams, J. F., *Problems in Counseling: A Case Study Approach.* New York: Macmillan, 1962 (paperback).
2. Adler, A., *Understanding Human Nature.* New York: Greenberg, 1927.
3. Allport, G. W., *Pattern and Growth in Personality.* New York: Holt, Rinehart and Winston, 1961.
4. Allport, G. W., J. S. Bruner, and E. M. Jandorf, Personality under social catastrophe: ninety life-histories of the Nazi revolution, *Character and Personality*, 1941, 10, 1–22.
5. Allport, G. W., The use of personal documents in psychological science. New York: *Soc. Sci. Res. Council Bull.*, 1942, No. 49.
6. Almy, M., *Child Development.* New York: Holt, 1955.
7. Ansbacher, H. L., and R. R. Ansbacher (eds.), *The Individual Psychology of Alfred Adler.* New York: Basic Books, 1956.
8. Arnold, M., *Emotion and Personality.* New York: Columbia University Press, 1960.
9. Baldwin, A. L., *Behavior and Development in Childhood.* New York: Dryden Press, 1955.
10. Baldwin, A. L., Personal structure analysis: a statistical method for investigating the single personality, *J. abn. soc. Psychol.*, 1942, 37, 163–183.
11. Baughman, E. E., and G. S. Welsh, *Personality: A Behavioral Science.* Englewood Cliffs, N. J.: Prentice-Hall, 1962.
12. Berkowitz, L., *Aggression.* New York: McGraw-Hill, 1962.
13. Bettelheim, B., Individual and mass behavior in extreme situations, *J. abn. soc. Psychol.*, 1943, 38, 417–452.
14. Blake, R. W., and G. Ramsey, *Perception: An Approach to Personality.* New York: Ronald, 1950.
15. Bonner, H., *Psychology of Personality.* New York: Ronald, 1961.
16. Bordin, E. S., *Psychological Counseling.* New York: Appleton-Century-Crofts, 1955.

17. Bucklew, J., *Paradigms for Psychopathology: A Contribution to Case History Analysis.* New York: Lippincott, 1960.
18. Burton, A., and R. E. Harris, *Case Histories in Clinical and Abnormal Psychology.* New York: Harper, 1947.
19. Burton, A., and R. E. Harris, *Case Histories in Clinical and Abnormal Psychology.* Volume II. *Clinical Studies of Personality.* New York: Harper, 1955.
20. Butz, O., *The Unsilent Generation.* New York: Rinehart, 1958.
21. Callis, R., P. C. Polmantier, and E. C. Roeber, *A Casebook of Counseling.* New York: Appleton-Century-Crofts, 1955.
22. Carroll, H. A., *Mental Hygiene: The Dynamics of Adjustment* (4th ed.). Englewood Cliffs, N. J.: Prentice-Hall, 1964.
23. Cattell, R. B., *Personality and Motivation: Structure and Measurement.* Yonkers, N. Y.: World Book, 1957.
24. Christie, R., and M. Jahoda (eds.), *Studies in the Scope and Method of the Authoritarian Personality.* Glencoe, Ill.: Free Press, 1954.
25. Cole, L., *Psychology of Adolescence.* New York: Holt, Rinehart and Winston, 1960.
26. Coleman, J. C., *Abnormal Psychology and Modern Life* (2d ed.). Chicago: Scott, Foresman, 1956.
27. Coleman, J. C., *Personality Dynamics and Effective Behavior.* Chicago: Scott, Foresman, 1960.
28. Combs, A. W., and D. Snygg, *Individual Behavior.* New York: Harper, 1959.
29. David, H. P., and J. C. Brengelmann, *Perspectives in Personality Research.* New York: Springer, 1960.
30. Diamond, S., *Personality and Temperament.* New York: Harper, 1957.
31. Dollard, J., and N. E. Miller, *Personality and Psychotherapy.* New York: McGraw-Hill, 1950.
32. Erikson, E. H., Identity and the Life Cycle. *Psychol. Issues,* No. 1. New York: International Universities Press, 1959.
33. Erikson, E. H., *Childhood and Society.* New York: Norton, 1955.
34. Evans, J., *Three Men: An Experiment in the Biography of Emotion.* Introduction by G. W. Allport. New York: Knopf, 1954.
35. Eysenck, H. J., *The Scientific Study of Personality.* New York: Macmillan, 1952.
36. Festinger, L., *The Concept of Cognitive Dissonance.* Evanston, Ill.: Row, Peterson, 1957.

37. Ford, D. H., and H. B. Urban, *Systems of Psychotherapy*. New York: Wiley, 1963.
38. Fromm, E., *The Sane Society*. New York: Holt, Rinehart and Winston, 1947.
39. Gagne, R. M., and E. A. Fleishman, *Psychology and Human Performance*. New York: Holt, 1959.
40. Garraty, J. A., The interrelations of psychology and biography, *Psychol. Bull.*, 1954, 51, 569–582.
41. Geldard, F. A., *Fundamentals of Psychology*. New York: Wiley, 1962.
42. Goldstein, M. J., and J. O. Palmer, *The Experience of Anxiety*. New York: Oxford University Press, 1963 (paperback).
43. Gordon, I. J., *Human Development from Birth Through Adolescence*. New York: Harper, 1962.
44. Gordon, J. E., *Personality and Behavior*. New York: Macmillan, 1963.
45. Greenwald, H., *Great Cases in Psychoanalysis*. New York: Ballantine Books, 1959 (paperback).
46. Guilford, J. P., *Personality*. New York: McGraw-Hill, 1959.
47. Hall, C. S., and G. Lindzey, *Theories of Personality*. New York: Wiley, 1954.
48. Heath, C. W., *What People Are: A Study of Normal Young Men*. Cambridge, Mass.: Harvard University Press, 1945.
49. Hebb, D. O., *The Organization of Behavior*. New York: Wiley, 1949.
50. Heider, F., *The Psychology of Interpersonal Relations*. New York: Wiley, 1958.
51. Hilgard, E. R., *Introduction to Psychology*. New York: Harcourt, Brace & World, 1962.
52. Hurlock, E. B., *Child Development*. New York: McGraw-Hill, 1956.
53. Jahoda, M., *Current Concepts of Positive Mental Health*. New York: Basic Books, 1958.
54. Jourard, S. M., *Personal Adjustment: An Approach Through the Study of Healthy Personality*. New York: Macmillan, 1958.
55. Kelley, G. A., *The Psychology of Personal Constructs*. New York: Norton, 1955.
56. Kendler, H. H., *Basic Psychology*. New York: Appleton-Century-Crofts, 1963.
57. Kimble, G. A., and N. Garmezy, *Principles of General Psychology* (2d ed.). New York: Ronald Press, 1963.

58. Krech, D., R. S. Crutchfield, and E. L. Ballachey, *Individual in Society*. New York: McGraw-Hill, 1962.
59. Lazarus, R. S., *Adjustment and Personality*. New York: McGraw-Hill, 1961.
60. Lecky, P., *Self-Consistency: A Theory of Personality*. New York: Island, 1945.
61. Leeper, R. W., and P. Madison, *Toward Understanding Human Personalities*. New York: Appleton-Century-Crofts, 1959.
62. Lehner, G. F., and E. Kube, *The Dynamics of Personal Adjustment*. Englewood Cliffs, N. J.: Prentice-Hall, 1955.
63. Leuba, C. L., *Man: A General Psychology*. New York: Holt, Rinehart & Winston, 1961.
64. Lewis, D. J., *Scientific Principles of Psychology*. Englewood Cliffs, N. J.: Prentice-Hall, 1963.
65. Lindgren, H. C., *Psychology of Personal and Social Adjustment*. New York: American Books, 1953.
66. MacKinnon, D. W., The nature and nurture of creative talent, *Amer. Psychologist*, 1962, *17*, 484–495.
67. McCandless, B. R., *Children and Adolescents*. New York: Holt, Rinehart & Winston, 1961.
68. McClelland, D. C., J. W. Atkinson, R. A. Clark, and E. L. Lowell, *The Achievement Motive*. New York: Appleton-Century-Crofts, 1953.
69. McClelland, D. C., *Personality*. New York: Sloane, 1951.
70. McKinney, F., and R. Wertheimer, A case history blank as a projective technique, *J. consult. Psychol.*, 1952, *16*, 49–60.
71. McKinney, F., Case history norms of unselected students and students with emotional problems, *J. consult. Psychol.*, 1947, *11*, 258–269.
72. McKinney, F., *Teaching Personal Adjustment: An Instructor's Manual*. New York: Wiley, 1960, pp. 10–13.
73. McKinney, F., *Psychology of Personal Adjustment*. New York: Wiley, 1960.
74. McKinney, F., *Counseling for Personal Adjustment*. Boston: Houghton Mifflin, 1958.
75. Maccoby, E. E., T. M. Newcomb, and E. L. Hartley (eds.), *Readings in Social Psychology* (3d ed.). New York: Holt, 1958.
76. Maslow, A. H., *Toward a Psychology of Being*. New York: D. Van Nostrand, 1962.
77. May, R., *Existential Psychology*. New York: Random House, 1961.

78. Mead, G. H., *Mind, Self and Society.* Chicago: University of Chicago Press, 1934.
79. Mednick, M. T., and S. A. Mednick (eds.), *Research in Personality.* New York: Holt, Rinehart & Winston, 1963.
80. Morgan, C. T., *Introduction to Psychology.* New York: McGraw-Hill, 1961.
81. Morris, C. W., *Varieties of Human Value.* Chicago: University of Chicago Press, 1956.
82. Moustakas, C. E. (ed.), *The Self: Explorations in Personal Growth.* New York: Harper, 1956.
83. Mowrer, O. H., *Learning Theory and Behavior.* New York: Wiley, 1960.
84. Munn, N. L., *Introduction to Psychology.* Boston: Houghton Mifflin, 1962.
85. Murphy, G., *Human Potentialities.* New York: Basic Books, 1958.
86. Murphy, G., *Personality: A Biosocial Approach to Origins and Structure.* New York: Harper, 1947.
87. Murray, H. A., et al., *Explorations in Personality.* New York: Oxford University Press, 1938.
88. Mussen, P. H., and J. J. Conger, *Child Development and Personality.* New York: Harper, 1956.
89. Muuss, R. E., *Theories of Adolescence.* New York: Random House, 1962.
90. Patterson, C. H., *Counseling and Psychotherapy: Theory and Practice.* New York: Harper, 1959.
91. Pennington, L. A., and I. A. Berg (eds.), *An Introduction to Clinical Psychology* (2d ed.). New York: Ronald Press, 1954.
92. Riesman, D., *The Lonely Crowd.* New Haven, Conn.: Yale University Press, 1950.
93. Rogers, C. R., A Theory of Therapy, Personality, and Interpersonal Relationships, as Developed in the Client-Centered Framework, in S. Koch (ed.), *Psychology: A Study of a Science,* Vol. 3. New York: McGraw-Hill, 1959.
94. Rogers, C. R., and R. F. Dymond (eds.), *Psychotherapy and Personality Change.* Chicago: University of Chicago Press, 1954.
95. Rosenzweig, S., The place of the individual and of idiodynamics in psychology: a dialogue, *J. individ. Psychol.,* 1958, *14,* 3–21.
96. Ruch, F. L., *Psychology and Life.* Chicago: Scott, Foresman, 1958.

97. Sanford, R. N., *The Authoritarian Personality*. New York: Harper, 1950.
98. Sappenfield, B. R., *Personality Dynamics*. New York: Knopf, 1954.
99. Sarnoff, I., *Personality Dynamics and Development*. New York: Wiley, 1962.
100. Sartain, A. Q., A. J. North, J. R. Strange, and H. M. Chapman, *Psychology: Understanding Human Behavior*. New York: McGraw-Hill, 1962
101. Sawrey, J. M., and C. Telford, *Dynamics of Mental Health: The Psychology of Adjustment*. Boston: Allyn & Bacon, 1963.
102. Sells, S. B., *Essentials of Psychology*. New York: Ronald Press, 1962.
103. Shaffer, L. F., and E. J. Shoben, *The Psychology of Adjustment*. Boston: Houghton Mifflin, 1956.
104. Sheldon, W. H., and S. S. Stevens, *The Varieties of Temperament*. New York: Harper, 1942.
105. Sherif, M., and M. O. Wilson, *Group Relations at the Crossroads*. New York: Harper, 1953.
106. Smith, H. C., *Personal Adjustment*. New York: McGraw-Hill, 1961.
107. Snyder, W. U., *The Psychotherapy Relationship*. New York: Macmillan, 1961.
108. Snyder, W. U., *Casebook of Non-directive Counseling*. Boston: Houghton Mifflin, 1947.
109. Stagner, R., *Psychology of Personality*. New York: McGraw-Hill, 1948.
110. Standal, S. W., and R. J. Corsini, *Critical Incidents in Psychotherapy*. Englewood Cliffs, N. J.: Prentice-Hall, 1959.
111. Stephenson, W., *The Study of Behavior*. Chicago: University of Chicago Press, 1953.
112. Stone, L. J., and J. Church, *Childhood and Adolescence*. New York: Random House, 1957.
113. Terman, L. M., and M. H. Oden, *The Gifted Child Grows Up*. Stanford, Calif.: Stanford University Press, 1947.
114. Thorne, F. C., *Principles of Personality Counseling*. Brandon, Vt.: *Journal of Clinical Psychology*, 1950.
115. Thorpe, L. P., B. Katz, and R. T. Lewis, *The Psychology of Abnormal Behavior* (2d ed.). New York: Ronald Press, 1961.
116. Torrence, E. P., *Guiding Creative Talent*. Englewood Cliffs, N. J.: Prentice-Hall, 1962.

117. Tyler, L. E., *The Work of the Counselor* (2d ed.). New York: Appleton-Century-Crofts, 1961.
118. Wallin, J. E. W., *Minor Mental Maladjustments in Normal People*. Durham, North Carolina: Duke University Press, 1939.
119. Weinberg H., and A. W. Hire, *Casebook in Abnormal Psychology*. New York: Knopf, 1956.
120. Wertham, F., *The Show of Violence*. Garden City, N. Y.: Doubleday, 1949.
121. White, R. W., *The Abnormal Personality* (2d ed.). New York: Ronald Press, 1956.
122. White, R. W., *Lives in Progress*. New York: Dryden Press, 1952.
123. Wickens, D. D., and D. R. Meyer, *Psychology* (2d ed.). New York: Holt, Rinehart & Winston, 1961.
124. Williams, R. J., *Biochemical Individuality*. New York: Wiley, 1956.